"The Devil's to Pay"
John Buford at Gettysburg

A History and Walking Tour

Eric J. Wittenberg

Savas Beatie
California

Library of Congress Cataloging-in-Publication Data

Wittenberg, Eric J., 1961-
The Devil's to pay : John Buford at Gettysburg : a history and tour guide / Eric J. Wittenberg.
pages cm
Includes bibliographical references and index.
ISBN 978-1-61121-208-2
1. Gettysburg, Battle of, Gettysburg, Pa., 1863. 2. Buford, John, 1826-1863. 3. Pennsylvania—History—Civil War, 1861-1865—Cavalry operations. 4. United States—History—Civil War, 1861-1865—Cavalry operations. 5. Gettysburg National Military Park (Pa.)—Tours. I. Title.
E475.53.W756 2014
973.7'349—dc23
2014032494

SB

Published by
Savas Beatie LLC
989 Governor Drive, Suite 102
El Dorado Hills, CA 95762

Phone: 916-941-6896
(E-mail) customerservice@savasbeatie.com

05 04 03 02 01   5 4 3 2 1
First edition, first printing

Savas Beatie titles are available at special discounts for bulk purchases in the United States by corporations, institutions, and other organizations. For more details, please contact Special Sales, P.O. Box 4527, El Dorado Hills, CA 95762, or you may e-mail us at sales@savasbeatie.com, or visit our website at www.savasbeatie.com for additional information.

Proudly published, printed, and warehoused in the United States of America.

Buford is dead!
No more to follow his daring form
Or see him dash through the battle's storm;
No more with him to ride down the foe.
And behold his falchion's crushing blow.
Nor hear his voice, like a rushing blast.
As rider and steed went charging past—
Buford is dead!

Rock Island Argus, March 10, 1896

Other works by Eric J. Wittenberg

We Have it Damned Hard Out Here: The Civil War Letters of Sgt. Thomas W. Smith, Sixth Pennsylvania Cavalry (1999)

One of Custer's Wolverines: The Civil War Letters of Brevet Brigadier General James H. Kidd, 6th Michigan Cavalry (2000)

Under Custer's Command: The Civil War Journal of James Henry Avery (2000)

At Custer's Side: The Civil War Writings of James Harvey Kidd (2001)

Glory Enough for All: Sheridan's Second Raid and the Battle of Trevilian Station (2001)

With Sheridan in the Final Campaign Against Lee (2002)

Little Phil: A Reassessment of the Civil War Leadership of Gen. Philip H. Sheridan (2002)

The Union Cavalry Comes of Age: Hartwood Church to Brandy Station, 1863 (2003)

The Battle of Monroe's Crossroads and the Civil War's Final Campaign (2006)

Plenty of Blame to Go Around: Jeb Stuart's Controversial Ride to Gettysburg (with J. David Petruzzi, 2006)

Rush's Lancers: The Sixth Pennsylvania Cavalry in the Civil War (2007)

One Continuous Fight: The Retreat from Gettysburg and the Pursuit of Lee's Army of Northern Virginia, July 4-14, 1863 (with J. David Petruzzi and Michael F. Nugent, 2008)

Like a Meteor Blazing Brightly: The Short but Controversial Life of Colonel Ulric Dahlgren (2009)

The Battle of Brandy Station: North America's Largest Cavalry Battle (2010)

Gettysburg's Forgotten Cavalry Actions: Farnsworth's Charge, South Cavalry Field and the Battle of Fairfield (Second Edition, 2011)

The Battle of White Sulphur Springs; Averell Fails to Secure West Virginia (2011)

Protecting the Flank at Gettysburg: The Battles for Brinkerhoff's Ridge and East Cavalry Field (Second Edition, 2013)

Table of Contents

Author's Preface and Acknowledgments
ix

Foreword
xii

Chapter 1:
John Buford and his Troopers
1

Chapter 2:
Marching to Pennsylvania
26

Chapter 3:
June 30, 1863
42

Chapter 4:
The Night Before the Battle: June 30-July 1, 1863
62

Chapter 5: Opening the Ball:
Early Morning, July 1, 1863
74

Chapter 6:
The Devil's to Pay: Buford Holds On
103

Chapter 7:
Gamble Saves the First Corps
132

Chapter 8:
Unshaken and Undaunted
148

Table of Contents (continued)

Chapter 9:
The Night of July 1-2, 1863
157

Chapter 10:
Devin's Brigade Skirmishes in Pitzer's Woods
163

Chapter 11:
Buford Departs the Battlefield
172

Conclusion:
An Assessment of John Buford's
Performance in the Battle of Gettysburg
181

Epilogue
197

Appendix A:
Order of Battle, Morning, July 1, 1863
205

Appendix B:
The Myth of the Spencers
208

Appendix C:
What was the Nature of John Buford's Defense at Gettysburg?
213

Appendix D:
Did James Lane's Confederate Brigade form Infantry Squares
in Echelon on the Afternoon of July 1, 1863?
218

Table of Contents (continued)

A Walking and Driving Tour
225

Bibliography
247

Index
263

Author's Preface

Like so many other Pennsylvania school children, I made my first visit to Gettysburg as a third-grader. Like most impressionable children, the giant boulders of Devil's Den left a prominent mark on my imagination. But so, too, did the heroic stand by the dismounted cavalrymen of Brig. Gen. John Buford's First Cavalry Division. The three most prominent memories I have of that first visit are of Devil's Den, the story of John Buford's stand on the first day, and the death of Maj. Gen. John Fulton Reynolds that bloody, fateful morning. I have vivid memories of being fascinated by the story of how Buford's badly outnumbered horse soldiers successfully held off the bulk of an entire corps of Confederate infantry for several hours, steadfastly resisting the Confederate advance until Reynolds and the Army of the Potomac's First Corps arrived on the field just in the nick of time. Hence, my fascination with the exploits of Buford's troopers dates back to my very first visit to Gettysburg as a 9-year-old.

I carry that fascination with me well into middle age. I have spent my adult life chronicling the exploits of the horse soldiers of the Civil War. I have written 17 books and dozens of articles on the topic, but in the end, I always come back to my first fascination, the story of Buford and his troopers. In the intervening years, I have periodically revisited Buford's command and its exploits with a number of articles and several books that touch on these men and what they accomplished. However, until now, I have never tried to do a monograph on the critical role of Buford's division at Gettysburg. Having documented the remaining cavalry actions at Gettysburg, I realized that my efforts to document all of the engagements involving the cavalry in this critical campaign would not be complete unless I filled that gap. Accordingly, I came to the conclusion that the time had come to do so. This is the story that I have waited my entire life to tell.

In this volume, I will introduce the reader to John Buford and the men he led, including his outstanding brigade commanders, Colonels William Gamble and Thomas C. Devin, as well as to Lt. John H. Calef, the talented young West Pointer who commanded the battery of horse artillery assigned to Buford's division. A brief overview of Buford's role in the Gettysburg Campaign to date, from its beginning on June 3, 1863 to the night of June 29, follows. A detailed tactical discussion of Buford's prominent role in the Battle of Gettysburg then follows, covering the events beginning on June 30, 1863 and ending with the withdrawal of the First Cavalry Division from Gettysburg on July 2. It concludes with an analysis of the critical role played by the quiet Kentuckian and his troopers. There are four appendices. The first is an order of battle timed for 9:15 a.m. on July 1, 1863. The second addresses the persistent myth that Buford's men were armed with repeating rifles at Gettysburg. The third addresses the question of the precise nature of the defense designed and conducted by Buford. The fourth addresses another persistent question, of whether Confederate infantry formed hollow squares to defend against a feinted mounted charge by Buford's two brigades. Finally, I include a driving/walking tour of sites associated with John Buford's stand at Gettysburg that includes GPS coordinates.

As with any project of this nature, I am grateful to any number of people for their assistance. I am especially grateful to my friend, co-author, and fellow cavalry historian, J. David Petruzzi, for writing the foreword that follows and for his invaluable assistance with sources and with reviewing this manuscript for me. My friend Daniel Mallock read the manuscript for me as to readability and as to coherence. William B. Styple of Kearny, New Jersey provided images from the dedication of the Buford monument on the battlefield at Gettysburg and some useful tidbits from the James E. Kelly papers. Marshall Krolick, the authority on all things pertaining to the 8th Illinois Cavalry, provided material and the image of Col. William Gamble that graces these pages. John Heiser and Greg Goodell, who are both rangers at Gettysburg, provided useful material, and so did Lauren Roedner, the archivist at the Adams County Historical Society. James Hessler, the authority on Dan Sickles at Gettysburg, gave me good and useful feedback on the three chapters that dealt with Buford's role on the second day of the battle, and I appreciate his assistance. Rick Wolfe and Joe Stahl both provided me with images that have never before been published but which appear here for the first time. Philip Laino drew the excellent maps that fill this volume, and Phil's maps make this a better book. Steve L. Zerbe and Bryce Suderow helped gather the research material that fills these pages.

I am pleased to continue my partnership with the good folks at Savas Beatie, LLC. This is now our sixth book together, and each time, working with Ted and his excellent staff has been a pleasure. I appreciate all that they do to make my work better.

Finally, I am endlessly grateful to my much loved but long-suffering wife, photographer, chauffeur, and battlefield assistant, Susan Skilken Wittenberg, without whose endless patience with my addiction to telling the stories of the cavalry soldiers of the American Civil War, none of this would be possible.

Eric J. Wittenberg
Columbus, Ohio

Foreword

Until the appearance of Michael Shaara's historical novel *Killer Angels* (which won the Pulitzer Prize for Fiction in 1975) and the resulting movie *Gettysburg* (Turner Pictures, 1993), many prominent historical characters that participated in the 1863 Battle of Gettysburg were well-known only to the most diehard Civil War historians and students. One of these was the gruff, no-nonsense commander of the Federal cavalrymen who opened the battle against the Confederate incursion upon the town on the morning of July 1–John Buford.

Played on the big screen by veteran actor Sam Elliott, Buford became an immediate "hit" among the main characters of the novel and movie, and for many viewers Elliott is forever identified for that particular role. Elliott's on- and off-screen demeanor actually seems to match that of the historical Buford – slow and deliberate of speech, contemplative, and a presence that suggests that fools are never suffered for long – indicating that the role was cast well.

For a small and dedicated subset of those who have long studied this bellwether conflict of our Nation's history, including Eric J. Wittenberg and me, Buford and his wartime exploits had been fascinating long before the appearance of the movie *Gettysburg*. As Eric explains in his Preface, one of his earliest memories of his initial visit to the Gettysburg battlefield was the story of Buford's and his troopers' performance during the opening phases of the battle, as it had been for this writer. Subsequent visits and studies often concentrated on the horse soldiers' role during the Gettysburg Campaign, until Eric has become, through sheer hard work and deep research, one of the foremost experts on the role of cavalry during the Civil War in general, and that of John Buford and his men in the Gettysburg Campaign in particular.

It is interesting to wonder what Buford would have thought of all this attention paid to him in the last couple of decades. He likely would have found it amusing, if not a little embarrassing. He was surrounded on all sides –indeed among the Federal and Confederate armies alike–by pompous, showy, attention-starved officers (most of which seemed to gravitate toward the cavalry) while Buford was quiet, all business, and let his saber do his talking. Buford wouldn't use five words when three would suffice. What a stark contrast to names and personas so familiar to us today such as Jeb Stuart, Alfred Pleasonton, George A. Custer, and Judson Kilpatrick—all of whom Buford fought for, with, or against during the war. While Confederate cavalry chieftain Jeb Stuart made a memorable presence on every battlefield with his crimson cape and feathered hat, Buford was quite content donning his comfortable old hunting jacket. As Federal Cavalry Corps commander Alfred Pleasonton courted newspapermen and plied them with oysters and the finest champagne, Buford threw reporters from his camps. Kilpatrick traveled with a hand-picked entourage so large it could nearly have been a brigade unto itself, but Buford kept only a small contingent of trusted aides by his side, all of whom became enamored with their leader to their last days. Little needs to be said about the famous dandy George Custer, whom one trooper, upon first seeing the newly-minted young general, remarked that in his new custom-tailored uniform Custer looked like nothing short of "a circus rider gone mad." Nothing is recorded of Buford's first impression of the golden-locked cavalier, but he likely looked upon him with guarded suspicion and hoped only that his battlefield performances would be as memorable as the copious gold braid that adorned his velvet attire.

Raised in Illinois but born roots-deep among the blue grasses of Kentucky, the pre-war Army officer Buford chose to remain loyal to the Union in those dark days of early 1861 as he watched the vast majority of his southern-heeled compatriots cast their lots with the Confederacy. Indeed, most of his immediate and extended family would end up fighting for the gray, including that of his wife Patsy, a distant cousin of his prior to their marriage.

Buford was in command of a brigade of Regular cavalry early in 1863, and these Regulars remained with him through various field posts. These were the troopers he trusted most, and they in turn would have gladly ridden at full speed through the gates of Hell itself if only Buford would have pointed the way. To open the Gettysburg Campaign, the Regulars (augmented by the 6th Pennsylvania Cavalry, whom Buford complimented by baptizing them as his "seventh Regulars") rode under his command at the June 9 Battle of Brandy Station, then in several massive cavalry brawls in and around the Loudoun Valley later that month. Inarguably, however, for all his activities before and after Gettysburg, Buford is best-known even among the casual war student for his opening of the Battle of Gettysburg on July 1, 1863.

There, Buford lamented, he did not have his beloved Regulars. He did, however, have his other two brigades, consisting of mostly veteran volunteers. In Buford's experienced hands they masterfully conducted a textbook dismounted delaying action that protected the ground surrounding the town of Gettysburg that soon became the world-famous main battlefield. That is the John Buford of Gettysburg that most students and visitors know and are told of. What most do not know or hear, however, is how Buford deployed his mounted volunteers later that afternoon to help clinch the final Federal defensive position atop Cemetery Hill and Ridge, the gradual yet sturdy perch upon which the Union would make a stand for two more bloody days that would slake the thirst of any self-respecting god of war. Two more risings and settings of the sun during which Robert E. Lee and his venerable Rebels would try and fail to crack that line, but during which heroes and cowards alike would carve their names into the annals of war.

Even much less known is the participation of a contingent of Buford's people on the morning of the second day of the battle, July 2. It was actually these cavalrymen, in concert with riflemen of the United States Sharpshooters, who discovered the growing Confederate line on the southern portion of Seminary Ridge and engaged the Rebels there, thus opening the conflict that day. The shooting and casualties at Gettysburg on July 2, then, started there and much earlier than the massive infantry assault on the southern and central portions of the Federal line led by Lt. Gen. James Longstreet that afternoon, or the ponderous bloodletting atop Culp's Hill. Before any general engagement got underway that morning, however, Buford and his men (save for two cavalry companies left with the III Corps for the remainder of the day) were ordered off the field, and the cavalrymen could only listen to the sounds of the battle they had personally started the prior day as they marched for Maryland.

It is this full story of Buford and his men at Gettysburg, then, that needs to be told in detail. For the very first time you hold it in your hands, masterfully crafted in its proper context by Wittenberg. Herein you will learn the strategy and tactics of Buford's opening of the battle on the morning of July 1, and how, why, and where the fighting began and progressed as it did during those sultry summer days of 1863. For the first time, too, the indispensable participation of Buford and his men in the securing of Cemetery Hill late on the afternoon of July 1 is related here in detail. Many know the story of the legendary Dan Sickles and that Federal corps commander's exploits on July 2, but herein for the first time is the narrative of the opening of that day's fighting by Buford's men, and how it fits into

Sickles' decision-making that fully opened the curtain on the bloodiest of the three days of the Battle of Gettysburg.

Buford didn't live to see the end of the war in which he fought to mend the Union he so loved. The insipid bug of typhoid fever did what a bullet couldn't do–it killed him before the third year of the war was over. He was in no shape to fight it off. Only 37 that summer, by the Gettysburg Campaign, he was already so wracked with debilitating arthritis due to hard riding and exposure, he couldn't even get into the saddle without a hand. Neither Buford nor his men had hardly a rest during the campaigns of 1863. When word of his death spread throughout the army's camps that December, and especially among those with whom he had personally served—his troopers and his Regulars in particular—the men took it hard. Buford didn't dress for respect, he earned it. He didn't try to get his name in the newspapers, instead he led with deeds that caused his men to follow his guidon with confidence and the full expectation of success.

I noted previously that it may be hard to tell what Buford would think now of all the recent attention paid to him. Like any other person who shuns the limelight and simply does his duty the best he can, he likely never would have called for such a book to be written—or at the very least, that it be focused on the men that he led instead of him. But I believe that those men, if they could, would tell us that the true story indeed was that short but powerful Kentuckian. The one with the steely gray eyes that could twinkle during a light moment, but narrow in deep concentration when a fight loomed. The one who would hang a spy from a tree in an instant, yet would silently cry as he watched the light fade from one of his badly wounded troopers. The one that men could and would follow, without reservation, and willingly place their lives in his hands for the cause they believed in, because their leader said simply "go there."

I believe Buford would be pleased. Very pleased indeed.

J. David Petruzzi
Brockway, Pennsylvania

Chapter 1

John Buford
and his Troopers

"*John* Buford was the best cavalryman I ever saw," declared Buford's longtime friend, Gen. John Gibbon, many years after the end of the Civil War.[1] That was high praise from a man who fought in the thick of the War of the Rebellion before spending years fighting Indians on the Great Plains. Who was this soldier that had earned Gibbon's undying admiration?

John Buford, Jr., was born in Woodford County, Kentucky, on March 4, 1826. The Buford family had a long martial tradition dating back to the family's roots in France. He could trace his French Huguenot stock back to the time of the Norman Conquest, when the family name was "Beaufort." Young John was the first child of John and Anne Bannister Watson Buford. His father was a Democratic state legislator in Kentucky and the son of Capt. Simeon Buford, a prominent Virginia veteran of the Revolutionary War. John's mother was the daughter of Capt. Edward Howe of the United States Navy. John was born into a large family that included two full brothers—Thomas Jefferson Buford and James Monroe Buford—and 13 half-brothers and sisters from the first marriages of both of his parents. By the time he was a teenager he was "a splendid horseman, an unerring rifle shot and a person of wonderful nerve and composure."[2]

---

1 John Gibbon, "The John Buford Memoir," John Gibbon Papers, Pennsylvania Historical Society, Philadelphia, Pennsylvania.

2 Simeon Buford served in the Culpeper Minutemen during the Revolutionary War. He served as the Marquis de Lafayette's quartermaster and in 1781 was promoted to captain and commanded a company of the Culpeper Minuteman until the end of the War of Independence.

Maj. Gen. Napoleon Bonaparte Buford, the older half-brother of John Buford. He briefly commanded a division under U. S. Grant until being exiled to garrison duty.
Library of Congress

Like many other American families, the Civil War divided the Buford clan, which contributed more than its share to fighting the conflict. John's older half-brother, Napoleon Bonaparte Buford, graduated sixth in his class at West Point in 1827 and commissioned into the Regular Army as a brevet second lieutenant of engineers. He studied law at Harvard, resigned in 1835 with the permission of the War Department, and served a stint at the academy as an assistant professor of Natural and Experimental Philosophy. Napoleon rejoined the army and was elected colonel of the 27th Illinois on August 10, 1861. After serving in the early Western campaigns, he was commissioned a brigadier general of volunteers on April 15, 1862, immediately after the battle of Shiloh. He was given command of a brigade in Brig. Gen. William S. Rosecrans' Army of the Mississippi and served in that capacity during the early phases of the Vicksburg campaign. "He would scarcely make a respectable hospital nurse if put in petticoats and certain—is unfit for any other military position," thought Maj. Gen. Ulysses S. Grant in February 1863. The future president despised Buford, and had

---

Simeon's oldest brother, Thomas Buford, served as a sergeant on Brig. Gen. James Braddock's expedition toward Pittsburgh during the French and Indian War, 1754-1756. He served as a lieutenant under George Washington in 1758. Later, he was elected captain of a company of militia from Bedford County, Virginia, and served in Lord Dumore's War. Captain Thomas Buford was killed on October 10, 1774, at the Battle of Point Pleasant. The combat took place at the confluence of the Kanawha and Ohio rivers in what is today West Virginia against an Indian force under the command of the Shawnee war chief Cornstalk. Marcus Bainbridge Buford, *History and Genealogy of the Buford Family in America* (LaBelle, Missouri, 1903), 27-28. For a detailed discussion of Lord Dunmore's War and, in particular, of Thomas Buford's role in it, see Warren Skidmore and Donna Kaminsky, *Lord Dunmore's Little War of 1774: His Captains and Their Men Who Opened Up Kentucky & The West To American Settlement* (Berwyn Heights, MD: 2002); Buford, *History and Genealogy of the Buford Family in America*, 307; Gibbon, "The John Buford Memoir."

accused him of disobeying his orders at the 1861 Belmont fight. "He has always been a dead weight to carry, becoming more burdensome with his increased rank." Napoleon was exited to garrison command at Cairo, Illinois, a position he held until September 12, 1863, when he took command of the garrison of Helena, Arkansas, a post he held until the end of the war. On March 13, 1865, he was promoted to brevet major general of volunteers and mustered out of the service five months later.[3]

John Buford's first cousin, Abraham Buford, also saw extensive service in the army. Abraham graduated 51st (second to last) in West Point's Class of 1841.[4] From there, Abraham Buford was commissioned into the First Dragoons, where he served for 13 years. He saw duty in the American West and also served with distinction during the Mexican War, eventually rising to the rank of captain in the Regular Army. After that conflict, Abraham served along the Mexican border, attended the Cavalry School for Practice at Carlisle, Pennsylvania, and finally resigned his commission in 1854. A man of great physical size and strength, he was known as a fighter and something of a hell-raiser. "Buford, as you may suppose, is hardly calculated to shine in any ballroom except a Mexican fandango, where he seems in his element," observed future Confederate general Richard S. Ewell, who served with Abe in the First Dragoons. "Here the natives call him 'Hell-roaring Buford.' He is over six feet tall and out of proportion, large in other respects."[5] Henry Heth, another future

3 N. B. Buford's West Point classmates included Confederate Lt. Gen. Leonidas K. Polk, who was killed during the 1864 Atlanta Campaign, and Brig. Gen. Philip St. George Cooke, who became John Buford's mentor in the Regular Army. Cooke was also Confederate cavalry commander Maj. Gen. J. E. B. Stuart's father-in-law; Ulysses S. Grant to Abraham Lincoln, February 9, 1863, quoted in Robert I. Girardi, comp., *The Civil War Generals: Comrades, Peers, Rivals in Their Own Words* (Minneapolis: 2013), 39; George W. Cullum, *Biographical Register of the Officers and Graduates of the U.S. Military Academy*, 2 vols. (New York: 1868), 1:310-11; Buford, *Genealogy of the Buford Family*, 311.

4 Abraham Buford had some very famous classmates. Among the members of his West Point class were future Union generals Horatio G. Wright, Thomas Rodman, Albion P. Howe, Nathaniel Lyon, John F. Reynolds, Don Carlos Buell, Alfred Sully, and Israel B. Richardson. Lyon, Reynolds, and Richardson were all killed or mortally wounded. Future Confederate generals included Josiah H. Gorgas (the Confederate chief of ordnance), Samuel Jones, Robert S. Garnett, and Richard S. Garnett. The Garnett cousins were both killed in action, the latter on the third day at Gettysburg leading his brigade in Pickett's Charge.

5 Percy Gatlin Hamlin, ed., *The Making of a Soldier: Letters of General R. S. Ewell* (Richmond, 1935), 77. Lieutenant Colonel Arthur Fremantle, a British officer sent to observe the American Civil War, described a "Mexican fandango:" "A Mexican fandango resembles a French ducasse, with the additional excitement of gambling. It commences at 9:30, and continues till daylight.

Brig. Gen. Abraham Buford, John Buford's first cousin, who commanded a division of cavalry under Nathan Bedford Forrest. *NARA*

Confederate general who would play a major role with John Buford at Gettysburg, and who knew Abe in the antebellum Regular Army, noted, "Buford was the most accomplished swearer I had ever seen up to that time—I had not [yet] met General [William S.] Harney."[6] After resigning his commission, Abe settled in Woodford County, Kentucky, where he bred and sold thoroughbred horses and served as president of the Richmond & Danville Railroad.

After much contemplation, Abraham Buford cast his lot with the Confederacy, joining Brig. Gen. John Hunt Morgan's Raiders in Kentucky in 1862. He was appointed brigadier general and with a brigade of raw recruits helped cover Gen. Braxton Bragg's October 1862 retreat from Perryville into East Tennessee by way of the Cumberland Gap. After a dispute with Maj. Gen. Edmund Kirby Smith, Abraham was transferred south to command a brigade of cavalry. In 1864, he joined Nathan Bedford Forrest's cavalry, where he assumed command of a mounted division. He participated in the battles of Brice's Cross Roads and Tupelo, prompting Forrest to seek Buford's promotion to major general. "It is true that Genl Buford has only served with me a short time, long enough, however, to fully establish his reputation and display his ability as an energetic and efficient cavalry commander and if any promotion are or can be made, in this department to the rank he desires," wrote

---

The scene is lit up by numerous paper lanterns of various colors. A number of benches are placed so as to form a large square, in the centre of which the dancing goes on, the men and women gravely smoking all the time. Outside the benches is the promenade bounded by the gambling-tables and drinking-booths…Monte is the favorite game, and the smallest silver coin can be staked, or a handful of doubloons." Arthur Fremantle, *Three Months in the Southern States April-June 1863* (New York: 1864), 19-20.

6   James L. Morrison, ed., *The Memoirs of Henry Heth* (Westport, CT: 1974), 82.

Forrest. "I respectfully recommend his appointment and promotion to Major General [Provisional Army of the Confederate States]."[7]

Buford's command covered the retreat of the Army of Tennessee during the 1864 Nashville campaign. During that action, he killed a Union major with his pistol after that officer struck him in the head with his sword while shouting, "Surrender, you damn big rebel!" Somehow Abraham escaped with but a slight wound in the leg. After the end of the Civil War, Abe Buford returned to Kentucky and became one of the best-known and most sought-after breeders of thoroughbred horses in America.[8]

Against this martial backdrop, it is no surprise that young John Buford become a soldier. After his mother died during the great cholera epidemic that swept across Kentucky in 1833, the family moved to Rock Island, Illinois. "Rock Island was his home, if he had one, and here are clustered memories of his boyhood days," recalled several friends years after his death. The earliest reference to this domicile is found in the 1840 United States Census, which indicates that the John Buford family of six persons resided in the town. Young John would have been 14 years old at that time. In 1842, his father was elected state senator for Rock Island County, and the next year was commissioned appraiser of the real estate belonging to the State Bank of Illinois. He remained in public service for the rest of his life. John Buford, Sr. was a staunch Democrat and supporter of Stephen C. Douglas. His sons shared his political leanings.[9]

7   Nathan Bedford Forrest to James A. Seddon, May 26, 1864, Abraham Buford Compiled Service Records, RG 109 Compiled Service Records of Confederate and Staff Officers and Non-regimental Enlisted Men, NARA, Washington, D.C.

8   Abraham Buford Compiled Service Records; Cullum, *Biographical Register*, 2:37; Buford, *Genealogy of the Buford Family*, 329-31. Unfortunately, after his wife and son died of disease, Abraham Buford committed suicide on June 9, 1884. Ironically, Abe Buford committed suicide on the 21st anniversary of his more famous cousin John's outstanding day at the Battle of Brandy Station. Buford, *Genealogy of the Buford Family*, 238.

9   From 1832-1835, a great cholera epidemic struck nearly every part of Kentucky. Ten percent of the population of Lexington died in just a few weeks because medical science had not yet made the connection between cholera and sanitation. Nearly every family was affected by this epidemic. Anne Buford was not alone. She was buried in the Mt. Pisgah Church cemetery in Woodford County alongside her first husband and his family. John E. Kleber, ed., *The Kentucky Encyclopedia* (Lexington: 1992), 184; "Honors Its Hero: Grand Army Post Has a Memorial Entertainment," *Rock Island Argus*, March 10, 1896; U.S. Census for the Year 1840, Rock Island County, Illinois, 254; Election Papers, Illinois State Archives, Springfield, Illinois.

In 1842 young John was "a fine promising young man, well grown for his age, and of excellent mind and morals." That year, the 16-year-old was nominated for an appointment to West Point, but the application was denied because his half-brother Napoleon had attended the academy. At that time, War Department policy prohibited two brothers from both obtaining a free education by attending either West Point or the Naval Academy. The denial sparked a flurry of letter writing on young John's behalf, including one from Napoleon that stated, "[h]e has all of the qualities for making a good soldier, and is well prepared to enter in the course of studies at the Academy." With his denial firm in hand, John enrolled for the 1842-43 academic year at Knox College in Galesburg, Illinois. After one year there, John moved to Cincinnati, Ohio, where he lived with Napoleon Buford and attended college.[10]

With his half-brother Napoleon leading another vigorous letter writing campaign, John was once again nominated for an appointment to West Point in 1843, was accepted in 1844, and entered West Point that fall. The place suited him well and Cadet Buford thrived in the regimented environment. "Rather slow in speech, [Buford] was quick enough in thought and apt at repartee," recalled his friend Gibbon. "He was not especially distinguished in his studies, but his course in the Academy was marked by a steady progress, the best evidence of character and determination." Another comrade said, "Buford did not display any great military talent in the limited field at West Point, not having been selected as a cadet officer until late in his career at the Military Academy. But this was not uncommon in those who, subsequently, greatly distinguished themselves in high military command."[11]

Buford stood 28th in his class at the end of the first year (38th in mathematics and 19th in French). He accumulated 49 demerits, placing him 86th out of 204 total cadets. By the end of his second year he was 25th in class

---

10 Thomas Ford letter of recommendation to Representative J. C. Spencer, February 16, 1843, John Buford, Jr. Cadet Records, Archives, United States Military Academy, West Point, New York; Napoleon B. Buford to Representative J. C. Spencer, January 14, 1863, Buford Cadet Records; *Catalogue of the Corporation, Officers, and Students of Knox Manual Labor College, July 1842* (Peoria, Iowa: 1843), 6; Napoleon B. Buford to J. C. Spencer, January 14, 1863, Buford Cadet Records.

11 John Buford, Jr. to W. Wilkins, Secretary of War, April 20, 1844, Microfilm M1064, Letters received by the Commissions Branch of the Adjutant General's Office, 1863-1870, roll 9, file no. B 1115 CB 1863, National Archives; Gibbon, "The John Buford Memoir"; Col. Joseph C. Clark to the Buford Memorial Association, April 20, 1894, *The Proceedings of the Buford Memorial Association* (New York: privately published, 1895), 37.

Martha "Patsy" McDowell Duke Buford, John
Buford's third cousin and wife.
Filson Club

standing (34th in mathematics, 14th in
French, 31st in English grammar, and
24th in drawing). That year he had but
14 demerits, placing him 46th out of
213 cadets. For his third year, 1846-
1847, Buford rose to finish 17th in his
class (24th in philosophy, 14th in
chemistry, and 12th in drawing). He
earned 45 demerits year, placing him
92nd out of 218 cadets. He graduated
16th out of 42 in the Class of 1848,
with future Civil War generals William
E. "Grumble" Jones, John C. Tidball, Nathaniel H. McLean, William N. R.
Beall, Nathan G. "Shanks" Evans, George H. Steuart, Jr., and Hugh B. Ewing.
He was commissioned, at his request, into the First Dragoons as a brevet
second lieutenant, and transferred to the Second Dragoons six months later.[12]

Buford was a superb horseman. "His boyhood was spent in close
communion with the horse and he acquired an intimate knowledge of him, his
nature and his powers, what he could do and what he could not do," observed
John Gibbon. "He thus acquired in his boyhood the first essential of a good
cavalryman in the knowledge of the character and capacity of the cavalryman's
co-worker in the field. Buford was one of the best horsemen I ever saw. He

12 *Official Register of the Officers and Cadets of the U.S. Military Academy, West Point, New York, June
1845* (Washington, D.C.: 1845), 13, 19; *Official Register of the Officers and Cadets of the U.S. Military
Academy, West Point, New York, June 1846* (Washington, D.C.: 1846), 11, 17; *Official Register of the
Officers and Cadets of the U.S. Military Academy, West Point, New York, June 1847* (Washington, D.C.:
1847), 9, 20; *Official Register of the Officers and Cadets of the U.S. Military Academy, West Point, New
York, June 1848* (Washington, D.C.: 1848), 7. He finished 15th in engineering, 19th in ethics,
12th in artillery, 10th infantry, and 16th in geology. Ibid. Buford had 70 demerits that year,
finishing 124th out of 230 cadets. Ibid, 7-8, 21. Buford and his classmate Jones, also a
cavalryman, would fight numerous times in 1863, including most of the day at Brandy Station
on June 9, 1863, and again at Upperville on June 21—both while on the way to Gettysburg. See
also, Wilson oration, 174.

delighted in the horse, was fond of riding, and it is said of him that 'as a boy he was the greatest dare-devil of a rider in the whole county.'" During the Civil War, Buford rode a handsome Kentucky thoroughbred named Grey Eagle. The horse was a gift from his Confederate cousin Gen. Abraham Buford, named for the Mississippi River steamboat commanded by John Buford's brother, Thomas Jefferson Buford.[13]

In the early stages of his career Buford served along the Mexican border and was promoted to second lieutenant in 1849 and to first lieutenant in 1853. On May 9, 1854, Lieutenant Buford married his third cousin, 24-year-old Martha McDowell Duke of Georgetown, Kentucky, known to friends and family as Patsy.[14] A "great favorite" and "a most estimable woman," Patsy was the granddaughter of Col. Abraham Buford, the Revolutionary War hero and brother of John's grandfather Simeon, and the one who was responsible for bringing the Bufords to Kentucky.[15] By all accounts they had a happy marriage. John and Patsy Buford had two children, James Duke Buford ("Duke"), born on July 26, 1855, and Pattie McDowell Buford ("Little Patsy"), born on October 14, 1857. In a tragedy all too common in those times, neither child would live to see adulthood.

John served as quartermaster of the Second Dragoons from 1855 through the beginning of August 1858, fighting in several Indian battles along the way. One of these was the Sioux Punitive Expedition under Brig. Gen. William S. Harney, which culminated in the Battle of Ash Hollow in 1856 where a young subaltern named Lt. Henry Heth commanded a detachment of mounted infantry that played an important role in the decisive victory. Colonel Philip St. George Cooke, the commanding officer of the Second Dragoons, cited Lieutenant Buford for his "good service" at Ash Hollow, as did Harney himself.[16] While he served as quartermaster, the Second Dragoons was

---

13 Gibbon, "The John Buford Memoir."

14 Buford, *Genealogy of the Buford Family*, 212. Besides being John Buford's cousin, Patsy was also a second cousin of Brig. Gen. Irvin McDowell, the commander of the Union forces at First Bull Run. Through her maternal grandmother, she was also related to some of the most prominent Virginia families, including the Marshalls, Randolphs, and Jeffersons.

15 *Paris Kentuckian-Citizen*, October 5, 1903, Patsy Buford obituary, *Georgetown News*, October 7, 1903. She was also a first cousin of Confederate cavalryman Brig. Gen. Basil W. Duke.

16 For a detailed discussion of the roles played by both Heth and Harney at Ash Hollow, see R. Eli Paul, *Blue Water Creek and the First Sioux War 1864-1856* (Norman: 2004).

stationed at Fort Riley, Kansas, where Buford participated in quelling the disturbances in "Bleeding Kansas" in 1856 and 1857.

The Second Dragoons went west under the command of Col. Albert Sidney Johnston to participate in the Utah Expedition against Brigham Young and his Mormon followers during 1857 and 1858. Buford won high praise from Cooke for his service during the arduous march west, and was posted at Camp Floyd, Utah. "I was stationed at Camp Floyd with General Buford at the commencement of the Rebellion," recounted an old friend. "I then considered him a model officer, whose distinguishing quality was a large fund of good, practical, common sense." Buford was promoted to captain on March 9, 1859, instructed recruits at the Army's Cavalry School of Practice at the Carlisle Barracks for a year, and returned to frontier duty, where he was given the task of conducting recruits to Oregon. Buford went on to serve at Fort Crittenden, Utah, with the Second Dragoons until the beginning of the Civil War.[17]

Buford was torn between his loyalty to his native Kentucky and his loyalty to the government he had faithfully served for 13 years. The difficult choice deeply troubled him. John Gibbon, who had three brothers who would serve in the Confederate army, decided to remain loyal to the Union. He recalled, "One night after the arrival of the mail we were in his [Buford's] room, talking over the news . . . when Buford said in his slow and deliberate way, 'I got a letter by the last mail from home with a message in it from the Governor of Kentucky. He sends me word to come to Kentucky at once and I shall have anything I want.'" An anxious Gibbon asked his friend, "What did you answer, John?" Buford's reply came as quite a relief: "I sent him word I was a captain in the United States Army and I intend to remain one."[18]

17 For a detailed discussion of the Mormon War and the role played by the Second Dragoons, see David L. Bigler and Will Bagley, *The Mormon Rebellion: America's First Civil War, 1857-1858* (Norman: 2011); Clark to the Buford Memorial Association, 37; Cullum, *Officers and Graduates of the U.S. Military Academy*, 2:215; Brian C. Pohanka, "Unsurpassed in Dash": Keogh in the American Civil War," in John P. Langellier, Hamilton Cox, and Brian C. Pohanka, eds., *Myles Keogh: The Life and Legend of an "Irish Dragoon" in the Seventh Cavalry*, Montana and the West Series (El Segundo, 1991), 9:70. As Carlisle is only a little more than 30 miles from Gettysburg, one cannot help but wonder whether Buford had explored the countryside and was familiar with the terrain features before the July 1863 battle.

18 Gibbon, "The John Buford Memoir." Cooke and Harney—two of Buford's heroes—were Southerners who remained loyal to the Union. Harney was from Tennessee and Cooke was a Virginian. Both continued to serve in the United States Army, with Cooke declaring, "I owe Virginia nothing, I owe my country everything."

Capt. John Buford, 2nd Dragoons, pictured in early 1861. Not long after this photograph was taken, Buford was promoted to major and was transferred to the inspector general's office.

Dennis Buttacavoli

Buford and his regiment of Regulars, having been re-designated the 2nd U.S. Cavalry, traveled from Fort Leavenworth, Kansas, to Washington, D.C., where they arrived in October of 1861. There, Buford requested and received an appointment as a major in the inspector general's office. He served in that position until June of 1862, a role that did not fully suit his temperament and abilities. Simply put, Buford languished there until Maj. Gen. John Pope learned of his plight. Pope had served with Buford in the "old" army, knew him well, and was surprised to find Buford deskbound in the nation's capital. He asked the dragoon how he could remain in such a position with a war raging, and inquired whether Buford had any objection to being assigned to a field command. Buford "seemed hurt" that Pope could doubt his desire to take the field, and he told Pope "he had tried to get a command, but was without influence enough to accomplish it." In what was perhaps his best decision as an army commander, Pope rescued Buford from oblivion as a staff officer and ordered him to report for assignment to the Army of Virginia on July 27, 1862. The move resulted in a promotion to brigadier general of volunteers and an assignment to command the reserve cavalry brigade attached to Maj. Gen. Nathaniel P. Banks' infantry corps.[19]

Buford served with distinction during the Second Bull Run campaign, which included a large-scale engagement with Confederate cavalry at the Lewis Ford on Bull Run creek on August 30, 1862, during the closing hours of Second Bull Run. Buford covered the army's chaotic retreat and led a bold mounted charge that drove several regiments of Confederate cavalry before a Rebel counterattack routed Buford's troopers. This was John Buford's first important contribution as a cavalry commander, and it also represented the first time the blue cavalry stood up to Maj. Gen. James E. B. Stuart in a toe-to-toe fight. Unfortunately, a spent ball struck Buford on the right knee. The severe contusion that resulted forced him to go on sick leave for a few days to recover.[20]

19 See Buford's Appointments, Commissions, and Pension File from the National Archives ("ACP File"). It is interesting to note that the first entries in the service record are from May of 1862, leading to the conclusion that Buford did little of note during the opening phases of the war; Maj. Gen. John Pope, "The Second Battle of Bull Run," in Robert U. Johnson and C. C. Buel. eds., *Battles and Leaders of the Civil War*, 4 vols. (New York: 1884-88), 2:491; Buford ACP File.

20 Much of the discussion of Buford's role in the Second Bull Run campaign goes well beyond the scope of this article and will not be addressed here. For more information on

Buford learned much from his experiences at Second Bull Run, including perhaps his most important lesson: he did not commit his entire force to the fight at Lewis Ford, and ultimately lost as a result. This defeat reinforced his dragoon training that mounted charges were not always the most effective means of employing cavalry. These lessons stuck, and he made good use of them throughout the remainder of his career.

Buford's greatest service during the Second Bull Run campaign, his outstanding work gathering intelligence, passed largely unnoticed. Some of his men came within a whisker of nabbing Stuart himself, but had to content themselves with capturing his famed plumed hat. On August 29, Buford observed the passage of James Longstreet's command through Thoroughfare Gap and reported this fact. The intelligence was forwarded to Pope's second-in-command, Maj. Gen. Irvin McDowell, who failed to forward the dispatch on to Pope. The news established beyond a doubt that Longstreet's divisions were on hand at Manassas and prepared to enter the fight. If Pope had properly interpreted the neglected dispatch, the ensuing disaster that befell his army the next day may well have been averted. That others ignored Buford's warning was not his fault. Nevertheless, Buford learned once more the importance of scouting and the delaying effect dismounted cavalry could have against advancing infantry.[21]

Buford was one of but a handful of Pope's senior commanders to remain in good standing after the ill-fated army commander's downfall following his Second Bull Run defeat. Buford's connection with the short-lived Army of Virginia, however, probably prevented him from attaining the high rank he deserved. Less than a month after being wounded at Second Bull Run he was appointed chief of cavalry of Maj. Gen. George B. McClellan's Army of the Potomac and led the army's mounted arm during the ensuing Antietam campaign. Unfortunately, the assignment was a purely administrative position and did not entail a field command. Buford once again found himself riding a desk. He was attached to the Army of the Potomac's headquarters at Antietam on September 17, 1862, and was present when Maj. Gen. Joseph Hooker was

---

Buford's role there, see John J. Hennessy, *Return to Bull Run* (New York: 1992), 430-34; Myles Keogh, "Etat de Service of Major Gen. Jno. Buford from his promotion to Brig. Gen'l. to his death," Archives, United States Military Academy, West Point, New York, Cullum, *Officers and Graduates of the U.S. Military Academy*, 2:354.

21 Ibid., 233-234.

Brig. Gen. John Buford, commander, 1st Division, Cavalry Corps, Army of the Potomac.
Library of Congress

wounded early in the battle. When he heard Hooker announce that it was his wish that Maj. Gen. George G. Meade command his corps in his absence, Buford rode back to army headquarters and informed McClellan, who issued the necessary orders.[22]

Following the tactical stalemate along Antietam Creek, Buford was assigned to McClellan's staff until that officer was relieved of command on November 7, 1862, in favor of Buford's old friend Maj. Gen. Ambrose E. Burnside. Buford once again served briefly as chief of cavalry from December 1862 until February 28, 1863, and retained this position during the army's winter encampment at Falmouth, Virginia, after the disastrous Fredericksburg campaign.[23]

In February 1863, General Burnside was removed and Joe Hooker elevated to command the Army of the Potomac. Hooker ordered that all of the cavalry forces assigned to the army be massed into a single corps. Buford's old and close friend, Maj. Gen. George Stoneman, assumed command of the newly formed Cavalry Corps. To his displeasure, Buford was serving on court-martial duty in Washington, D.C., that month, an unpleasant responsibility that would not end until the third week of March despite his repeated requests to be released. On February 9, Buford penned a revealing letter to his old friend Stoneman. "I have heard that all of the cavalry of the Army of the Potomac is to be massed under your command. I take it for granted that I am to have a command under you," he candidly acknowledged. "Being absent while you are making your organizations, I am a little afraid that the different brigade commanders being on the ground may succeed in getting the fighting regiments leaving me the less desirable ones. There is a great difference in the Reg'ts—some will stay while others will not under any circumstances. If I can have my choice I would prefer Western troops," he continued. "If the Regulars

---

22 Gibbon, "The John Buford Memoir."

23 Cullum, *Officers and Graduates of the U.S. Military Academy*, 2:354. See Buford's ACP File for references to his various commands and postings with the Army of the Potomac. The ACP File shows his two brief stints as cavalry chief for the Army of the Potomac, but this service was limited by the promotion of Maj. Gen. George Stoneman to command of the Army of Potomac's Cavalry Corps, as well as by the nature of the Fredericksburg campaign and the fact that the Army of the Potomac went into its winter quarters shortly after completion of the campaign.

are to be put together, I believe they would prefer me to either of the other cavalry commanders."[24]

Buford got his wish. When he was finally released from the unwelcome court-martial duty, Stoneman assigned the old dragoon to command the Reserve Brigade. Buford's new outfit consisted of the four regiments of U.S. Army Regular cavalry assigned to the Army of the Potomac, which included Buford's former regiment, the 2nd U.S. Cavalry. The Reserve Brigade began as an independent command, but became a permanent part of the First Cavalry Division in May of 1863.

Stoneman led the Cavalry Corps on a long and unsuccessful raid during the Chancellorsville campaign. The operation drew the ire of General Hooker, who tried to make Stoneman the scapegoat for his disastrous defeat at Chancellorsville in early May. Stoneman left the Army of the Potomac on medical leave on May 15 and never returned. Brigadier General Alfred Pleasonton, the senior subordinate and commander of the First Division, succeeded Stoneman in command of the Cavalry Corps. With Pleasonton's ascension to corps command, Buford became commander of the First Division.[25]

By the end of May 1863, John Buford was poised to play a significant role in the coming Gettysburg campaign. By the time of the great battle Buford was 37 years old and one of the best cavalry officers in the Union army. "A dashing officer, he inspired his men," recalled a friend. "His cry was go ahead booming."[26]

The hardships of many years of service, however, had taken their toll on Buford. "He suffered terribly from rheumatism," explained Gibbon, "and for days could not mount a horse without help, but once mounted, he would remain in the saddle all day." He was also a man of few words, full of energy, and as Army of the Potomac artillerist Col. Charles S. Wainwright later wrote, was "never looking after his own comfort, untiring on the march and in the supervision of his command, quiet and unassuming in his manners." One of Buford's West Point classmates recalled that "he had a good deal of

24 John Buford to George Stoneman, February 9, 1863, Letters Sent and Received, First Cavalry Division, Army of the Potomac, National Archives, Washington, D. C.

25 For a detailed discussion of these events, see Eric J. Wittenberg, *The Union Cavalry Comes of Age: Hartwood Church to Brandy Station 1863* (Dulles, VA: 2003), 236-238.

26 "A Present to the Post," *Rock Island Argus*, May 26, 1897.

A previously unpublished image of Col. William Gamble, taken in 1862, when he was the lieutenant colonel of the 8th Illinois Cavalry. He commanded Buford's 1st Brigade at Gettysburg.

Marshall Krolick

humor—not of the funny kind, but a little sarcastic. If he saw something humorous, he would smile, look at it, and make some passing remark about it."[27]

"He is one of the best officers of [the Union cavalry] and is a singular-looking party . . . a compactly built man of middle height, with a tawny mustache and a little triangular gray eye, whose expression is determined, not to say sinister," wrote Lt. Col. Theodore Lyman, who left one of the best descriptions of the cavalryman about to enjoy the finest day of his career. Lyman, who joined Maj. Gen. George G. Meade's staff during the fall of 1863, continued: "His [Buford's] ancient corduroys are tucked into a pair of ordinary cowhide boots and his blue blouse is ornamented with holes; from one pocket thereof peeps a huge pipe, while the other is fat with a tobacco pouch. Notwithstanding this get-up, he is a very soldierly looking man. He is of a good natured disposition but not to be trifled with." Lyman offered a prime example of the latter observation: "[Buford] caught a notorious spy last winter and hung him to the next tree, with this inscription: 'This man is to hang three days; he who cuts him down before shall hang the remaining time.'"

---

27 Gibbon, "The John Buford Memoir"; Allan Nevins. ed., *A Diary of Battle, The Personal Journals of Colonel Charles S. Wainwright, 1861-1865* (New York: 1962), 258; William B. Styple, ed., *Generals in Bronze: Interviewing the Commanders of the Civil War* (Kearny, NJ: 2005), 111.

Lyman went on to note that Buford had "a great reputation for cool daring, and is good-hearted withal.[28]

"Probably no officer of the Cavalry Corps was more honored, respected, and loved than he; a most gallant and efficient officer, of a pleasant and genial nature, cool in action, and always quick to see mistakes of the enemy and to take advantage of them," recalled Capt. Jerome B. Wheeler of the 6th New York Cavalry. "His movements were planned with deliberation and executed most brilliantly, but never coupled with rashness."[29]

"Everyone knows that he 'in his day' was first and foremost," declared Lt. Aaron B. Jerome, who served as Buford's signal officer at Gettysburg. Another of his soldiers described Buford as "straight forward, honest, conscientious, full of good common sense, and always to be relied upon in any emergency . . . decidedly the best cavalry officer in the Army of the Potomac." While no match for his rival Jeb Stuart in flair, Buford, in his tattered old hunting shirt and worn corduroys, was popular with his men and trusted as a competent leader. Perhaps most tellingly, Buford's comrades regularly referred to him as either "Old Steadfast" or "Honest John."[30]

The First Division Buford now commanded consisted of three brigades. The First Brigade, under Col. William Gamble, included some of the finest volunteer cavalrymen in the Union army. Colonel Gamble was born at Duross, County Tyrone, Ireland, on January 1, 1818, and spoke with the distinctive brogue of the Emerald Isle for the rest of his life. He studied civil engineering and from age 15 to 20 worked in the Queen's surveying office mapping Northern Ireland. He practiced his trade until he immigrated to the United States in 1838. One year after arriving he enlisted in the 1st U.S. Dragoons as a private and was quickly promoted to sergeant major. Gamble served for five

---

28 George R. Agassiz, ed., *Meade's Headquarters 1863-1865: Letters of Colonel Theodore Lyman from the Wilderness to Appomattox* (Boston: 1922), 21; David W. Lowe, ed., *Meade's Army: The Private Notebooks of Lt. Col. Theodore Lyman* (Kent, OH: 2007), 34.

29 Hillman A. Hall, ed., *History of the Sixth New York Cavalry* (Worcester, 1908), 377.

30 David L. Ladd and Audrey J. Ladd, eds., *The Bachelder Papers: Gettysburg in Their Own Words*, 3 vols. (Dayton, OH, 1995), 1:202; Edward G. Longacre, *The Cavalry at Gettysburg: A Tactical Study of Mounted Operations During the Civil War's Pivotal Campaign, 9 June-14 July 1863* (East Rutherford, NJ: 1986), 51. A trooper of the 8th Illinois Cavalry declared, "General Buford . . . many of us claim, was the best cavalry officer ever produced on this continent." James A. Bell to Gusta Ann Halluck, July 11, 1863, Bell Papers, Huntington Library, San Marino, California. Lieutenant Colonel Lyman called him the "model commander." Agassiz, *Meade's Headquarters*, 21; Buford, *Genealogy of the Buford Family*, 313.

years, participated in the Seminole Wars in Florida and against Indians at Forts Leavenworth and Gibson, and was honorably discharged in 1843. Two years earlier in 1841 Gamble married Sophia Steingrandt. The couple produced either 13 or 15 children, depending upon which account is accepted.[31]

When he left the army, Gamble settled in Chicago and resumed his former career in civil engineering as an employee of the Chicago Board of Public Works, where he was involved with the Chicago canal and river system. He also helped found the Indiana Street Methodist Church, which was the first church of that denomination north of the Chicago River. In 1859 the Gamble family moved to Evanston, where the home Gamble built currently houses the Anthropology Department of Northwestern University. While living in Evanston, he became involved with the Methodist church established by the founders of Northwestern University.

The day after the surrender of Fort Sumter in April 1861, an abolitionist group held a meeting in that church. Congressman John F. Farnsworth, an Illinois Republican and Abraham Lincoln's personal friend, was recruiting at the president's request. Many of the men in attendance enlisted to help put down the rebellion, forming the nucleus of what would become known the 8th Illinois Cavalry. Gamble knew his military experience would be valuable, and he left his lucrative business to enlist as a drill sergeant in the new regiment. "His services in drilling the 8th were of great value, and did much to make it what it became, a model of discipline and terribleness," noted an early biographer. Gamble's son George also enlisted and was commissioned a lieutenant.[32]

Gamble was commissioned lieutenant colonel of the 8th Illinois Cavalry on September 5, 1861, and often led the regiment, gaining notoriety as both a fearless and capable leader. In an order to his regiment, Gamble set forth his leadership philosophy. "The first duty of a soldier is a prompt and cheerful obedience to all lawful orders," he declared, "and no one is fit to command in any capacity, that is not himself willing to obey." Not everyone who served

---

31 Ezra J. Warner, *Generals in Blue: Lives of the Union Commanders* (Baton Rouge, 1964), 165; T. M. Eddy, *The Patriotism of Illinois*, 2 vols. (Chicago, 1865), 1:557; Warner, *Generals in Blue*, 165.

32 Eddy, *The Patriotism of Illinois*, 1:557. The 8th Illinois Cavalry became one of the finest mounted units in the entire Union service. Three of its original complement of officers—John F. Farnsworth, Gamble, and Elon J. Farnsworth—became full rank brigadier generals of volunteers during the Civil War, and another five—John L. Beveridge, Daniel Dustin, David Clendennin, John Waite, and George A. Forsyth—received brevets to brigadier general of volunteers. The talent pool for this regiment was wide and deep.

Col. Thomas C. Devin, commander of Buford's 2nd Brigade. The New York-born Devin
was a house painter with no formal military training, but proved to be one of the
most effective cavalrymen in the Army of the Potomac.

Library of Congress

under Gamble admired him. "Col Gamble [is] an inefficient old fool," groused
a trooper of the 3rd Indiana Cavalry not long after the end of the Gettysburg
campaign. This was not, however, the majority view of the old dragoon.[33]

33 Order no. 14, November 11, 1861, in 8th Illinois Order and Log Books, RG94, National
Archives; Edward C. Reid, Diary, July 22, 1863, Edward C. Reid Papers, Illinois State Historical
Society, Springfield, Illinois.

When Col. John J. Farnsworth, the organizer of the 8th Illinois, was promoted to brigadier general in 1862, Gamble was promoted to colonel of the regiment. He led his Illinois troopers through the Peninsula campaign of 1862, and was badly wounded with a round in the chest leading a charge at Malvern Hill on August 5, 1862. The serious injury disabled the Irishman until December of that year. Gamble returned to duty just in time to participate in the disastrous battle of Fredericksburg that month, though he suffered from regular hemorrhages from his lungs, and would for the rest of his life. By January 1, 1863, he was in command of a brigade, but took ill again in the spring of 1863 and could not return to duty until shortly after the June 9, 1863, Brandy Station combat, when he assumed command of the 1st Brigade. Gamble's extensive experience with dragoon tactics would pay huge dividends at Gettysburg.[34]

Gamble's First Brigade consisted of the 8th New York Cavalry, the 8th Illinois Cavalry, half of the 3rd Indiana Cavalry (Companies A, B, C, D, E, and F, otherwise known as the regiment's Right Wing), and four companies of the 12th Illinois Cavalry. These veteran troopers had seen combat throughout the war, and three of its units—the 8th New York, the 8th Illinois, and the 3rd Indiana—fought hard at Brandy Station.[35]

Colonel Thomas C. Devin of New York commanded Buford's Second Brigade. Devin was born in New York City to Irish immigrant parents on December 10, 1822. Following an education in the city's public schools, Devin formed a partnership with his brother painting homes and selling varnish, paint, and oils. Since his boyhood, Devin was enamored with the martial life and watched wide-eyed with other lads as local militia marched in parades and provided pomp for public ceremonies. When of sufficient age, Devin joined the neighborhood's company of militia cavalry and eventually rose through the ranks to command it as captain. An accomplished horseman, he garnered a reputation as an ideal cavalryman even though he had, as yet, no practical

---

34 Jack D. Welsh, M.D., *Medical Histories of Union Generals* (Kent, 1997), 122.

35 The Left Wing of the 3rd Indiana Cavalry—Companies G, H, I, K, L, and M—served in the Western Theater. The two wings never served together during the war. Likewise, the 12th Illinois Cavalry had been split up. A portion of the regiment was part of the Union garrison that occupied Yorktown, Virginia, during the summer of 1863. Frederick H. Dyer, *A Compendium of the War of the Rebellion*, 2 vols. (Des Moines, 1908), 1:1029.

battlefield experience. On March 4, 1861, Devin was promoted to lieutenant colonel and to the command of the 1st New York State Militia Cavalry.[36]

A staunch patriot, Devin ached to play an active role in the Civil War the moment it broke out. On July 12, he sought out strong-arm New York political boss Thurlow Weed. If anyone could get him into the action, Devin reasoned, it was Weed. He found him one evening on the steps of one of the city's landmarks, the Astor House, and although a stranger to the well-connected and powerful politico, Devin boldly approached him and asked for his support. The episode made an impression on Weed, who later recalled that Devin "informed me that he desired to raise a company of cavalry, which, if he could obtain the authority, should be organized and ready to march in three days." Devin obviously had his own militia in mind, which was already outfitted and well drilled. "I was so favorably impressed with his bearing and manner that I immediately telegraphed Governor [Edwin] Morgan, earnestly asking his authority for Thos. C. Devin to organize a cavalry corps."

At the time, however, Devin refused to leave Weed's presence. "[Devin] remained at my room until a favorable response from the Governor, two hours afterward, was received," continued Weed, "and he was also faithful to his promise, for in three days, with a full company of men, he was on his way to the front." On July 19, 1861, Devin was mustered in for three months as captain of Devin's Independent Company of New York State Militia Cavalry. The 100 mounted men from his former regiment preferred to call themselves the "Jackson Horse Guards," and took pride in the distinction of being the first unit of volunteer cavalry to arrive in Washington for service in the field.

Following a short stint on the staff of Brig. Gen. Isaac Stevens, Devin was commissioned colonel of the 6th New York Cavalry, also known as the 2nd Ira Harris Guards, on November 18, 1861. The 6th New York performed good service during the Antietam campaign, and following the Fredericksburg defeat Devin assumed command of a brigade under Alfred Pleasonton, who regularly and fruitlessly urged his promotion to brigadier general. Devin's "command was long known in the Army of the Potomac as one of the few cavalry regiments which in the earlier campaigns of that Army, could be deemed thoroughly reliable," observed an early historian of the Cavalry Corps. A

36 "General Thomas C. Devin," *New York Times*, April 5, 1878.

A previously unpublished image of Capt. Seymour Beach Conger, the Ohio-born commander of the detachment of the 3rd West Virginia Cavalry assigned to Devin's brigade. Conger was killed in action in 1864.

Rick Wolfe

healthy mutual respect and attachment developed between John Buford and Devin.[37]

"I can't teach Col. Devin anything about cavalry," Buford once said. "He knows more about the tactics than I do." Buford trusted Devin implicitly and often placed his troopers in the toughest spots. Another said of Devin that he was "of the school of Polonius, a little slow sometimes in entrance to a fight, but, being in, as slow to leave a point for which the enemy is trying." The modest Devin inspired the highest regard in those who knew him, and often understated his role in his reports, which probably held him back from richly-deserved promotions.[38]

"To see him on the battlefield, absolutely self-poised, to see the look of determination on his face as he placed himself in command of his regiment when the charge was to be made, to hear his clear, ringing tones amid the clash of sabers and the rattle of carbines and musketry, was to understand something of his value as a soldier," recalled a sergeant of the 6th New York Cavalry. "Among the brilliant officers who led our cavalry squadrons to victory, few, if any, excelled our beloved commander."[39]

---

37 Warner, *Generals in Blue*, 124. That promotion did not come until the spring of 1865, and was long overdue when it finally happened; Henry Edwin Tremain, *The Last Hours of Sheridan's Cavalry* (New York, 1904), 37. The fact that Devin was not a West Pointer undoubtedly impeded the progress of his military career.

38 Longacre, *The Cavalry at Gettysburg*, 51; Frederic C. Newhall, *With General Sheridan in Lee's Last Campaign* (Philadelphia: J. B. Lippincott, 1866), 228; Styple, *Generals in Bronze*, 109.

39 Alonzo Foster, *Reminiscences and Record of the 6th New York V.V. Cavalry* (New York: privately published, 1892), 129.

Lt. John H. Calef, commander, Battery A, 2nd U.S. Artillery. Calef, who was 23 years old on July 1, 1863, served in the U.S. Army for nearly 40 years.

USAHEC

"His manner was at times brusque and stern, but he possessed a kind heart and was always just, tender and sympathetic to those who merited such consideration," recalled one of his officers of the 6th New York. "He despised a shirk, or one tainted with the least hypocrisy or dishonesty, but was quick to redress the wrongs of any officer or enlisted man in his command. A Democrat politically, he was grandly loyal to his country and its flag."[40]

Perhaps the finest accolade paid to him was that "Colonel Devin knew how to take his men into action and also how to bring them out." At 40, Devin was older than most of the other Union cavalry commanders, but he had experience and was always reliable under fire. "His blunt soldiership, sound judgment, his prompt and skillful dispositions for battle, his long period of active service, his bulldog tenacity, and his habitual reliability fully entitled him to the sobriquet among his officers and soldiers of the old 'war horse,' 'Sheridan's hard hitter,' and the like," observed one of Maj. Gen. Philip H. Sheridan's staff officers after the end of the war. Devin, explained Pleasonton, "was a good soldier and a hard fighter." By the time the war ended, Tom Devin participated in 72 skirmishes and battles. Devin's veteran brigade consisted of his 6th New York, the 8th Pennsylvania, the 17th Pennsylvania, and two companies, A and C, of the 3rd West Virginia Cavalry commanded by Ohioan Capt. Seymour Beach Conger.[41]

40 Hall, *History of the Sixth New York Cavalry*, 392.

41 Warner, *Generals in Blue*, 124; Tremain, *The Last Hours of Sheridan's Cavalry*, 39; Styple, *Generals in Bronze*, 116; "General Thomas C. Devin." Conger's brother, Everton J. Conger, was also

Buford also had a battery of horse artillery attached to his command. Lieutenant John H. Calef commanded Battery A, 2nd U.S. Artillery, which consisted of six 3-inch ordnance rifles, a light but highly accurate gun tube that could easily keep up with cavalry. The battery was organized into three sections of two guns each. John H. Calef was born in Gloucester, Massachusetts, on September 24, 1841. He hailed from a long line of Calefs who had settled in New England in the 1700s. His grandfather, Col. John Calef, of Kingston, New Hampshire, led a unit in the Continental Army during the Revolutionary War.[42]

At 17, Calef entered West Point as a cadet and graduated 22nd in the Class of 1862. Ironically, he finished just five slots from the bottom of his class in artillery tactics, but he soon proved that, in spite of his low grade, he had learned his lessons well. He was commissioned a second lieutenant in the 5th Artillery on June 17, 1862. Calef quickly demonstrated a real talent for artillery, serving in the 1862 Peninsula campaign, at Second Bull Run, and and at Antietam during the 1862 Maryland campaign. On October 6, Calef, who was also a skilled horseman, was transferred to the 2nd Artillery and officially joined the horse artillery. By the spring of 1863 he was in command of Battery A, 2nd U.S. Artillery. The talented and well-liked professional artillerist earned the respect of everyone who served with him, and would ultimately spend nearly four decades in the Regular Army.[43]

John Buford's new command had 2,704 officers and men and another 81 horse artillerists. With 1,596 officers and men Gamble had the larger of the two brigades that would participate at Gettysburg on the first day of July, with

---

commissioned as an officer in the 3rd West Virginia Cavalry. He was later commissioned lieutenant colonel of the 1st District of Columbia Cavalry. He was badly wounded in battle in 1864, which rendered him incapable of further service in the field. Everton Conger joined Gen. Lafayette Baker's intelligence service as a detective. It was in this role that he tracked John Wilkes Booth into Virginia after the assassination of Abraham Lincoln in April 1865. Conger set fire to the barn where Booth was trapped, and was present when Sgt. Boston Corbett mortally wounded Booth.

42 With conventional, or mounted, artillery, teams of horses or mules pull the guns, caissons, and limber chests. The men who man those guns either walk or they ride on the limber chests or the caissons. With horse artillery, each member of the gun crew has his own horse or mule and rides that animal so the artillerists can keep up with cavalry. Some refer to horse artillery as "flying artillery." The tubes for the 3-inch ordnance rifles weighted only 800 pounds each, which made them highly mobile and appropriate for use with cavalry. J. David Petruzzi, "Faded Thunder," http://petruzzi.wordpress.com/2007/02/23/faded-thunder/.

43 James S. Robbins, *Last in Their Class: Custer, Pickett and the Goats of West Point* (New York, 2006), 235; Cullum, *Officers and Graduates of the U.S. Military Academy*, 2:582.

Devin's smaller brigade fielding 1,108 officers and men. As noted earlier, Buford was missing his favorite brigade, Wesley Merritt's Reserve Brigade, which would have added another 1,317 veteran Regular Army horse soldiers to the force that was about to meet its fate on the hills north and west of Gettysburg.[44]

44 J. David Petruzzi and Steven Stanley, *The Gettysburg Campaign in Numbers and Losses: Synopses, Orders of Battle, Strengths, Casualties, and Maps, June 9-July 14, 1863* (El Dorado Hills, CA, 2013), 117.

Chapter 2

Marching
to Pennsylvania

After thrashing Maj. Gen. Joseph Hooker's Army of the Potomac at Chancellorsville by utilizing a risky maneuver—splitting his army in the face of a numerically superior enemy—Gen. Robert E. Lee met with other members of the Confederate high command in a series of meetings in Richmond to discuss how best to follow up the victory. After three days of extremely intensive dialogue, Lee persuaded President Jefferson Davis that the time had come to seize the operational initiative once again. It was time for a greater gamble than dividing his army and launching another bold flanking attack. The time had come for a second invasion of the North. Confederate Secretary of War James A. Seddon later reported that Lee's opinion "naturally had great effect in the decisions of the Executive."[1]

Lee's bold arguments rested on the basic assumption that a northward thrust would serve a variety of purposes. First, it held the potential of relieving Federal pressure on the beleaguered Southern garrison at Vicksburg. Second, it would provide the people of Virginia with an opportunity to recover from "the ravages of war and a chance to harvest their crops free from interruption by military operation"; Third, it would to draw Hooker's army away from its base at Falmouth, giving Lee an opportunity to defeat it in the open field on Northern soil. Finally, Lee wanted to spend the summer months in Pennsylvania in the hope of leveraging the political gain that would come with a successful invasion. Once Davis approved Lee's audacious plan to invade

---

1 Jeffry D. Wert, *Cavalryman of the Lost Cause: A Biography of J.E.B. Stuart* (New York: 2008), 234.

Robert E. Lee, commander of the Army of Northern Virginia.
Library of Congress

Pennsylvania, the Southern commander began planning to shift troops west for a strike north down the Shenandoah Valley. The operation commenced on June 3, when his infantry begin quietly slipping away from the area around Fredericksburg on their way to the Valley. Before the march began, Jeb Stuart arrived in Culpeper County on May 20 and established his headquarters there to oversee the concentration of the Confederate cavalry in preparation for the operation.[2] Within a few days, three brigades of Southern horse soldiers arrived and established their camps in the county's lush fields. On June 9, General Pleasonton led the entire Army of the Potomac Cavalry Corps into Culpeper County to destroy or disperse the concentration of Southern cavalry. The move culminated in the Battle of Brandy Station, by far the largest cavalry battle ever fought on the North American continent. John Buford, in command of the First Division of the Cavalry Corps, was in charge of the right wing of the Union force.

Buford performed extremely well in the bloody and brutal action, where his troopers bore the brunt of the 14-hour fight and one of his brigade commanders was killed during the opening moments. Ultimately, the day's fighting proved inconclusive and the Union troopers withdrew from the field, leaving Stuart's large force bloodied but still intact. The bold surprise attack had failed.[3]

On the morning after the Brandy Station fight, Lt. Gen. Richard S. Ewell's Second Corps marched toward Winchester. The Third Corps under Lt. Gen. A. P. Hill and the First Corps under Lt. Gen. James Longstreet followed in Ewell's wake. On June 12, Ewell passed through Chester Gap and closed in on Winchester. After a sharp battle there, half of the Union garrison surrendered on June 14 and Ewell pressed on across the Potomac River into Maryland. On June 22, Ewell's leading elements crossed the Mason-Dixon Line and entered Pennsylvania. Longstreet, meanwhile, began moving up the Loudoun Valley on

---

2 Eric J. Wittenberg, *The Battle of Brandy Station: North America's Largest Cavalry Battle* (Charleston, 2010), 22.

3 A detailed discussion of the specifics of the Battle of Brandy Station strays far beyond the scope of this book. For a detailed study of this important engagement, see Wittenberg, *The Battle of Brandy Station*. One cannot help but wonder what might have happened had Lee's invasion of the north begun on June 9 as planned. It is possible that his army would have occupied Gettysburg on June 30, depriving the Army of the Potomac of the strong defensive position it assumed there.

Lt. Gen. Richard S. Ewell, commander of the Army of Northern Virginia's 2nd Corps. Gettysburg was Ewell's first major battle as a corps commander, and he did not perform well.

Library of Congress

June 15, feinting toward Leesburg. Elements of Ewell's Corps occupied Carlisle on June 27 and York the following day.[4]

Once Ewell captured Winchester, Hooker finally realized Lee had shifted his army into the Valley and was about to invade the North. Hooker began

4   For readers interested in learning more about this aspect of the campaign, see Scott Mingus, Sr., *Flames Beyond Gettysburg: The Confederate Expedition to the Susquehanna River, June 1863* (El Dorado Hills, CA: 2011).

shifting his troops in response between June 14 and 17, all the while keeping his Army of the Potomac interposed between Lee's Army of Northern Virginia and the national capital at Washington, D.C. The blue-clad infantry cautiously pursued Lee's army north and east, uncertain of Lee's intentions or destination. The Cavalry Corps served as the tip of the Union spear as it began pursuing the moving Confederate enemy.

Civil War cavalry had three main missions: scouting, screening, and intelligence gathering. Scouting entailed finding routes of march for the army. Screening, a harder task, required interposing the cavalry between the main body of the army and the enemy in an effort to keep the enemy from finding that main body. These were important missions, but no mission was more important than intelligence gathering. "There are no more important duties, which an officer may be called upon to perform, than those of collecting and arranging the information upon which either the general, or daily operations of a campaign must be based," succinctly declared Dennis Hart Mahan, the West Point instructor who had taught John Buford.[5] How well Mahan's former student would perform this duty during the Gettysburg campaign remained to be seen.

The competing cavalry forces spent the period from June 10-21 jousting continuously, with Stuart doing his best to keep the active and probing Union cavalry away from the main body of Lee's army. The first significant engagement occurred at Aldie in Virginia's Loudoun Valley on June 17, and the second outside Middleburg a few miles west just two days later. On June 21, the Union Cavalry Corps scored its first significant battlefield victory over Stuart's veteran troopers at Upperville, assisted by a reinforcing brigade of infantry that delivered the decisive blow. Buford's division carried the bulk of the fight at Upperville, besting two brigades of Confederate cavalry and horse artillery in a hard day-long fight.[6]

"Hooker, following up Lee's movements, with the mountains intervening, covered his left flank with his cavalry and horse batteries," wrote Buford's West Point classmate and friend, Capt. John C. Tidball, the commander of a battalion of horse artillery. "These two opposing cavalry forces were in constant

---

5 Dennis H. Mahan, *An Elementary Treatise on Advanced-Guard, Out-Post, and Detachment Service of Troops, and the Manner of Posting and Handling Them in the Presence of an Enemy* (New York: 1861), 105.

6 For specifics on the battle of Aldie, Middleburg, and Upperville, see Robert F. O'Neill, Jr., *The Cavalry Battles of Aldie, Middleburg and Upperville: Small but Important Riots, June 10-27, 1863* (Lynchburg, 1993).

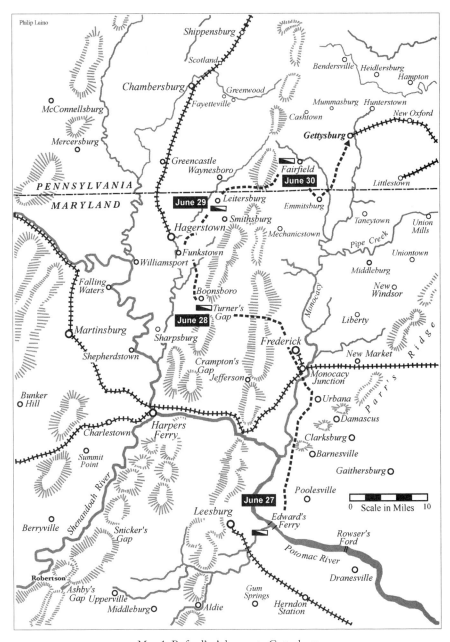

Map 1: Buford's Advance to Gettysburg

collision, resulting in many skirmishes and combats, some of which, as those of Beverly Ford, Aldie and Upperville, approximated the dignity of battle."[7] Stuart's horsemen did fine service keeping the active and probing Union cavalry away from Lee's army as it advanced down the Shenandoah Valley toward the Potomac River.

On June 22, the day after the fighting at Upperville, Pleasonton ordered his Cavalry Corps to give up the ground for which it had fought so hard and withdraw to Aldie. There, Pleasonton gave his command some much-needed rest. Although Tom Devin's brigade spent the afternoon of June 22 skirmishing with Confederate cavalry near Snickersville, Virginia, for the most part Pleasonton's troopers spent the next few days resting and refitting around Aldie. After nearly constant marching and fighting since the beginning of the Stoneman Raid on May 1, the weary blue-clad troopers welcomed the brief respite. While the cavalry rested, Hooker set his army in motion northward in earnest. While the Federal cavalry rested and refitted, however, much of Stuart's cavalry slipped past them, starting what would be a very controversial eight-day expedition.[8]

The bulk of the Army of the Potomac crossed the Potomac at Edwards Ferry, near Leesburg, on June 25-26. By June 29, the last elements had crossed over into Maryland. When Lee learned from a spy employed by Longstreet that the entire Union army was in Maryland, he recalled Ewell's Second Corps from near Harrisburg, Pennsylvania, and ordered the concentration of his army at Cashtown. Longstreet's First Corps entered the Shenandoah Valley through Ashby's and Snicker's gaps and crossed the Potomac at Williamsport on June 25-26. His corps marched through Chambersburg and arrived in Fayetteville on June 27 and Cashtown two days later. A. P. Hill's Third Corps, meanwhile, left Culpeper on June 18, crossed the Potomac at Shepherdstown on June 23, and then crossed into Maryland. His command marched from Boonsboro to Fayettsville, where it arrived on June 27.

Elements of Lee's army entered a crossroads town near the Mason-Dixon Line named Gettysburg on June 26. There, troopers of the 35th Battalion of

---

7 John C. Tidball, *The Artillery Service in the War of the Rebellion 1861-1865*, ed. Lawrence M. Kaplan (Yardley, PA: 2011), 157-158.

8 For a detailed discussion of the controversy surrounding Stuart's expedition during the Gettysburg Campaign, see Eric J. Wittenberg and J. David Petruzzi, *Plenty of Blame to Go Around: Jeb Stuart's Controversial Ride to Gettysburg* (El Dorado Hills, CA: 2006).

Virginia Cavalry and soldiers of Maj. Gen. Jubal A. Early's division of Ewell's Second Corps looted the town and terrorized its inhabitants, scattering a scratch force of emergency militia troops in the process. While this took place, Pleasonton dispatched Buford's division north from Aldie, Virginia, to the mouth of the Monocacy River with orders to cross the Potomac at Edwards Ferry. Buford and his troopers made it as far as Leesburg, where the division camped for the night.[9] At 6:00 a.m. on June 27, Buford's division broke camp and forded the Potomac, passing the old Balls Bluff battlefield along the way. As one member of the 9th New York Cavalry of Devin's brigade recalled, "We were again off Virginia soil, and in 'my Maryland.'"[10]

Entering familiar territory in loyal Maryland, Buford's troopers rode north, crossed the Monocacy River, and camped at the foot of South Mountain near Jefferson. "We had been marching and counter-marching, camping and fighting on the slave-accursed and God-forsaken soils of old Virginia," recorded Lt. Marcellus E. Jones of the 8th Illinois Cavalry, "desolation and death marked the track of both armies, the country was nearly deserted, the inhabitants who could not get away never recognized our presence, hostile and bitter, they regarded us as invaders of their soil and enemies of them and their sacred rights."[11]

"On Sunday, June 28, we mounted early, and, under a summer Sabbath morning sun, shining alike upon lands at peace and at war, upon kneeling worshippers and mounted troopers, rode up the eastern slope of the Catoctin Range," was the fond recollection of Maj. John L. Beveridge, the commander of the 8th Illinois Cavalry. "From the summit a magnificent prospect met our view." Beveridge likened the panoramic sight to the view that Moses and Aaron saw of Canaan from Mt. Pisgah after 40 years of wandering the desert.[12] Buford's tired troopers were happy to be back on friendly soil. At the same

9   Abner N. Hard, *History of the Eighth Cavalry Regiment Illinois Volunteers, During the Great Rebellion* (Aurora, IL: privately published, 1868), 254; Newell Cheney, History of the Ninth Regiment, New York Volunteer Cavalry (Poland Center, NY: privately published, 1901), 132.

10 Newell Cheney, *History of the Ninth Regiment, New York Volunteer Cavalry* (Poland Center, NY: privately published, 1901), 132

11 The Marcellus E. Jones Journal, Perrin-Wheaton Chapter, National Society of the Daughters of the American Revolution, Wheaton, Illinois, June 27, 1863.

12   John L. Beveridge, "The First Gun at Gettysburg," *War Papers, Military Order of the Loyal Legion of the United States, Illinois Commandery* (Chicago: 1894), 2:87-88.

time, they recognized what was likely to be one of the most important fights of the war awaited them somewhere north of the Potomac River, and they grimly went about preparing for the task.

That same day John Harvey of Company M of the 9th New York Cavalry captured (and inexplicably released) a Rebel spy. Trooper Charles Whitney of Company F, also of the 9th New York, recaptured the spy the next day and took the man to Buford's headquarters in the Catoctin Valley near Frederick, Maryland. The cavalry commander was just then grappling with the news that three young captains, Wesley Merritt, Elon J. Farnsworth, and George A. Custer, had been promoted several grades to brigadier general, jumping past numerous officers much more senior to themselves. These young officers quickly became known as the three "boy generals."[13] The spy, a man named Will Talbot, was placed before Buford for a drum-head court-martial. On the way to Buford's headquarters, the spy attempted to talk his way out of his predicament by spinning an impressive yarn about the large family he supported. Buford's provost marshal, Lt. John Mix, smiled when he heard the tale and pointed out a lone tree to the man. When Talbot acknowledged seeing it, Mix blandly predicted the Rebel sympathizer would be hanging from one of its branches within five minutes.

After papers found on his body betrayed his intentions, Talbot admitted he was a member of Confederate Elijah V. White's 35th Battalion of Virginia Cavalry, and that he was scouting for General Lee. Buford promptly pronounced the spy guilty and, turning to Mix, said, "I guess you had best hang him." He also ordered the body be left to dangle for three days as a message to other potential spies. Talbot was hanged from the same tree Mix had pointed out on the way to Buford's headquarters.[14]

A number of the townspeople complained to Buford about the hanging of the spy, which they viewed as barbaric. Instead of summarily executing him, they asked, why not send the spy back to Washington where he could have been interrogated? Perhaps Buford was exhausted, or maybe a bit bitter about the promotion of the three "boy generals" after his own difficulties in obtaining a field command. Whatever the reason, Buford flashed some of his sarcastic

13 Cheney, *History of the Ninth Regiment*, 132.

14 Thomas J. Smith, "Two Spies Instead of One," *National Tribune*, May 1, 1884; John Kelly, "The Spy at Frederick, Maryland," *National Tribune*, February 9, 1888.

Gen. Alfred Pleasonton, commander, Cavalry Corps, Army of the Potomac.
Pleasonton ordered Buford to go to and hold Gettysburg. *Library of Congress*

humor and informed the citizens that "the man was a spy and he was afraid to send him to Washington because he knew that the authorities would make [the spy] a brigadier general."[15] Buford had little tolerance for civilians or spies, and

15 Henry P. Moyer, *History of the Seventeenth Regiment, Pennsylvania Volunteer Cavalry* (Lebanon, 1911), 58; J. McGardner, "Fighting Them Over," *National Tribune*, May 24, 1885 ("[O]n June 27 in Frederick City, Maryland. Buford stopped there long enough to hang a rebel spy or two."). John Kelly of Company F of the 2nd U.S. Cavalry recalled that Buford's comment about not sending the spy back to Washington was, "Well, if we send him a prisoner up to Washington, it's ten to one that he will be back inside of a month with a commission in his pocket." "The Spy at Frederick, Maryland," *National Tribune*, February 9, 1888. For more on the issue of

probably wanted to dispatch the callers as quickly as possible. His darkly humorous reply was his means of doing so. Most of the Army of the Potomac passed the corpse on its march north into Pennsylvania. The gruesome sight left quite an impression on them.

"I have always believed that if Talbot had got to Gen. Lee's headquarters with the information he had of our army," Charles Whitney of the 9th New York, the man who captured the spy, observed, "there never would have been a Battle of Gettysburg. Lee would have cut off our trains and gone to Baltimore." Buford would encounter Whitney in Gettysburg on the morning of July 1, where the trooper asked for permission to find a carbine and join the fighting west of town. Buford instead told Whitney to fall back, and that "I had done my country more service by capturing the spy than if I killed a whole brigade of rebels."[16]

Also on June 28, Hooker ordered "that the cavalry be sent well in advance of Frederick in the direction of Gettysburg and Emmitsburg and see what they can learn of the movements of the enemy."[17] In response, General Pleasonton deployed his three divisions of cavalry to feel for the enemy. He ordered Brig. Gen. David M. Gregg's Second Division to guard the army's right flank, and Brig. Gen. Judson Kilpatrick's Third Division to cover the army's center. Pleasonton instructed Buford to move from Middletown, Maryland, by way of Emmitsburg to Gettysburg, with orders to cover the army's left flank, and "hold Gettysburg at all hazards until supports arrive."[18]

Buford's men spent a quiet day near Middletown, shoeing their mounts and refitting equipment. Citizens reported that the Confederate army had crossed the Potomac at Williamsport and was in very strong force. One man reported counting nearly 100 pieces of artillery.[19] Late that day, word reached Buford's

---

Buford's treatment of spies during the Gettysburg Campaign, see Eric J. Wittenberg, "And Everything is Lovely and the Goose Hangs High: John Buford and the Hanging of Confederate Spies during the Gettysburg Campaign," *The Gettysburg Magazine: Articles of Lasting Historical Interest*, (January 1998), 18:5-14.

16 Thomas J. Smith, "Two Spies Instead of One."

17 Joseph Hooker to Maj. Gen. E. D. Townsend, September 28, 1875, Civil War Collection, Musselman Library, Gettysburg College, Gettysburg, Pennsylvania.

18 Walter Kempster, M.D., "The Cavalry at Gettysburg," Military Order of the Loyal Legion of the United States, Wisconsin Commandery, Read October 1, 1913, 399.

19 *The War of the Rebellion: A Compilation of the Official Records of the Union and Confederate Armies*, 128 volumes (Washington, D.C.: United States Government Printing Office, 1880-1901), vol.

camp that Hooker had asked to be relieved, and that Pennsylvanian George G. Meade, the commander of Fifth Corps, had replaced him.[20] The response throughout the army was mixed; Buford's response is not recorded.[21]

Buford's sarcastic side surfaced once again during that day's march. "During the march to Gettysburg," wrote Lt. James Wade of the 6th U.S. Cavalry, "General Buford led his command past a roadside hotel/tavern (in Maryland, I believe), and sitting out on the front porch were several secesh gentlemen. Gen. Buford," continued Wade, "knew the hard-marching Confederates would soon be in need of footwear, and asked where the nearest shoe factory was located. The seated secesh said, 'Wouldn't tell you if we knew.' Gen. Buford then turned to a sergeant and said, 'All-right, sergeant.' And then quicker than spit, each secesh gentleman had a cavalryman sitting upon his chest, while another trooper began pulling off the offender's boots."[22] It would be difficult to argue Buford was unwilling to do whatever it took to obtain the intelligence he needed about the location and disposition of the Army of Northern Virginia.

On the morning of June 29, Buford detached the Reserve Brigade, now commanded by his protégé, the newly promoted Wesley Merritt and, pursuant to Pleasonton's orders, sent it to Mechanicsville (modern-day Thurmont, Maryland) to escort the division's wagon trains and to protect the rear and bring up stragglers.[23] The First and Second Brigades left at 9:00 a.m., riding out along

27, part 1, 926, hereinafter referred to as *OR*. All further references are to Series 1 unless otherwise noted; Henry Norton, *Deeds of Daring: or History of the Eighth New York Volunteer Cavalry* (Norwich, NY: 1889), 68.

20 Hall, *History of the Sixth New York Cavalry*, 132.

21 Secretary of War Edwin M. Stanton called Hooker's bluff. Hooker threatened to resign if he was not given authority over the Federal garrison at Harpers Ferry. When Stanton refused the request, Hooker's request to be relieved of command was granted. President Lincoln ordered Meade to assume command of the army. Although Meade did not desire the command, he was a good soldier and obeyed the order.

22 Interview with Benjamin F. Wade, included in the James E. Kelly Papers, Archives, New York Historical Society, New York, New York.

23 The Reserve Brigade suffered 319 casualties at Brandy Station and took 63 additional losses at Upperville on June 21. It still had about 1,700 men present for duty on June 29, but its officer corps had been decimated. The brigade lost 21 of its 52 officers during this period, leaving only one officer per company. In short, attrition left it combat ineffective for a few days, and it needed time to reorganize and become accustomed to its new commander. Don Caughey, the historian of the Reserve Brigade, did an analysis of the reasons why the Regulars were sent to Mechanicsville over Buford's objections. "Why was the Reserve Brigade guarding wagon

the National Road. While it probably never registered in Buford's mind (he had more important things to occupy his thoughts), he was riding along the precise route used by his great-uncle Capt. Thomas Buford, who had helped build the road during the disastrous Braddock expedition of 1754. The irony probably would have struck Buford, had he known of it. His command passed over South Mountain via Turner's Gap at Boonsboro.

Buford's column headed for Cavetown and Monterey Springs, Maryland, following along the base of South Mountain heading toward Pennsylvania via the Monterey Pass. Major Beveridge declared, "this day's march was the most delightful of my army life. The day was perfect; the roads were good. We passed over the mountains twice, and had charming views." When the long column of dusty horsemen reached the Mason-Dixon Line, the guidon carrier of Company G of the 17th Pennsylvania of Devin's brigade sat astride the line, announcing to each company as it passed that it was entering the soil of their home state of Pennsylvania. The men of the 17th "raised their caps and lustily cheered, again and again, for the old Keystone State and Old Glory." "We crossed the Pennsylvania line in the afternoon, soon coming again into the mountains, beholding some wild and beautiful scenery, and receiving cordial expressions of pleasure from the inhabitants along the route," recounted a member of the 8th New York Cavalry. "We heard of the movements of the enemy all the way, they having passed through two or three days previous, seizing all the valuable horses they could find, but doing little other damage." The march north through Maryland was almost joyous. "As we came along up from the Potomac, each town we passed through had flags flying and citizens crowding the streets," recalled Eli Ditzler of the 8th Illinois Cavalry. "The ladies waved their handkerchiefs and the air was rent with cheer after cheer. Made me feel homesick to see how happy free people were."[24]

---

trains? The answer is simply attrition, of officers even more than enlisted men," he wrote. "By the end of June 1863, the brigade was simply fought out, and needed a day or two to reorganize before returning to the fight. During the preceding two months, each of its regiments averaged losses in excess of 15% of their enlisted strength and nearly half of their officers." By July 3, the Reserve Brigade, having had an opportunity to rest and reorganize itself, was ready to go into action, and it fought long and hard on South Cavalry Field at Gettysburg and at Fairfield that day. See Don Caughey, "Reserve Brigade Attrition in the Gettysburg Campaign," http://regularcavalryincivilwar.wordpress.com/2013/06/20/reserve-brigade-attrition-in-the-gettysburg-campaign/.

24 Beveridge, "The First Gun at Gettysburg," 88; Moyer, *History of the Seventeenth Regiment*, 48; "Genesee," "From the 8th Cavalry—List of Killed and Wounded," *Rochester Daily Union and*

Interestingly, Buford did not obey Pleasonton's orders for the march into Pennsylvania. Pleasonton had directed Buford to ride from Middletown through Beallsville, Wolfsville, and then Emmitsburg. Instead, Buford traveled a route father west through Boonsboro and Cavetown, Maryland, and then on to Monterey Springs and Fountaindale. Buford never explained why he diverged from Pleasonton's prescribed route, and Pleasonton never mentioned the lack of compliance with his orders.[25] Pleasonton and Buford knew each other very well, having served together in the old Second Dragoons for more than a decade before the Civil War. In all likelihood, Pleasonton trusted Buford to carry out the spirit, if not necessarily the letter, of his orders.

As the First Division drew closer to Gettysburg, Buford's attention turned to his primary mission of gathering as much intelligence as possible about the disposition of the enemy. The command rode on to the village of Fountaindale, situated at the eastern end of the important South Mountain route known as the Monterey Pass.[26] Buford's troopers happily found the area abounded "in forage and water for our jaded horses."[27] The tired men led their horses up "the long ascending road, winding its way around the sides of the rocky cliffs for over two miles until we reached the summit of the pass, and here we passed an institution of health called Monterey Springs."[28] They camped at the base of South Mountain after riding nearly 40 miles that day.[29]

Advertiser, July 9, 1863; Winfield Scott Hall, *The Captain: William Cross Hazelton* (Riverside, IL: privately published, 1994), 40-41.

25 *OR* 27, pt. 3, 400-401, and pt. 1, 926.

26 Just the day before, a detachment of Union cavalry from the 1st Potomac Home Brigade Cavalry, also known as Cole's Cavalry, encountered Confederate cavalry at Fountaindale, where they had a brief scrap. Lieutenant William A. Horner "went right through them, and came out at Boonsboro and from there to Waynesboro then over to Fountain Dale, where he encountered a squad of Johnnies gathering up horses and provisions. He charged them, captured several and ran the rest in Fairfield and from there to Emmitsburg." Captain Albert M. Hunter's account of the War between the States, Archives, Emmitsburg Historical Society, Emmitsburg, Maryland. For more about the little-known skirmish at Fountaindale on June 28, 1863, see John A. Miller, "The Skirmish of Fountaindale," http://southmountaincw. wordpress.com/2010/ 03/23/the-skirmish-of-fountaindale/.

27 Abner B. Frank, 12th Illinois Cavalry, Diary, June 30, 1863, U.S. Army History and Education Center, Carlisle, Pennsylvania.

28 Anonymous letter by a member of the 8th Illinois Cavalry, Aurora Beacon, August 20, 1863.

29 George H. Chapman Diary, June 29, 1863, Indiana Historical Society Library, Indianapolis, Indiana.

Many troopers recorded seeing an old man standing with his hat in his hand and tears streaming down his face as the Federal troopers trotted past. Buford and some of his staff rode to the top of nearby Jack's Mountain, where he took in the spectacular view of the Cumberland Valley sprawling below. His long gaze into gathering dusk convinced Buford that a major battle would soon take place, for stretched out in the valley below him was a carpet of flickering Confederate campfires. Speaking to no one in particular, Buford announced, "Within forty-eight hours the concentration of both armies will take place on a field within view and a great battle will be fought."[30] "By the examination of a local map obtained in the neighborhood, the remarkable convergence of broad highways at Gettysburg was first clearly disclosed to the officers in command, and indicated the approximate field of the coming conflict," recalled Lt. Col. Theodore W. Bean of the 17th Pennsylvania Cavalry. "To this point, under general instructions, Buford hastened and directed his next day's march."[31]

Once down from the mountain, Buford and his troopers camped about two miles from the town of Fairfield, Pennsylvania. Lieutenant Calef described the day's march as "very long and fatiguing, adding horses very much used up." Both men and animals welcomed the opportunity to rest.[32] The regimental historian of the 17th Pennsylvania described the rigors of the march north as the men of his regiment prepared to bed down for the night. "The division had been marching and picketing for almost a week with no rest for man or beast. They had marched all night to reach this point. . . . The column halted before the light of day with orders to dismount and stand to horse," he wrote. "[A]n hour passed and the gray dawn . . . lighted up a picture I can never forget. The men, who were completely exhausted, had slipped the bridle rein over their arms and lay down in a bed of dust (8 inches deep) that almost obscured them from sight. Their jaded steeds seemed to know they should not move, and propping

---

30 Col. George H. Sharpe to J. Watts DePuyster, August 15, 1867, quoted in J. Watts DePuyster, *Decisive Conflicts of the Civil War* (New York: 1867), reprinted as *Gettysburg and After* (Gaithersburg, MD: 1987), 30; Lt. Col. Theo. Bean, "Address at the Dedication of the 17th Pennsylvania Cavalry Monument of September 11, 1889," *Pennsylvania at Gettysburg*, 2 vols. (Harrisburg: 1904), 2:858.

31 Lt. Col. Theodore W. Bean, "Address at the Dedication of the 17th Pennsylvania Cavalry Monument of September 11, 1889," *Pennsylvania at Gettysburg*, 2:876.

32 John H. Calef, "Gettysburg Notes: The Opening Gun," *Journal of the Military Service Institute of the United States*, Vol. 40 (1889), 47.

themselves with extended necks and lowering heads, stood like mute sentinels over their riders dead in sleep."[33]

Company G of the 17th Pennsylvania had been raised in the area around Waynesboro, and its men requested that they be allowed to visit their homes on the night of June 29. Devin granted their request—with the proviso they return in time for morning roll call. Not a man of Company G missed roll call the next day.[34]

33 DePuyster, *Decisive Conflicts*, 57-58.

34 Moyer, *History of the Seventeenth Regiment*, 48-49.

Chapter 3

June 30, 1863

John Buford roused his men at 2:00 a.m. on June 30. "Soon after 3 we got the men in the saddle and moved out," recalled Col. George H. Chapman of the 3rd Indiana Cavalry.[1] The Yankee troopers struggled through dense fog toward Fairfield via the Jack's Mountain Road (which parallels the south side of Jack's Mountain) with the 8th Illinois Cavalry in the lead. A small portion of his command—a detachment of the 6th New York Cavalry—took the parallel Iron Springs Road on the north side of Jack's Mountain, covering Buford's flank. After half an hour's ride and reaching the foot of Jack's Mountain, the Illinois troopers unexpectedly encountered enemy infantry from Maj. Gen. Henry Heth's division—the 42nd Mississippi of Brig. Gen. Joseph Davis' Mississippi Brigade and Company B of the 52nd North Carolina of Brig. Gen. James J. Pettigrew's North Carolina Brigade. One Unionist described the location as "a strong outpost of the enemy" on the Peter Musselman farm near a bridge over the swift moving Tom's Creek.[2] At the same time, troopers of Devin's 6th New York Cavalry clashed with Confederate pickets along the Iron Springs Road.[3] Captain Benjamin Little of the 52nd North Carolina claimed the rest of his regiment

---

1 Chapman, Diary, June 30, 1863.

2 Cheney, *History of the Ninth New York Cavalry*, 101-102. See History of Cumberland and Adams Counties (Chicago, 1886), 445, for the identification of Peter Musselman as the owner of the farm where this encounter occurred.

3 Walter Clark, ed., *Histories of the Several Regiments and Battalions from North Carolina in the Great War, 1861-65* (Goldsboro, 1901), 3:236; David G. Martin, *Gettysburg, July 1* (Conshohocken, 1995), 40; Sarah Sites Thomas, Tim Smith, Gary Kross, and Dean S. Thomas, *Fairfield in the Civil War* (Gettysburg, 2011), 42.

came up to support Company B, skirmished with the enemy at Fairfield, and swept them away.[4]

This unexpected and chance encounter could have been avoided if the local citizenry been more forthcoming with information. These Confederate soldiers were there for two reasons: they were guarding the mouth of the Fairfield Gap, which provided the direct route to Fountaindale and the Monterey Pass, and protecting Tom's Creek, a fast-moving stream that provided an excellent water source. The picket post manned by the Tar Heels, commanded by Lt. W. E. Kyle, was about five miles from the rest of the regiment and from the rest of their brigade, which was camped at Cashtown. The North Carolinians believed Buford's horse soldiers were part of a Union picket post, and not a large force of cavalry patrolling the south-central Pennsylvania countryside gathering intelligence about the disposition of the Army of Northern Virginia.[5]

An officer of Buford's experience realized that an isolated force of Confederate infantry without a cavalry screen so far north of the Mason-Dixon Line was simply part of a much larger infantry command operating nearby. "I determined to feel it and drive it, if possible," he wrote. He briefly considered unlimbering Calef's guns and having them open on the Confederates, but he did not want to bring on a general engagement, fearing the sounds of artillery fire might be heard at Lee's headquarters.

"[W]e encountered the Rebels the next morning; as they were in force here we were about to open against infantry," recalled one of Buford's troopers, "but as we were dismounting orders came which were to the effect that we should tumble back and take the branch road to Emmitsburg."[6] During those brief minutes, however, a ricocheting Confederate ball struck Pvt. Thomas Withrow of the 8th Illinois in the abdomen and knocked him from his saddle. Fortunately, the ball did not break his skin or the wound may have been fatal. Infuriated at being unhorsed, Withrow swore revenge. The bruised trooper took cover behind a barn and began popping away at the Confederates with his carbine. He was close enough to overhear a Confederate officer direct his men to search the barn, so he hid in the hay pile. The Southern infantrymen thrust their bayonets into the stack, probing to make sure nobody was hiding there. The steel points narrowly missed Withrow. A colonel passed by so close that Withrow could have easily killed him, but he valued his own life "more than that

---

4 Account of Capt. Benjamin F. Little, Co. F, 52nd North Carolina Infantry, copy in files, Gettysburg National Military Park, Gettysburg, PA.

5 Clark, *Histories of the Several Regiments*, 3:236.

6 *Aurora Beacon*, August 20, 1863.

of a rebel colonel." The Southerners left when they failed to find the Union trooper. The farmer upon whose land the brief exchange occurred got quite a surprise when he came out to make sure nothing had been stolen and found Withrow occupying his barn. Relieved that the trespasser was a Yankee, the farmer invited the Illinois native into his home for dinner. Withrow gratefully accepted before setting off toward Gettysburg on foot.[7]

After the "brief skirmish," Buford ordered his men to disengage and countermarch south towards Emmitsburg. A light drizzle accompanied the riders. The Tar Heels also withdrew from their exposed position that night.[8] And so the opposing forces, wrote one Unionist, "mutually recoiled from each other."[9] The North Carolinians and Buford's troopers would meet again the next day in a much larger affair.

Buford made a prudent choice. He did not know the strength of the Confederate force nor the number of artillery pieces supporting it, and he was under orders to observe and not to engage Heth's infantry. Despite Withrow's light wound Buford did not report any casualties, while the Rebels lost one Mississippian killed and three wounded.[10]

After the encounter with Heth's infantry at Fairfield, Buford jotted a quick report to his wing commander, Maj. Gen. John F. Reynolds of the First Corps, whose headquarters were at Emmitsburg, and sent it off with a courier. "The enemy has increased his forces considerably," reported Buford. "His strong position is just behind Cashtown. My party toward Mummasburg met a superior force, strongly posted. Another party [the detachment of the 6th New York Cavalry] that went up the road due north, 3 miles out, met a strong picket; had a skirmish, and captured a prisoner of [Robert] Rodes' division. Another party that went toward Littlestown heard that Gregg or Kilpatrick had a fight with Stuart, and drove him to Hanover."[11] This concise yet detailed report

---

7 Hard, *History of the Eighth Cavalry Regiment*, 256.

8 *OR 27*, pt. 1, 926.

9 DePuyster, 52.

10 Hard, *History of the Eighth Cavalry Regiment*, 255-256.

11 *OR 27*, pt. 1, 922. Here, Buford refers to the beginning phases of the June 30, 1863, battle of Hanover, which evolved into a day-long slug match with Brig. Gen. Judson Kilpatrick's Third Cavalry Division. For a detailed discussion of these events, see Eric J. Wittenberg and J. David Petruzzi, *Plenty of Blame to Go Around: Jeb Stuart's Controversial Ride to Gettysburg* (El Dorado Hills, 2006).

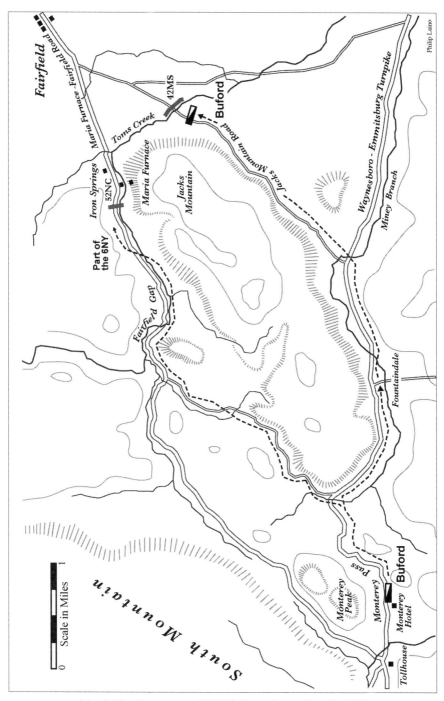

Map 2: The Encounter at Fairfield, Pennsylvania, June 30, 1863

accurately described the whereabouts of the Confederate troops around Fairfield and Cashtown while reporting the proximity of Jeb Stuart's troopers.

Buford arrived at Emmitsburg, about seven miles away, about 10:00 a.m. to consult with Reynolds in person.[12] The cavalryman recounted the Fairfield skirmish to Reynolds, who as an informal wing commander led about one-half of the Army of the Potomac.[13] It was imperative that Reynolds fully understand all that Buford had discovered, and that a large force of enemy infantry was close to his headquarters, so he sent a staff officer along with Buford who would ensure that the most current intelligence was relayed back to the wing commander.[14] After the brief meeting with Reynolds, Buford turned his brigades north and rode the eight miles to Gettysburg along the Emmitsburg Road, passing marching Federal infantry moving in the same direction.

Given his later reporting on the subject, there is little doubt that Buford stewed over his Fairfield experience as he rode toward Gettysburg. "The inhabitants knew of my arrival and the position of the enemy's camp, yet no one gave me a particle of information, nor even mentioned the fact of the enemy's presence," complained the Union cavalry commander. "The whole community seemed stampeded, and afraid to speak or act, often offering as excuses for not showing some little enterprise, 'The rebels will destroy our houses if we tell anything.' Had any one given me timely information, and acted as a guide that night," he concluded, "I could have surprised and captured this force, which proved the next day to be two Mississippi regiments of infantry and two guns.[15] Buford's frustration is understandable, but some of this criticism seems unfair. Whether the local citizenry even knew of the presence of Buford's troopers, for example, has never been determined. Fair or not, the silence of these

---

12 There is some question as to whether Buford and Reynolds met. A dispatch by Buford to Reynolds written at 11:30 that morning repeats the information about the camps of the Confederates at Cashtown. However, it seems highly unlikely Buford would pass by Reynolds' headquarters and not stop to update his old friend.

13 Marcellus Jones Journal, June 30, 1863.

14 Harry W. Pfanz, *Gettysburg: The First Day* (Chapel Hill, 2001), 39.

15 *OR* 27, pt. 1, 926. According to Thomas, Smith, Kross, and Thomas, *Fairfield in the Civil War*, 43, the local citizenry does not deserve blame on this issue. "Over the years, many historians have given credence to Buford's comments, but in reality, the citizens of Fairfield had no knowledge of Buford's arrival at Fountaindale and Monterey that night. And the idea that Buford's cavalry could have, or would have even attempted, to capture or destroy a force of Confederate infantry is highly questionable."

Pennsylvania farmers drew the Kentuckian's ire—and he had little enough tolerance for civilians as it was.

Jubal Early's visit to Gettysburg on June 2 had been reported to another force of Federal cavalry that reached the town two days later. Detailed intelligence about the size and location of the Rebel force was passed to the commander of that detachment (a brigade of four regiments of Michigan cavalry under Brig. Gen. Joseph Copeland, who relayed the information to army headquarters). A large Confederate camp had also been spotted on the Chambersburg Pike above Cashtown and another near Fairfield (the latter likely the same one Buford had blundered into on the morning of June 30). Buford expected to find Copeland's Michigan horse soldiers in possession of Gettysburg when he arrived. What he did not know was that these Wolverines had moved on and were even then engaged with Jeb Stuart's troopers at Hanover under their new commander, Brig. Gen. George A. Custer.

As Buford's troopers crossed the Mason-Dixon Line and approached Marsh Creek, they passed the camps of Reynolds' First Corps. "They had plenty of news for us, and it was of an exciting character," recalled a First Corps artillerist. "They would sing out as they rode by, 'We have found the Johnnies; they are just above and to the left of us, and the woods are full of 'em.'" The men of the 6th New York Cavalry reported they had tried to go to Gettysburg by the shorter route that morning, but had encountered Confederate infantry in sufficient number to compel them to turn back and approach by the Emmitsburg route. The same artillerist also overheard Maj. William E. Beardsley, the commander of the 6th New York Cavalry, tell his battery commander that Lee's entire army was in front of them and that the cavalry was advancing to bring on an engagement.[16]

At 11:00 a.m. on June 30, the lead elements of Buford's column clattered into Gettysburg. The first to arrive were scouts from the 3rd Indiana and 8th Illinois of Gamble's brigade led by Capt. Harry B. Sparks of Company C of the 3rd Indiana. These men dashed into town, surprising and capturing several Confederate soldiers who "seemed to be straggling through the streets and mingling with the citizens."[17]

16 Augustus C. Buell, "Story of a Cannoneer," part 3, *The National Tribune*, October 24, 1889.

17 Martin, *Gettysburg, July* 1, 42.

Lieutenant A. H. Moore of the 7th Tennessee, part of Brig. Gen. James J. Archer's brigade of Heth's division (Hill's Third Corps) had orders to take 40 men east toward Gettysburg to picket the road from Cashtown. Cavalry normally performed this sort of critical duty, but there were no horse soldiers available to screen the advance that morning, meaning infantry, which was not well suited to this sort of duty, had to perform this important duty. As a result, Lieutenant Moore and some of his fellow Tennesseans found themselves well in advance of Hill's Corps on the road to Gettysburg. "Here, about mid-day, I observed some Federal cavalry ride to the top of an eminence, and after reconnoitering they retired," Moore remembered. "This was the first appearance of the enemy yet seen by any of Hill's Corps. These appeared to be scouts, and not of any regular command—at least they did not come in any force. As they retired, I sent a man back to report to General Archer; I remained with my command for the rest of the day and night."[18] These cavalry scouts were probably troopers from Captain Sparks' command.

The Federals received a hero's welcome from the townspeople, who flooded them with food, drinks, and rumors about the Confederates. The column halted in the streets while Buford and his commanders reconnoitered the area. A citizen rode along with the advancing Federals, telling all who would listen that 6,000 Rebel cavalry was waiting for them on the other side of town.[19] A local couple invited Capt. William C. Hazelton of the 8th Illinois into their home for a meal. When they asked, "Can't we do something for you?" Hazelton replied, "You will have the opportunity to do something for us tomorrow." The startled citizens naively responded, "Why? Will there be a battle?"[20]

"As we advanced on Gettysburg, the Rebels fell back and, oh, how glad the people were!" declared Eli Ditzler of the 8th Illinois Cavalry. "On street corners fair misses collected and sang 'Star Spangled Banner' for us as we passed, and there were roaring cheers." Later, after the 8th Illinois established its camp, Ditzler rode back into town to buy some small articles. "Ladies on the streets with baskets filled would give us all the pies, cakes, and goodies we wanted . . . I stopped at a house where seminary girls boarded. They gave me a bouquet and

---

18 A. H. Moore, "Heth's Division at Gettysburg," *Southern Bivouac* (May, 1885), vol. 3, No. 9, 384.

19 *Aurora Beacon*, August 20, 1863.

20 W. C. Hazelton, "An Address Made at a Regimental Reunion," *Gettysburg Star and Sentinel*, September 1, 1891.

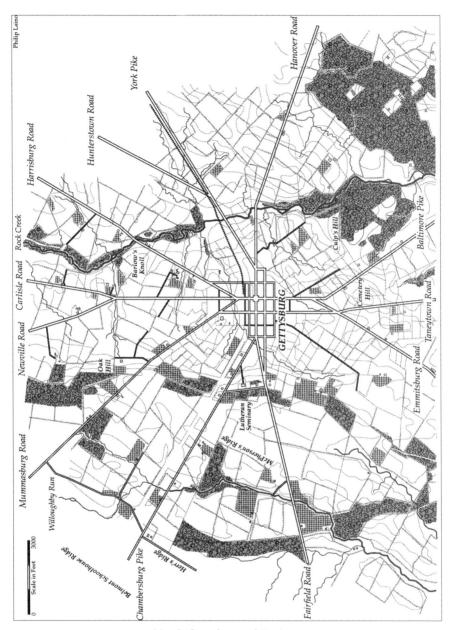

Map 3: Gettysburg and Environs

sang songs to the accompaniment of the piano—all for my benefit, dirty and rough as I was. How sweet it sounded!"[21] Private Thomas B. Kelley of the 8th

21 Hall, *The Captain*, 41.

Illinois had similar fond recollections of that day when he wrote, "The women brought out bread, coffee, milk and cake for us, and I can tell you that nothing ever tasted better. It was the first time in 18 months that soft bread had passed my lips."[22]

"That reception was a good deal of a surprise to us," recalled an officer of the 6th New York Cavalry of Devin's brigade.[23] Captain William H. Redman in the 12th Illinois Cavalry watched as "young Ladies came out in the streets by the hundreds—handing us bouquets and singing to us as we passed along, 'My Lover has Gone to War'—a very beautiful song which us all feel good." Redman liked the town, noting, "the people are truly loyal and look upon us . . . as . . . rescuers." These horse soldiers were filthy after days on the march, but they were a sight for sore eyes after Early's Rebels had swept through four days earlier.[24]

Tate's Blue Eagle Hotel, which served as John Buford's headquarters
on the night of June 30, 1863. The hotel burned down in 1960.
Adams County Historical Society

22 "Opened the Fight at Gettysburg," *Boston Sunday Globe*, December 5, 1909.

23 Gettysburg Honor to Girls of '63," *New York Times*, July 1, 1913.

24 William H. Redman to his mother, July 1, 1863, William H. Redman Papers, Special Collections, Alderman Library, University of Virginia, Charlottesville, Virginia.

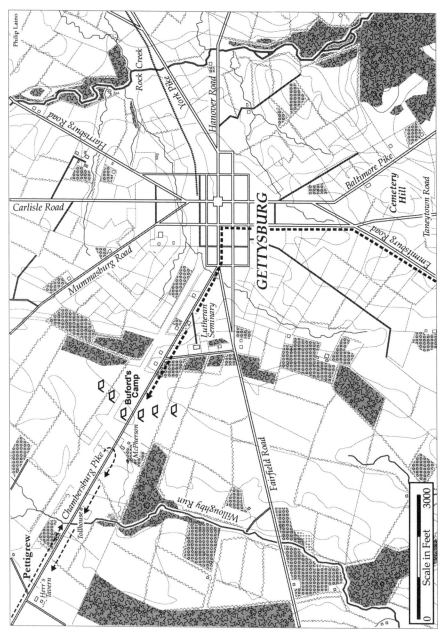

Map 4: Buford Enters Gettysburg and Encounters Pettigrew's Brigade

Teenager Tillie Pierce, a 15-year-old Gettysburg native, watched the columns of Buford's troopers pass through town on their way toward the Chambersburg Pike. "It was to me a novel and grand sight," she recalled. "I had never seen so many soldiers at one time. They were Union soldiers and that was enough for me, for I knew we had protection, and I felt they were our dearest friends." Tillie and her friends gathered on the corner of Washington and High streets to watch the novel event. "Desiring to encourage them, we, as we were told, would before long be in battle, my sister started to sing the old war song 'Our Union Forever.'" The appreciative men responded with smiles and waves, but it soon became obvious that the girls did not know the song well because they kept repeating the chorus. The repetition prompted one of the soldiers to tell Tillie that the soldiers enjoyed the singing very much, but wanted to hear more than just the chorus to the song. We don't know whether anyone else was on hand to make sure the men heard more than the chorus, but we do know the townsfolk were beginning to feel a bit nervous. The presence of so many soldiers in town increased the likelihood that war was about to visit their homes.[25]

Buford established his headquarters at Tate's Blue Eagle Hotel, west of the town square, about one mile from a prominent Lutheran Seminary, and atop a commanding ridge just west of town.[26] After establishing his headquarters, Buford scrawled another update to Reynolds. "The main force—Anderson's Division—encamped last night 9 miles NW of Gettysburg on Chambersburg Pike—at base of South Mountain 1 mile beyond Cashtown," he reported at 11:30 a.m. "One Regt of Infty came near Gettysburg at 11 a.m. and retired as I advanced. The main force is believed to be marching north of Gettysburg through Mummasburg, Hunterstown, Hampton & towards Berlin & York. I will send parties out on roads towards the supposed position of the enemy." He signed the note with a simple "Buford." The cavalrymen sent another galloper with this important intelligence to Reynolds, who was less than 10 miles distant, but for reasons that remain unexplained, the report apparently did not reach Reynolds' headquarters until nearly three that afternoon.[27] Before he received this critical intelligence, Reynolds contemplated taking up a position on Marsh

---

25 Tillie Pierce Alleman, *At Gettysburg, or What a Girl Saw and Heard of the Battle* (New York, 1889), 28-29.

26 John Blosher to John B. Bachelder, December 8, 1890, copy in files, Gettysburg National Military Park.

27 John Buford to John F. Reynolds, June 30, 1863, Army of the Potomac Bureau of Military Information, RG 393I, Entry 3980, Box 11, NARA, Washington, D.C. This dispatch does not appear in the *Official Records*.

The Lutheran Seminary, as it appeared a few days after the Battle of Gettysburg. Note the cupola that Jerome and Buford occupied during the fighting on the morning of July 1.

Library of Congress

Creek between Gettysburg and Emmitsburg as the spot for the army to make its stand. Buford's reports persuaded Reynolds to instead shift farther north to Gettysburg.[28] Buford also scribbled a quick note to General Pleasonton at 12:20 p.m., "My extreme left reports a large force coming toward Fairfield, in a direction to strike the Emmitsburg road this side of Marsh Creek. Reliable."[29]

While Buford was passing along his intelligence to his superiors, he was also declaring martial law in the town. The hard-nosed trooper jailed a suspected spy, issued strict orders prohibiting local tavern owners from selling alcohol to his troops, and had leaflets printed to that effect. In addition to everything else he had learned, Buford discovered a citizen for whom Robert E.

28 OR 27, pt. 3, 417-418. Reynolds told Meade, "it might be necessary to dispute the enemy across (Marsh) Creek, in order to take up position behind Middle Creek."

29 OR 27, pt. 1, 922.

Lee had signed a pass that morning in Chambersburg—solid evidence of the whereabouts of the Confederate commander's headquarters. The armies were now in proximity, and major fighting could break out at any time. The last thing he needed was for his troopers to be impaired by alcohol.[30] Buford directed Gamble and Devin to establish their camps near the Lutheran Seminary, and set about planning his defense of Gettysburg.

Gettysburg, a town of about 2,000 residents, was the county seat of Adams County. The town rests in a basin surrounded by mountains between 10 to 20 miles of the town square. A series of ridges and hills extend to the north and west. About a mile west of the town square, Seminary Ridge extends on a north-south axis with Lutheran Seminary, the most prominent point on the eponymous ridge. Seminary Ridge was heavily wooded south of the seminary complex. About half a mile farther west was the more open McPherson's Ridge that features twin crests. A wealthy local businessman named Edward McPherson owned the farm and most of the ridge that carried his name.[31] Two barns and a large farmhouse sat between the crests of McPherson's Ridge south of the Chambersburg Pike.

A small creek called Willoughby Run flows south along the western base of McPherson's Ridge. Beyond it, roughly two miles from the town square, are the highest elevations of Herr's Ridge and Belmont Schoolhouse Ridge, the latter of which merges into the former on a northwesterly diagonal angle just below the Chambersburg Pike. Herr's Tavern there provided accommodations and food for travelers. Another valley lay to the west of Herr's Ridge, with Knoxlyn Ridge rising another mile or so farther west. Ephraim Wisler's blacksmith shop sat atop the crest of Knoxlyn Ridge overlooking March Creek, a wide, swift brook running through the valley beyond. These terrain features would play a critical role in a drama John Buford was about to script.

Like any good soldier, Buford took note of the terrain to the south and east of Gettysburg as he approached the town. With large hills at both ends (Cemetery Hill in the north and the Round Tops in the south) and a prominent ridge connecting those hills, Buford understood the ground offered an excellent defensive position for the army. Knowing that a large force of the

---

30 Gerald R. Bennett, *Days of Uncertainty and Dread* (Camp Hill, 1994), 18; Edwin C. Fishel, *The Secret War for the Union: The Untold Story of Military Intelligence in the Civil War* (Boston, 1996), 506.

31 Edward McPherson did not live in or work on the farm that bore his name. He leased the farm to a man named John Slentz, who resided there when the war arrived in his yard on June 30, 1863.

Lt. Gen. A. P. Hill, commander, Third Corps, Army of Northern Virginia. Hill's cavalier
dismissal of reports of Union cavalry in Gettysburg did much to bring
about the Battle of Gettysburg. *Library of Congress*

enemy was situated near Cashtown and that it might advance on Gettysburg
from the west, Buford decided to conduct a delaying action north and west of
the town—called a covering force action in modern military parlance—wherein
Buford's troopers would hold successive defensive positions until Reynolds'
infantry, six miles away at Emmitsburg, could arrive and occupy the strategic
high ground.

Around 4:00 p.m. on June 30, Gettysburg resident Daniel Skelly spotted Buford at the corner of the Chambersburg Pike and Washington Street, in front of the Blue Eagle Hotel. The cavalryman, "sat on his horse in the street in front of me, entirely alone, facing to the west, and in profound thought. . . . It was the only time that I ever saw the General and his calm demeanor and soldierly appearance, as well as the fact that his uniform was different from any general's I had ever seen, struck me forcibly," he continued. "He wore a sort of hunting coat of blouse effect. It is possible that from that position he was directing through his aides the placing of his two brigades of cavalry . . . to the west and northwest of town."[32]

Having carefully chosen the ground, Buford saw to it that "arrangements were made for entertaining" the Confederates.[33] He ordered Gamble to proceed through the town, past the seminary, and select the best lines of defense along the Chambersburg Pike.[34] Buford and Devin, meanwhile, climbed to the top of a nearby belfry—perhaps the cupola of the Lutheran Seminary—to reconnoiter the ground from a different perspective.[35]

It was at this time that Buford's lead elements encountered Confederate infantry advancing from the west along the Chambersburg Pike. Corps leader A. P. Hill had sent Brig. Gen. James Johnston Pettigrew's large brigade of North Carolina infantry, part of Maj. Gen. Henry Heth's division, east to Gettysburg with 15 wagons to forage for supplies.[36] Heth gave Pettigrew specific verbal instructions for his expedition, which Lt. Louis G. Young, one of Pettigrew's staff officers, later recalled. "General Early had levied on Carlisle,

---

32 Daniel A. Skelly, *A Boy's Experiences During the Battles of Gettysburg* (Gettysburg, 1932), 10.

33 *OR* 27, pt. 1, 923-927.

34 William Gamble to William L. Church, March 10, 1864, copy in files, Gettysburg National Military Park.

35 Hall, *History of the Sixth New York Cavalry*, 377.

36 Brigadier General James Johnston Pettigrew, known as Johnston to his friends and family, was 34 years old on June 30, 1863. A brilliant student during his college days, Pettigrew had found success as an author, lawyer, diplomat, linguist, and legislator. He was born into a wealthy North Carolina family and rose through the ranks during the Civil War to become colonel of the 12th North Carolina in 1861. "Pettigrew seemed to have every attribute of a great soldier," recalled a friend, "uniting with the brightest mind and an active body a disposition which had him the idol of his men, and a courage which nothing could daunt." Pettigrew was mortally wounded during the last hours of fighting during the withdrawal into Virginia. Larry Tagg, *The Generals of Gettysburg: The Leaders of America's Greatest Battle* (Mason City, 1998), 343-344.

Brig. Gen. James J. Pettigrew, commander, Pettigrew's Brigade, Heth's Division. The North Carolinian's troops were the first to make contact with Buford's command at Gettysburg. *NARA*

Chambersburg, and Shippensburg, and had found no difficulty in having his requisitions filled," recalled Young. "It was supposed that it would be the same in Gettysburg. It was told to General Pettigrew that he might find the town in possession of a home-guard, which he would have no difficulty in driving away; but, if, contrary to expectations, he should find any organized troops capable of making resistance, or any portion of the Army of the Potomac, he should not attack it. The orders to him were peremptory, not to precipitate a fight," insisted the staff officer. "General Lee with his columns scattered, and lacking the information of his adversary, which he should have had from his cavalry, was not ready for battle—hence the orders."[37]

Pettigrew had approximately 2,000 men with him from three of his four North Carolina regiments (the 11th, 26th, and 47th), as well as the Donaldson artillery battery of Louisiana for "intimidating" purposes.[38] About 9:30 a.m., a line of Pettigrew's soldiers "at least a mile and a half in length" moved along the Chambersburg Pike toward Gettysburg. A local physician on his way to visit a patient told Pettigrew there were four or five thousand Union soldiers in the area, news that naturally made the North Carolinian brigadier that much more cautious. These Confederates stopped short of Willoughby Run to await word from the skirmishers sent out well to the front to signal that there was a clear

37 Louis G. Young, "Pettigrew's Brigade at Gettysburg, 1-3 July 1863," in Clark, ed., *Histories of the Several Regiments and Battalions from North Carolina,* 5:115.

38 His fourth regiment, the 52nd North Carolina, was left at Cashtown, perhaps because of the detachment of the troops that had skirmished with Buford at Fairfield that morning.

line of march into the town.[39] The approach of so many Confederates worried many of the town's residents. "We had a good view of them from our house," recalled Gettysburg resident Sarah Broadhead, "and every moment expected to hear the booming of cannon, and thought they might shell the town."[40]

The Confederate pickets interrogated other local residents and continued advancing as far east as Seminary Ridge, where Pettigrew and many of his men spent about an hour, reconnoitering and interviewing local residents. It was about then that his pickets saw something in the distance that brought them up short: a column of enemy troopers was entering the town from the south. What the Rebels did not yet know was that the riders were part of Buford's cavalry column. Within a short time the news was reported to Pettigrew: "a large force of cavalry near the town, supported by an infantry force."[41]

Even though he was willing to fight Union cavalry, Pettigrew was unsure of the strength of the Federal force opposing him, and with only his own brigade up and available, he prudently withdrew west to the banks of Marsh Creek. Lieutenant Young confirmed the withdrawal. Under strict orders not to bring on a general engagement, he explained, they "did not enter the town . . . but examined it with their field glasses. Having learned of the approach of Meade's advance guard, they withdrew toward Cashtown, leaving pickets about four miles from Gettysburg."[42] Pettigrew placed a regiment on each side of the Chambersburg Pike and the third straddling the road in front, or east, of the other two. Apparently the brigadier was trying to lure Buford into something approximating a trap when he arranged his regiments. One eyewitness described the deployed as "two regiments defiled under cover of a hill, one to the right of the road, the other to the left, whilst a third was sent a short distance forward to induce a pursuit."[43]

If the Rebels could see the Union troopers, the reverse was also true. As Gamble's men rode through the town, they spotted Pettigrew's men. Companies D and E, commanded by Capt. Henry J. Hotopp of the 8th Illinois,

---

39 Professor Michael Jacobs, *Notes on the Rebel Invasion of Maryland and Pennsylvania and the Battle of Gettysburg, July 1st, 2nd, and 3rd, 1863* (Philadelphia, 1864), 21-22.

40 Sarah M. Broadhead, Diary, June 30, 1863, GNMP.

41 OR 27, pt. 2, 627.

42 The Journal of Marcellus E. Jones, June 30, 1863.

43 Jacobs, *Notes on the Rebel Invasion*, 22.

dashed forward to determine the intentions of the hostile infantry. "Buford's cavalry followed us at some distance, and Lieutenant Walter H. Robertson and I, of Pettigrew's staff, remained in the rear to watch it," recalled Lieutenant Young. "This we easily did, for the country is rolling, and from behind the ridges we could see without being seen and we had a perfect view of the movements of the approaching column. Whenever it would come within three or four hundred yards of us we would make our appearance, mounted, when the column would halt until we retired. This was repeated several times. It was purely an affair of observation on both sides," concluded the staff officer, "and the cavalry made no effort to molest us."[44]

Jaquelin Marshall Meredith served as the chaplain for Heth's division. That June 30 afternoon, the division surgeon, Dr. E. B. Spence, asked Meredith to ride into Gettysburg with him to procure much needed medical supplies. The two men rode about five miles without seeing any rebel or Union troops. They reached the town, dismounted, tied their horses up at the first apothecary they found, and went into the store. A few minutes later, they spotted one of Pettigrew's regiments coming from the direction of the town at a quick march. The two non-combatants hastily mounted and joined the regimental colonel at the head of the column, riding with him all the way back to Cashtown. "The Doctor and I were told that a superior force of the enemy were moving on Gettysburg," recalled Meredith. "We were not followed nor did any Federal cavalry attack, or even show itself in rear or flank during the one hour and a half, to two hours that this regiment took to proceed in orderly march back to Cashtown."[45]

Pettigrew waited about two hours, but Buford's troopers refused to aggressively advance into what surely would have been a one-sided killing zone. The brigadier withdrew west, but left the 26th North Carolina to picket Marsh Creek and pulled the 11th and 47th regiments back to a spot between the hamlets of McKnightstown and Seven Stars, where they could support the 26th if needed. He sent his fourth regiment, the 52nd North Carolina, the Donaldson artillery, and his wagons back to Cashtown.[46]

44 Young, "Pettigrew's Brigade at Gettysburg," 5:116.

45 Jaquelin Marshall Meredith, "The First Day at Gettysburg: Tribute to Brave General Harry Heth, Who Opened the Great Battle," *Southern Historical Society Papers* (1896), 24:182-183.

46 Earl J. Hess, *Lee's Tar Heels: The Pettigrew-Kirkland-MacRae Brigade* (Chapel Hill, 2002), 116.

Captain William W. Chamberlaine served on the staff of Maj. William J. Pegram, the commander of the battalion of artillery attached to A. P. Hill's Third Corps. Pegram's battalion was descending South Mountain after passing through the Cashtown Pass when the trudging column of Third Corps infantry suddenly halted, which, explained Chamberlaine, "usually indicates that the enemy has been seen." Although the enemy had indeed been seen, they were much farther east around Gettysburg. The column had stopped short because Pettigrew's brigade was returning along the same road after its near-encounter with Buford's troopers. News of the presence of Union soldiers in Gettysburg quickly spread through the ranks.[47]

On the other side of the lines, Buford reported the presence of Confederate infantry to General Pleasonton:

> I entered this place to-day at 11 a.m. Found everyone in a terrible state of excitement on account of the enemies' advance on the place. He had approached to within half a mile of the town when the head of my column entered. His force was terribly exaggerated by reasonable and truthful but inexperienced men. On pushing him back to Cashtown, I learned from reliable men that [Maj. Gen. Richard H.] Anderson's division was marching from Chambersburg by Mummasburg, Hunterstown, Abbottstown, on toward York. I have sent parties to the two first-named places, Cashtown, and a strong force toward Littlestown…My men and horses are fagged out, I have not been able to get any grain yet. It is all in the country and the people talk instead of working. Facilities for shoeing are nothing. Early's people seized every shoe and nail they could find…no reliable information could be obtained from the inhabitants. . . . P.S. The troops that are coming here were the same I found early this morning at Millersburg or Fairfield. General Reynolds has been advised of all that I know.[48]

Buford also sent a dispatch to General Reynolds: "I have pushed the pickets, or rather the rear guard of the Rebs, 6 miles toward Cashtown. I am satisfied that the force that came here this morning was the same that I found at Fairfield."[49] Buford was correct.

47 William W. Chamberlaine, *Memoirs of the Civil War Between the Northern and Southern Sections of the United States of America 1861-1865* (Washington, D.C., 1912), 64.

48 *OR* 27, pt. 1, 923.

49 John Buford to John F. Reynolds, June 30, 1863, 4:00 p.m., RG 393, Entry 3980, Army of the Potomac, 1861-1865, Miscellaneous Letters, Reports, and Lists Received, The National Archives, Washington, D.C.

Pettigrew also sent the news up his command chain. When he relayed the information to General Heth, however, the division leader refused to believe there was a large force of enemy cavalry in the town. The two officers were discussing this intelligence when General Hill rode up and asked Pettigrew to repeat his report. Pettigrew, who was by this time likely a bit frustrated, called up his staff officer, Lieutenant Young, to confirm what he saw and knew. Young's account exactly tracked Pettigrew's report, and both made it clear these were disciplined enemy troops and not members of a homeguard.[50] Like Heth before him, however, Hill dismissed the report out of hand. He believed Buford's command was still in the Loudoun Valley of Virginia, so he refused to accept the possibility that the First Division could be in his front. "I still cannot believe that any portion of the Army of the Potomac is up," he replied. After pausing a moment, Hill said, "I hope that it is, for this is the place I want it to be."[51]

50 Hess, *Lee's Tar Heels*, 116.

51 W. H. Swallow, "The First Day at Gettysburg," *Southern Bivouac* (December 1885), N.S. 1, 441.

Chapter 4

The Night Before the Battle:
June 30-July 1, 1863

In 1863, the U.S. Army published *Instructions for Officers and Non-Commissioned Officers on Outpost and Patrol Duty, and Troops in Campaign*, a field manual spelling out the U.S. Army's procedure for circumstances like those facing Buford's command at Gettysburg. John Buford spent the nighttime hours deploying his brigades in strict accordance with this doctrine.[1]

The manual required the officer in command to place videttes in positions where they could make a stand (always near a rock or a tree that could provide cover) in case of an attack long enough to permit the main body of the army to come up. Before that placement, however, the commanding officer had to carefully reconnoiter the terrain to determine the best locations for vidette posts to be established, positions from which they could see not only what was coming in front of them, but also see their fellow videttes on either side.[2] At night, continued the manual, the videttes and the vidette reserve would move two to three miles in advance of the main body, into the position on high ground with a commanding view from which they could make a firm stand in front of the main body and on its flanks, as needed. The videttes had instructions to put their ears to the ground from time to time in order to hear

---

1 *Instructions for Officers and Non-Commissioned Officers on Outpost and Patrol Duty, and Troops in Campaign*, 2 parts (Washington, D.C., 1863).

2 Ibid., 8-9. Videttes were mounted sentries. The picket reserve was also known as the grand guard. The grand guard was one of the posts of the second line belonging to a system of advance posts of an army. In other words, the picket reserve was the reinforcements to the original line of videttes.

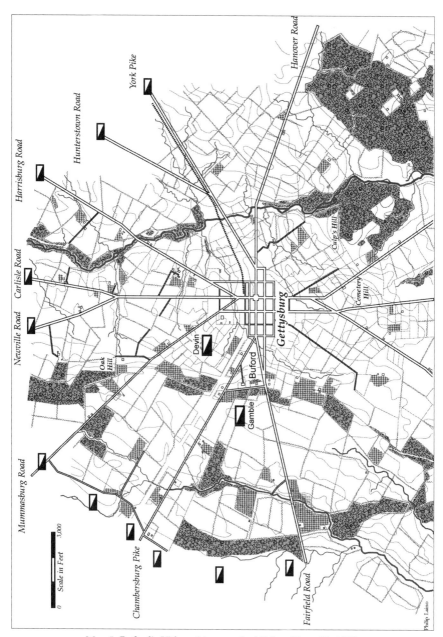

Map 5: Buford's Vidette Lines on the Night of June 30, 1863.

the movement of large bodies of men.[3] "When the videttes are posted in such a manner as to be able to overlook their front," explained the army manual, "and see each other and the ground between them, so as that nothing can pass them unperceived, they are placed as they ought to be."[4]

Once posted, if the videttes spotted evidence of the enemy's approach, they were to signal the commander of the grand guard, who would report the presence of the enemy: "If obliged to retire, he must do it as slowly as possible, endeavoring to gain all the time he can, for the corps in his rear to turn out. If he had previously fixed upon places where to make a stand . . . now is the time to make use of them."[5] Buford made his dispositions in accordance with these instructions, and his textbook deployment is still taught to soldiers on staff rides to this day.

Buford established vidette posts along a seven-mile front stretching from the Fairfield Road on the southern end of this line north and east to the Harrisburg Road on the northeastern end of the line. Well aware that the Confederates had a large camp along the Chambersburg Pike near Cashtown, Buford established vidette posts along the pike about four miles from the center of town so that he would have as much advance warning of any enemy approach as possible. Buford intended for his videttes to make their stand as far away from the defensible high ground to the south and east of the town as possible. His hope was that John Reynolds' infantry would arrive before his troopers were driven through the town and away from that good defensible ground.

Troopers of the 8th New York peeled off to the left and advanced through McPherson's Woods southwest of the Chambersburg Pike while a squadron of the 8th Illinois advanced about two miles out of the Chambersburg Pike, establishing one vidette post on the road, three posts south of the road, two posts north of the road, and one at the Wistler blacksmith shop on Knoxlyn Ridge, overlooking Marsh Creek. This last vidette post consisted of Pvts. Thomas Benton Kelley and James Hall, Sgts. Levi Shaffer and George Heim, and Lt. Alex Riddler of Company E, 8th Illinois Cavalry. The 12th Illinois and

---

3 Ibid.

4 Ibid., 13.

5 Ibid., 16-18.

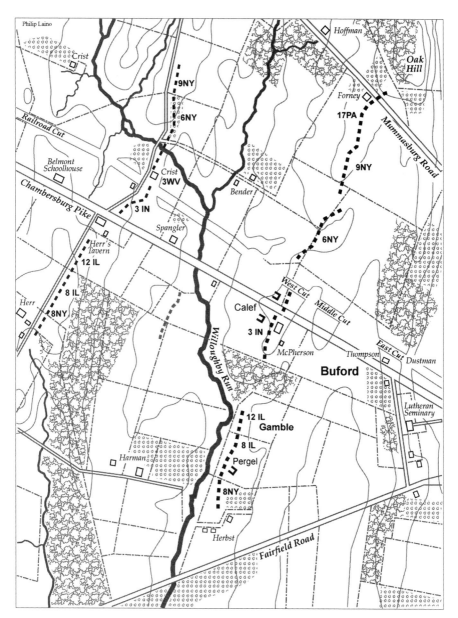

Map 6: The Plan for Buford's Covering Force Action Along the Western Front.

the 3rd Indiana fell into line north of the 8th Illinois. Devin's troopers deployed their videttes north and east of Gamble's thin line.

The McPherson farm buildings, atop McPherson's Ridge.
Adams County Historical Society

The videttes posted themselves at intervals of 30 feet, using fence posts and rail fences as shelter.[6] A typical vidette post consisted of four or five enlisted men with an officer or non-commissioned officer in charge, with a vidette reserve waiting close behind. "The order was for double posts, and two men were placed on each post with a corporal or sergeant," recalled Pvt. Thomas B. Kelley of the 8th Illinois. "We had several posts on or near the road, and others spread out on either side, along the creek."[7]

Half the command's horses were kept bridled at all times and the men slept in shifts, prepared to go into action at any moment. The men spent two hours on duty and four hours off.[8] No more than 200 of Gamble's troopers manned the vidette posts. The rest remained with the main line of battle atop McPherson's Ridge.[9] Devin made similar dispositions north and east of town. Devin's farthest left vidette post was stationed on the Chambersburg Pike commanded by Cpl. Alphonse Hodges of Company F, 9th New York. These videttes were ordered "not to fire on anyone approaching from the front, but to

6   Edwin B. Coddington, *The Gettysburg Campaign: A Study in Command* (New York, 1979), 266.

7   "Opened the Fight at Gettysburg."

8   Ibid.

9   Gary M. Kross, "Fight Like the Devil to Hold Your Own," *Blue & Gray* (February 1995), vol. 12, Issue 3, 12.

notify the pickets in each direction and the reserve."[10] Other Devin vidette posts were stationed among and around the Forney farm buildings on the Mummasburg Road.

H. O. Dodge of the 8th Illinois was on the picket line on the evening of June 30. "We remained there all night, and nothing occurred to break the monotony of the watching," he recalled. "We felt sure that a great battle was impending, for on the hillsides away down on the Chambersburg road we could plainly see the glowing campfires of the enemy, while now and then we could distinguish a soldier who walked between us and the fire."[11]

Morgan Hughes served in Company E of the 8th Illinois Cavalry. "I remember that night of having charge of a reserve picket-post out on a turnpike near a farmer's house, and how he invited us all in to supper, and wanted the man out on post to come in, too," he recalled years after the war. "And when I explained that he was on duty, the kind soul offered to take his place while he came and ate supper; and how the same old farmer came out and chatted with us till late at night." The men on the picket lines spent a long night alternating between stress and boredom as they kept a sharp eye out for the inevitable advance of the enemy.[12]

John Slentz, the tenant who farmed Edward McPherson's land along the Chambersburg Road, watched helplessly while Buford's troopers tore down his fences to remove impediments to battle and hungrily eyed his livestock. The troopers also used the fence rails for firewood. Concerned for his few worldly possessions, Slentz and his family hid what they could and took cover.[13]

Devin's and Gamble's brigades, supported by Calef's battery with its six three-inch rifles, awaited the Confederate attack. "[W]e of the artillery were not imbued with the idea that a great battle was pending," Calef admitted. [14] Others knew better. Trooper A. R. Mix of the 9th New York needed new boots, for his were "just about gone." He got permission to ride into town to look for new ones, found a decent pair that fit, but could not pick them up until the next

---

10 Cheney, *History of the Ninth Regiment*, 103.

11 H. O. Dodge, "Opening the Battle. Lieut. Jones, the 8th Ill. Cavalryman, Fired the First Shot at Gettysburg," *The National Tribune*, September 24, 1891.

12 Morgan Hughes, "People of Gettysburg. How They Inspired the Cavalry to Do Their Effective Work," *The National Tribune*, March 24, 1892.

13 John Slentz Claims Reparation Files, copy in files, Gettysburg National Military Park.

14 Calef, "Gettysburg Notes," 47.

Lt. Col. Joseph Dickinson, of Meade's staff. Dickinson visited Buford at the Blue Eagle Hotel on the night of June 30, 1863, and noted the cavalryman's calm demeanor.
Library of Congress

morning. When Mix approached Buford for permission to leave the ranks on July 1 to get the boots, Buford instructed one of his staff officers to give the trooper a pass, adding, "Mix, you take all of your belongings with you, for we'll be in line when you come back."[15] Buford harbored no illusions about what awaited his command later that morning.

Buford ordered numerous scouting parties to scatter to the four points of the compass in an effort to locate the precise dispositions of the enemy. Gamble sent out scouting parties to the west toward Cashtown while Devin's scouts headed north and east, reconnoitering the country and capturing enemy stragglers who provided critical information under interrogation. This was intelligence gathering at its best, and it quickly bore fruit because the reports sent back to Buford convinced him the entire Army of Northern Virginia was converging—and quickly—on Gettysburg.[16]

At 10:30 p.m. Buford sent a detailed intelligence report to Reynolds, as follows:

> The Reserve Brigade, under General Merritt, is at Mechanicstown with my trains. General Pleasonton wrote he would inform me when he relieved it. To-day I received instructions saying it would picket toward Hagerstown and south. I am satisfied that A.P. Hill's corps is massed just back of Cashtown, about 9 miles from this place. Pender's division of this (Hill's) corps came up to-day—of which I advised you, saying, "The enemy in my front is increased." The enemy's pickets (infantry and artillery) are within 4 miles of this place, on the Cashtown [Chambersburg] road. My parties have returned from Cashtown to Oxford in several places. They heard nothing of any force

---

15 A. R. Mix, "Experiences at Gettysburg," *The National Tribune*, February 22, 1904.

16 Samuel P. Bates, *The Battle of Gettysburg* (Philadelphia, 1875), 55.

having passed over it lately. The road, however, is terribly infested with prowling cavalry parties. Near Heidlersburg to-day, one of my parties captured a courier of Lee's. Nothing was found on him. He says Ewell's corps is crossing the mountains from Carlisle, Rodes' division being at Petersburg in advance. Longstreet, from all I can learn, is still behind Hill. I have many rumors of the enemy advancing upon me from toward York. I have to pay attention to some of them, which causes me to overwork my horses and men. I can get no forage nor rations; am out of both. The people give and sell the men something to eat, but I can't stand that way of subsisting; it causes dreadful straggling. Should I have to fall back, advise me by what route.[17]

This remarkably accurate intelligence report provided Reynolds with a rich and full picture of the disposition of Lee's army and enabled the wing commander to plan accordingly for the next day.

Once the message to Reynolds was in the hands of a rider, Buford penned a similar dispatch to General Pleasonton before asking, "When will the reserve be relieved, and where are my wagons? I have no need of them, as I can find no forage. I have kept General Reynolds informed of all that has transpired."[18] Buford, whose concern about the absence of his Regulars and the state of his horses is evident, knew his dispositions were good and that his veterans could hold off the advancing Confederates for a time. The question was for how long.

On the afternoon of June 30, George Gordon Meade summoned one of his staff officers, Lt. Col. Joseph Dickinson, to his tent. Dickinson, explained the general, was to ride to Emmitsburg to meet with Reynolds and share Meade's intentions with him, then to Gettysburg to meet with Buford, and then back to Reynolds to ensure that Reynolds had the benefit of Buford's observations and plans. Dickinson found Reynolds near Emmitsburg and the two officers talked for about 20 minutes before the staff officer rode on to Gettysburg. He located Buford at his headquarters at the Blue Eagle Hotel. Dickinson left a detailed account that is worth presenting at length:

The General had been engaged in thoroughly informing himself of the movements of the hostile forces, through the instrumentality of his own scouts and that of a number of patriotic citizens of Gettysburg, who were engaged voluntarily in scouring the country in every direction if possible . . . there sat General Buford, cool, calm, and serenely receiving the reports, quietly weighing in his military mind their value, but saying nothing. . . . This was indeed a trying time and position for a commander of two small brigades of cavalry to be placed in, and yet there was not wisdom enough existing

17 OR 27, pt. 1, 923-924.

18 Ibid., 924.

to have made a better choice. The modest yet brave, retiring yet efficient, quiet yet vigilant, unostentatious but prompt and persevering, gallant General John Buford was, at least for once, the right man in the right place . . . for I doubt, if ever the skill and courage of any officer were put to a sterner or more decisive test than upon that night of June 30, 1863, at Gettysburg, and yet show himself so fully equal to the emergency as did General John Buford. [19]

Dickinson departed on his long ride back to headquarters after midnight. Both Buford and Dickinson wanted to make sure Meade had the benefit of what the staff officer had learned consulting face-to-face with Reynolds and Buford. The primary conclusion was this: "that it was extremely essential, in order to secure and hold a choice of positions, that General Reynolds should be notified to proceed to Gettysburg, both agreeing that a battle has to be fought nearby." Dickinson sent a staff officer to Reynolds to brief him on the meeting with Buford and to instruct him to move his command to Gettysburg the next morning, and he then rode off to brief Meade. The die was cast: the Army of the Potomac would make its stand at Gettysburg.[20]

John Buford was not as calm as he appeared to Dickinson. In fact, he was quite concerned. The cavalryman recognized his small force faced potentially overwhelming odds—especially if the Confederate infantry advanced from more than one direction. Although his dispatches to Reynolds and Pleasonton requested that the Reserve Brigade be returned to him,[21] his requests fell upon deaf ears: the Reserve Brigade did not receive orders to ride to Gettysburg until the morning of July 3. When Dickinson set eyes upon Buford, he knew that it was more likely than not that he would face the Confederate infantry with only two of his three brigades, with his favorite brigade detached for less vital duty.

---

19 Bvt. Brig. Gen. Joseph Dickinson, "A Gettysburg Incident," *The Proceedings of the Buford Memorial Association*, 23-25.

20 Ibid., 25; Powell, *Officers of the Army and Navy Who Served in the Civil War*, 78. Dickinson, descended from Philadelphia blue bloods, including founding father John Dickinson who drafted the Articles of Confederation and who signed the U. S. Constitution, was 32 years old in June 1863. After setting the wheels in motion for the Army of the Potomac to concentrate at Gettysburg, Dickinson selected Lydia Leister's small house on the Taneytown Road for Meade's headquarters at Gettysburg. He was badly wounded on the third day of the battle when over shots by Confederate artillery during the great cannonade preceding Pickett's Charge exploded nearby. His wounds left him unable to serve in the field again, and he resigned his commission in January 1864 due to disability. In recognition of his outstanding service, Dickinson received a brevet to brigadier general of volunteers.

21 *OR* 27, pt. 1, 923-924.

Buford's anxiety was more visible during a meeting with his brigade commanders that night when he voiced concern that the upcoming fight might begin "in the morning before the infantry can come up." Tom Devin, who was always spoiling for a fight, announced that he would hold his position the next day. The pragmatic Buford shot back, "No, you won't. They will attack you in the morning and they will come booming—skirmishers three deep. You will have to fight like the devil to hold your own until supports arrive. The enemy must know the importance of this position and will strain every nerve to secure it, and if we are able to hold it we will do well."[22]

Buford ordered his signal officer, Lt. Aaron B. Jerome, to "seek out the most prominent points and watch everything; to be careful to look out for camp-fires, and in the morning, for dust." Jerome observed that, "Buford seemed anxious, more so than I ever saw him," as he fretted about his "arrangements for entertaining" the Confederates the next morning.[23] The worried cavalryman slept fitfully before rising around 3:00 a.m. He awakened Dr. Elias Beck, the regimental surgeon of the 3rd Indiana Cavalry, "and when the gray of the morning began to make its first appearance he was in the saddle, and watching for the approaching enemy."[24]

Buford's two brigades bivouacked in a large field near the Lutheran Seminary, where the men unsaddled their hungry horses and turned them out to graze. Companies C and M of the 9th New York Cavalry were directed to set up

22 Lt. Aaron B. Jerome, "Buford on Oak Hill," in DePuyster, *Decisive Conflicts of the Civil War*, 151-152. Lieutenant Jerome played a very important role in these events. Jerome, often known as A. Brainard Jerome, was from New Jersey. He enlisted in the 1st New Jersey Infantry in May 1861, was commissioned a second lieutenant on August 31, 1861, and promoted to first lieutenant in May 1863. On March 3, 1862, he was assigned to the newly created Signal Corps, in which he served during most of the Army of the Potomac's early major engagements. After Chancellorsville, Jerome was assigned as a signal officer for Buford's cavalry division, and had only served in this capacity for a few weeks by the beginning of the battle of Gettysburg. Jerome was brevetted to first lieutenant on June 18, 1867, for gallant and meritorious service throughout the Civil War, and to captain on the same date for his gallant and meritorious service in the Signal Corps. He was honorably discharged at his own request on December 1, 1870, and died April 17, 1881. There is some evidence that he had a serious drinking problem after the Civil War. Francis E. Heitman, *Historical Register and Dictionary of the United States Army*, 2 vols. (Washington, D.C., 1903), vol. 1, 578; J. Willard Brown, *The Signal Corps, U.S.A. in the War of the Rebellion* (Boston, 1896), 193.

23 DePuyster, *Decisive Conflicts of the Civil War*, 152.

24 J. H. S. "Washington Letter," *The Fort Wayne Journal-Gazette*, November 29, 1885.

Lt. Aaron B. Jerome, who served as Buford's signal officer at Gettysburg. Jerome carefully documented Buford's activities there, and his accounts provide much of the detail in this book. *Library of Congress*

their bivouac on the grounds of Pennsylvania (now Gettysburg) College, securing the college campus and its prominent cupola for Union use.

The Union mounts were exhausted after days of rapid marching and insufficient food, so the chance to graze and rest was a welcome one. "[We] fared luxuriously among the substantial farmers," boasted one of the cavalrymen, "procuring loaves of bread of fabulous size, milk, butter and eggs in abundance, so that we felt compensated for our extra march."[25] Trooper James Bell of the 8th Illinois rode into town on the evening before the battle and found that "every one wanted to talk and at every house they would ask me in to eat supper. It done me lots of good to go there."[26] Thomas G. Day of the 3rd Indiana was invited to come to town for dinner. He cleaned up his horse and himself as best he could and rode into Gettysburg for a delightful meal. The same family invited him back for breakfast, an invitation he readily accepted. Unfortunately, intervening circumstances would make that impossible.[27]

By the time the 2,700 officers and enlisted men of the First Division hunkered down for the night,[28] Confederate campfires were visible flickering in

---

25 "Genesee," "From the 8th Cavalry."

26 Bell to Hallock, July 1, 1863.

27 Thomas G. Day, "Opening the Battle. A Cavalryman's Recollections of the First Day's Fight at Gettysburg," *The National Tribune*, July 30, 1903.

28 OR 27, pt. 1, 924; John W. Busey and David G. Martin, *Regimental Strengths and Losses at Gettysburg* (Hightstown, 1994), 101-102.

the distance. They knew battle awaited them the next morning.[29] They made the most of that lovely early summer evening. "Thus picketed, thus bivouacked, beneath our own skies, on our own soil, with a sense of security and a feeling of homeness, thinking of the loved ones, and breathing prayer to Him who had blessed us and our arms, we lay down upon the greensward, pillowing our heads on our saddles, to rest and to sleep, little dreaming the morrow would usher in a battle so sanguinary which would determine the destiny of the Republic, and fix the fate of human liberty on the earth," declared an officer of the 8th Illinois Cavalry.[30]

An early historian of the town of Gettysburg waxed poetic about the night of June 30, 1863. "The vast details of the coming slaughter were complete, and the hills and valleys about Gettysburg were lit up by the extended camp-fires of two mighty armies, and night and quiet reigned over all," he wrote. "Many a poor, brave fellow, for the last time as he lay down to quiet sleep, looked upon the twinkling stars and thought and dreamed of his far-away home and the loved ones there, and wondered if he would ever be there with them again."[31]

The men of the 8th Illinois Cavalry—known as one of the finest regiments in the Union service—in particular faced a stern task, as its men had been assigned the critical positions along the Chambersburg Pike.[32]

A heavy task lay before Buford's two veteran brigades. Would they be up to it?

29 Edward C. Reid, Diary, June 30, 1863. Edward C. Reid Papers, Illinois State Historical Society, Springfield, Illinois.

30 Beveridge, "Address," 17.

31 *History of Adams and Cumberland Counties*, 156.

32 Confederate guerrilla leader Col. John S. Mosby had a great deal of respect for the 8th Illinois Cavalry, a regiment he would tangle with several times in 1864. When he wrote his postwar memoir, Mosby noted the 8th Illinois was "regarded as the finest regiment in the Army of the Potomac." John S. Mosby, *The Memoirs of Colonel John S. Mosby* (Boston, 1917), 286.

Chapter 5

Opening the Ball:
Early Morning, July 1, 1863

As day broke, Buford's anxieties were borne out with the discovery that Confederate infantry was marching east along the Chambersburg Pike toward Gettysburg.[1] The foot soldiers belonged to Maj. Gen. Henry Heth's division, who set out "to feel the enemy," as he would later put it. His division set out about 5:00 a.m.[2] with orders, as recounted by Lee's

---

1 General Henry Heth, age 37, had the unique distinction of being the only man in the Army of Northern Virginia that Robert E. Lee called by his first name—Harry. Heth also understood his own limitations and was not afraid to laugh at them. Handsome and charming, the West Point-trained Heth shared the same aristocratic Virginia roots as did Lee. He finished dead last in the West Point class of 1847, earning the distinction of being called one of "The Immortals," as those who finished last in each class were known. "My four years career at West Point as a student were abominable," he recalled. "My thoughts ran in the channel of fun. How to get to Benny Havens' occupied more of my time than Legendre or calculus. The time given to study was measured by the amount of time necessary to be given to prevent failure at the annual examinations." Heth admitted he barely cracked a book during his first six months at West Point. Morrison, *The Memoirs of Henry Heth*, 15, 16-17. He was the first colonel of the 45th Virginia Infantry, and made his way up the ranks to division command. When Heth's friend A. P. Hill was plucked from his six-brigade "Light Division" and promoted to lead the newly created Third Corps after Chancellorsville, Lee faced a difficult choice for Hill's replacement. Although he selected William Dorsey Pender for that position, he also believed Heth needed a division as well. "Of General Heth," wrote Lee, "I have to say that I consider him a most excellent officer, and gallant solider, and had he been with the Division through all its hardships, and acquired the confidence of the men, there is no man I had rather see promoted than he." Instead, Lee took two brigades from Hill's former division (John Brockenbrough's Virginians and James Archer's Tennesseans and Alabamans) and added them to a pair of brigades ordered up from the Carolinas (Johnston Pettigrew's North Carolinians and Joe Davis' Mississippians and North Carolinians) to form a new four-brigade division for Heth. As a result, July 1, 1863, was the first time Heth led a division in combat. Tagg, *The Generals of Gettysburg*, 340-341.

2 OR 27, pt. 2, 637.

Maj. Gen. Henry Heth, commander of Heth's
Division, Hill's Corps. Heth and Buford
served together in the Regular Army.
Library of Congress

military secretary Col. Walter Taylor,
"to ascertain what force was at
Gettysburg, and, if he [Heth] found
infantry opposed to him, to report the
fact immediately, without forcing an
engagement." In short, Heth was not to
bring on a battle.[3] Neither A. P. Hill nor
Heth expected a major fight that
morning. Heth (who was inexperienced
at division command) made sloppy
dispositions.

"The Battle of Gettysburg was by the result purely of an accident," claimed
Heth years after the end of the war, "for which I am probably more than anyone
else, accountable."[4] The Virginian made a number of critical errors that
morning. His first was ordering his column forward with no skirmishers leading
the way well to the front. Because he had no cavalry to screen his advance, Heth
should have deployed these skirmishers to avoid stumbling into a fight at a
disadvantage. This was a critical blunder because it meant that his column
would grope blindly for the enemy as it marched along.

His march order was also curious. Even though there was no Rebel cavalry
scouting in advance of the infantry, Heth placed his vulnerable artillery near the
head of his column, allowing it to lead the way. He compounded that error by
placing Brig. Gen. James J. Archer's brigade at the van of his infantry column.
Archer's brigade had been hit hard at Chancellorsville and was the smallest in
his division.[5] If a battle broke out, Archer's men would necessarily bear the

3   Walter H. Taylor, "The Campaign in Pennsylvania," *Annals of the War* (Philadelphia, 1879),
307.

4   Letter from General H. Heth, *Southern Historical Society Papers* (1877), 4:157.

5   Marylander James J. Archer was 45 at Gettysburg. He graduated from Princeton University
in 1835 and studied law at the University of Maryland. He was admitted to the bar and practiced
law until the outbreak of the Mexican War in 1846, when he joined the Regular Army as a

Brig. Gen. James J. Archer, commander, Archer's Brigade, Heth's Division. Archer was captured during the fighting with the Iron Brigade on July 1, 1863.

Museum of the Confederacy

brunt of the fighting. Heth's third error was putting Brig. Gen. Joseph R. Davis's brigade behind Archer. This command was the most inexperienced brigade in Hill's Third Corps, and Davis' primary qualification for command was that his uncle was Confederate President Jefferson Davis.[6] Davis should have been at the rear of the column, not second in line.

Jaquelin Marshall Meredith, Heth's divisional chaplain, rode east that morning with regimental colonel Robert M. Mayo of the 47th Virginia and his brigade commander, Col. John M. Brockenbrough. Marshall claimed he heard Capt. Stockton Heth, the general's brother and aide-de-camp, tell Brockenbrough, "General Heth is ordered to move on Gettysburg, and fight or not as he wishes." As Captain Heth rode away, Brockenbrough turned to Mayo

---

captain, winning a brevet for valor at Chapultepec. Archer resigned his commission after the war and returned to the practice of law, but rejoined the Army in 1855. He resigned in 1861 and accepted a commission in the Confederate service. Later that year, he was promoted to brigadier general and assumed command of a brigade. His brigade was a mainstay of A. P. Hill's famous "Light Division." Tagg, *The Generals of Gettysburg*, 349-351.

6 At 38, Joe Davis (like his men) was seeing his first combat on July 1, 1863. While "a very pleasant and unpretending gentleman," he was far outside his expertise. He attended Miami University in Oxford, Ohio, and returned to his home state of Mississippi to practice law. He was elected to the Mississippi state senate in 1860 as a States Rights advocate. With the coming of war he joined the Confederate army as a captain, and was promoted to lieutenant colonel of the 10th Mississippi Infantry and then to its colonel. Davis was assigned to serve on his uncle's staff in Richmond. Without ever having led troops in combat, he was promoted to brigadier general in September 1862, but the Confederate Senate refused to confirm the promotion. Once Jefferson Davis promised political rewards, the Senate confirmed the appointment two days later. In January 1863, he was assigned to command a large brigade of Mississippi troops in North Carolina. This brigade was one of the two brought north to make up part of the new division organized for Harry Heth. The brigade joined the Army of Northern Virginia at the end of May 1863. Tagg, *The Generals of Gettysburg*, 352-353.

Brig. Gen. Joseph R. Davis, commander, Davis' Brigade, Heth's Division. Davis, a nephew of Confederate President Jefferson Davis, was not competent to command a large body of troops.

USAHEC

and said, "We must fight them; no division general will turn back with such orders." As events would bear out, Heth was determined to bring on a fight—even if Marshall's recollection was not wholly accurate.[7]

Lieutenant A. H. Moore of the 7th Tennessee, part of Archer's command, rose that morning with the rest of his comrades before sunrise. They enjoyed "confiscated chicken" for breakfast, broke their crude camp, and headed east on the Chambersburg Pike toward Gettysburg. Their leisurely pace allowed them to enjoy the pleasant summer morning. General Archer had promised them that there were no Yankees nearby, so they plodded along blissfully unaware of the threat waiting up ahead.[8] Before long, Lieutenant Moore spotted Buford's videttes on the same distant ridgeline where he had spotted a handful of Union horse soldiers the day before. This time they were there in force. When Moore reported their presence to Archer, however, the brigadier ordered him to return to his regiment and continue the march. "Our corps, as well as the whole of Lee's army, was without cavalry," recalled the Tennessee lieutenant, "and, as every soldier knows, we were liable, unawares, to encounter the enemy."[9]

About five miles from town, west of the hamlet of Seven Stars and anticipating fighting, Col. Birkett D. Fry of the 13th Alabama of Archer's

---

7   Meredith, "The First Day at Gettysburg," 185.

8   William Thomas Venner, *The 7th Tennessee Infantry in the Civil War* (Jefferson, NC, 2013), 80.

9   Moore, "Heth's Division at Gettysburg," 384.

A previously unpublished image of Maj. Charles Lemmon, 3rd Indiana Cavalry. Lemmon was the highest-ranking officer of Buford's division to die at Gettysburg.

Indiana State Library and Archives

brigade ordered his regimental colors unfurled.[10] Fry, a capable commander, advanced cautiously with his skirmishers deployed, expecting contact with enemy forces known to be in the area.[11] When Pvt. E. T. Boland of the 13th Alabama spotted a group of Union cavalrymen holding their horses in a field south of the Chambersburg Pike, he realized things were about to get interesting.[12]

On the Union side of the line, 31-year-old Maj. Charles Lemmon of the 3rd Indiana Cavalry had a premonition that early morning. He called to fellow Hoosier Maj. William McClure to join him under a nearby tree, where Lemmon rested in the shade. When McClure approached, Lemmon said, "Major, take a drink with me; it will be the last one we will ever take together, as I will be a dead man before night." The two officers drank from the same canteen before McClure continued out to the picket line; Lemmon remained with the regiment.[13]

With dawn breaking over South Mountain, the 8th Illinois troopers holding the vidette post on the crest of Knoxlyn Ridge scanned the western horizon from the backs of their horses. "The weather had been terribly hot and dry, and

10 E. T. Boland, "Beginning the Battle of Gettysburg," *Confederate Veteran* (July, 1906), 14:308.

11 William Frierson Fulton, II, *The War Reminiscences of William Frierson Fulton, II* (Gaithersburg, MD, 1986), 76.

12 Boland, "Beginning the Battle of Gettysburg," 308.

13 Day, "Opening the Battle"; Thomas G. Day, "First Shot at Gettysburg," *The National Tribune*, October 30, 1902.

we wondered as we sat in our saddles if we were in for another scorching day," remembered Pvt. Thomas B. Kelley. "From our orders we did not expect to march that day, and believed we might come into contact with the enemy, though of course we troopers did not know where he was." Not long after, the Illinois horsemen spotted a cloud of dust billowing in the distance. They watched it for a few minutes until the head of a column of marching Confederate infantry broke out of the dust, their battle flags snapping in the morning breeze. Kelley set his spurs and set off to spread the word.[14]

Lieutenant Marcellus E. Jones of the 8th Illinois—a cousin of Private Kelley's— commanded the videttes of the 8th Illinois from his headquarters at Herr's Tavern near the spot where Belmont Schoolhouse Ridge and Herr's Ridge converge. Jones enjoyed the early minutes of the day, munching fresh bread he had just purchased in the town.[15] His pickets scanned to the west for signs of the Confederate advance. It was a misty morning and visibility was not good, so the videttes were particularly attentive. At that moment, Kelley breathlessly reined in his mount and cried, "The Johnnies are coming!" Jones yelled instructions to his first sergeant to call out the entire command, swung into the saddle, and rode west. Within minutes he was watching the giant dust cloud billowing above the trees on the next ridgeline, a sure sign that a large body of infantry was heading their way. Jones scribbled a quick report and sent it back to the main line.[16]

About 7:00 a.m., the head of the Confederate column under General Archer stepped into view on a hill west of Marsh Creek about one mile from Jones' position. When the Rebels spotted the vidette post, they threw out additional skirmishers and continued advancing. Jones sent most of his command to the rear with their horses, borrowed Sgt. Levi Schaffer's Sharps carbine, rested the weapon on a fence post, and squeezed off a single shot at a mounted officer (possibly Colonel Fry of the 13th Alabama). The distance was

<hr/>

14 "Opened the Fight at Gettysburg."

15 Jones, age 33, was raised in Vermont as the descendant of Revolutionary War veterans. He settled in the Chicago area in 1850 and became a prominent building contractor before the war. He was one of the first residents of Danby to enlist in 1861, joining Co. E of the 8th Illinois Cavalry. He originally declined to serve as an officer, but was commissioned a second lieutenant in the regiment in December of 1862. J. David Petruzzi, "Faded Hoofbeats—Marcellus Jones, 8th Illinois Cavalry," http://petruzzi.wordpress.com/2007/05/31/faded-hoofbeats-marcellus-jones-8th-illinois-cavalry/.

16 "Opened the Fight at Gettysburg."

A post-war view, looking west along the Chambersburg Pike from the crest of Knoxlyn Ridge, where Lt. Marcellus Jones fired the first shot of the Battle of Gettysburg. The Jacob Lott farm is on the left. Marsh Creek marks the lowest spot visible in the photograph.

Gettysburg National Military Park

about 600 yards, well beyond the carbine's effective range.[17] Jones' shot, which likely hit nothing, may have been the first shot of the battle of Gettysburg.[18]

The echoing crack of Jones' shot triggered a smattering of fire up and down the vidette line. One of Jones's men galloped off to report the Confederate advance to division headquarters. Captain Daniel Buck, who commanded the squadron of the 8th Illinois on vidette duty, sent word that the enemy was advancing in two columns, which prompted Major Beveridge to dispatch a

17 The Journal of Marcellus E. Jones, July 1, 1863.

18 The question of who fired the first shot at Gettysburg has been the subject of intense controversy for many years. Many claimed that Pvt. Alphonse Hodges of the 9th New York Cavalry fired the first shot, but the evidence does not support that claim. For a detailed discussion of this controversy, see J. David Petruzzi, "Opening the Ball at Gettysburg: The Shot that Rang for 50 Years," *America's Civil War* (July 2006), 30-36.

second squadron to reinforce Buck and send orderlies into Gettysburg to raise the alarm.[19] Lieutenant Henry E. Dana of the 8th Illinois rode out and spotted a continuous line of Confederate infantry advancing toward the Federal videttes. Dana called in the pickets, sent his horses to the rear, and scattered his dismounted men to the right and left at intervals of 30 feet, placing them behind fence posts and rails to create the illusion of greater strength. Dana "directed them to throw up their carbine sights for 800 yards, then taking rest on the top rail, we gave the enemy the benefit of long-range practice from a long, much attenuated line." This was the day's first formed line of battle. It consisted of 20 of the videttes, including Dana himself, a few hundred yards behind the initial picket posts in the valley between Knoxlyn Ridge and Herr's Ridge. Dana also noted, "Our first position proved to be well-taken—in our front there was a large open field. . . . The firing was rapid from our carbines, and, at the time, induced the belief of four times the number of men actually present, as we learned from prisoners taken soon afterward."[20]

As the fighting intensified, messengers found General Buford at his headquarters at the Blue Eagle Hotel. Buford ordered his signal officer, Lieutenant Jerome, to ascend to the cupola of the Lutheran Seminary to observe the Confederate advance. The signal officer obeyed and sent periodic updates to Buford of the fighting raging along the Chambersburg Pike.[21]

Dana and his videttes retired at a snail's pace. "The pickets fell back slowly, making all the resistance in their power," remembered the regimental historian of the 8th Illinois, "and arrangements were made to hold the rebels in check until the infantry could come up."[22] Private Kelley saw it differently. "When the fight actually began it was hot and heavy," he recalled. "We were outnumbered five to one, dismounted cavalry against infantry. We just had to fight for all that was in us until our infantry could come up."[23] When the Confederate infantry eventually realized that all they faced was a thin skirmish line of dismounted cavalry, they pressed forward against the front and flanks of the Union skirmish

19 Beveridge, "Address," 17.

20 Theodore W. Bean, "Who Fired the Opening Shots! General Buford at Gettysburg—the Cavalry Ride Into Pennsylvania and the Choice of the Field of Battle—the First Day on the Outposts Before the Arrival of the Infantry," *Philadelphia Weekly Times*, February 2, 1878.

21 Jerome, "Buford in the Battle of Oak Ridge," 152.

22 Hard, *History of the Eighth Cavalry*, 256.

23 "Opened the Fight at Gettysburg."

lines. "We retired, and continued to take new positions, and usually held out as long as we could without imminent risk of capture. We thought the [rest of the 8th Illinois Cavalry] was slow in coming to our support. We had been driving from three positions successively in less than one hour before support came."[24]

"Startled this morning by the report of the pickets that the rebs were advancing in force up the Chambersburg Road. Saddled in a hurry—and advanced towards the hills," a trooper of the 3rd Indiana Cavalry recorded in his diary that night.[25] Private Thomas G. Day, also of the 3rd Indiana, had intended to ride back into town for breakfast, but he had to water and feed his horse first. His mount was drinking from a trough by a house along the Chambersburg Pike when he heard two gunshots. The alarmed trooper looked up and to his surprise, spotted enemy infantry heading straight at him. The private leaped on his horse and galloped back to camp to spread the word. "Our company being the first to form, was rushed over the bridge and down to the house where I had watered my horse," he recalled. "Then we were deployed, and skirmished with the Johnnies as we could. Our orders were to hold them back. I suppose other companies were to help our company, but I do not know."[26] Another trooper from the 3rd Indiana, Pvt. Edward C. Reid, was detailed as a skirmisher under Major Lemmon. Lemmon and his skirmishers were driven back and rejoined the main body of the regiment. "Moved back and forward over the field between Getsbg and the Seminary avoiding exposure to shell with difficulty," was how Reid explained the event.[27]

"Boots and Saddles" sounded in the Union cavalry camps near Mcpherson's Ridge as the troopers prepared to meet the looming threat. "The bugles sounded in the clear summer air, and we awoke ready, as never before, to do or die," recalled Capt. William Hazelton of the 8th Illinois Cavalry. "Such a spirit animated our cavalrymen that morning—a spirit aroused by the demonstrations of the people of Gettysburg yesterday, and to-day finding expression in deeds of heroism."[28] The blue-clad horse soldiers quickly saddled and mounted their horses and advanced in line of battle along the ridge. The 3rd

---

24 Bean, "Who Fired the Opening Shots!"

25 Edward C. Reid, Diary, July 1, 1863.

26 Day, "Opening the Battle."

27 Edward C. Reid, Diary, July 1, 1863.

28 Hazelton, "An Address Made at a Regimental Reunion."

Indiana Cavalry took a position on the right north of the unfinished railroad cut, with the 12th Illinois Cavalry between the railroad cut and the Chambersburg Pike, the 8th Illinois Cavalry south of the road in and around McPherson's Woods, and the 8th New York Cavalry south of the Illinoisans, extending the line to the Fairfield Road. "Colonel Gamble made an admirable line of battle, and moved off proudly to meet him," reported an admiring Buford.[29]

While Gamble aligned his front, the surprised Confederates pressed forward. When their skirmishers reached Marsh Creek, "the place looked suspicious, the banks of that stream were covered with trees and underbrush, so the skirmishers halted." Part of their ranks deployed into line of battle in an apple orchard, while some advanced as skirmishers. Every man loaded his weapon.[30] "It was a slow, cautious drive," recalled an officer of the 7th Tennessee.[31]

Surprised by the stiff Union resistance, Heth called for the deployment of his artillery. The gunners did not appreciate their predicament as they rumbled along toward Gettysburg that morning. The artillery battalion "march[ed] behind our whole corps and were considered as in reserve but when the time came for fighting, we opened it,"[32] complained one of the gunners. Lieutenant John Marye of the Fredericksburg Artillery was not expecting a fight. He recalled that the "morning was lovely. A soft, fresh breeze rippled over ripe wheat fields stretching away on either side of us. We moved forward leisurely smoking and chatting as we rode along, not dreaming of the proximity of the enemy."[33]

While the infantry deployed, Maj. William J. Pegram, commanding Heth's artillery battalion, brought up Capt. Edward A. Marye's Fredericksburg Artillery and deployed it in the road near Blocher's Schoolhouse. "Load with shrapnel shell," barked Pegram.[34] Captain Marye recalled speculation that the opposing force were men from Confederate General Longstreet's First Corps.

---

29 OR 27, pt. 1, 927.

30 Chamberlaine, *Memoirs of the Civil War*, 66.

31 J. C. Bingham, "Undated Letter," *Confederate Veteran* (November 1897), 5:565.

32 Robert K. Krick, *The Fredericksburg Artillery* (Lynchburg, VA, 1986), 58.

33 Lt. John L. Marye, "The First Gun at Gettysburg, With the Confederate Advance Guard'," *The American Historical Register* (July 1895), 1,228.

34 Ibid.

Maj. William J. Pegram, commander of the artillery battalion assigned to serve with Hill's 3rd Corps. Although very young, Pegram was a very effective artillery commander.

Lee's Lieutenants

The rumor ended quickly when one man announced "he had passed Longstreet's corps and that it was two days' march in our rear."[35]

When 28-year-old Captain Marye gave the order to load his guns, the owner of the land upon which they had deployed came out and exclaimed, "My God, you are not going to fire here, are you?" The terrified man ran off, hands in the air, when the first lanyard was pulled and the gun recoiled. The round, recorded one eyewitness, "burst high above the line of [Yankees] on the hill."[36] Marye's gunners fired several more shells "in rapid succession, receiving no immediate response" while flushing Buford's troopers from the trees lining Marsh Creek.[37] "Their batteries rained upon our men showers of shot and shell," recalled an Illinois trooper.[38] These opening artillery shots by Marye's guns occupied only "a few minutes."[39]

Lieutenant Colonel John A. Kress of Maj. Gen. James Wadsworth's division arrived outside the Blue Eagle and met with Buford and his staff. "What are you doing here, sir?" Buford asked. Kress replied that he had come to get shoes for men in Wadsworth's First Corps division, which was marching fast to reach the fighting. Buford suggested Kress return to his command,

35 Peter S. Carmichael, *Lee's Young Artillerist: William J. R. Pegram* (Charlottesville, VA, 1995), 98.

36 Martin, *Gettysburg*, July 1, 66.

37 Marye, "The First Gun at Gettysburg," 1229.

38 Hard, *History of the Eighth Cavalry*, 256.

39 Krick, *The Fredericksburg Artillery*, 59.

prompting the staff officer to ask, "Why, what is the matter, General?" At that moment, Marye's opening gun boomed, and as he mounted his thoroughbred warhorse Grey Eagle, Buford tersely snapped, "That's the matter!"[40] Buford put spurs to Grey Eagle and headed for the sound of the guns.

When he arrived at the front lines, calmly puffing his pipe, Buford told one of his staff, "Give my compliments to Colonel Gamble, and tell him to move out with his command and meet the enemy; we must keep him out of the town as long as possible. Tell the colonel to keep me posted as to the enemy's movements from time to time."[41]

Asa Hardman of the 3rd Indiana Cavalry overheard Buford order "all poorly mounted men to the rear. Five men were ordered to turn out of our company, myself among them. Going to the rear, we turned our disabled horses into the corral and three of us returned."[42] Buford directed the horses be concealed in swales wherever possible to protect the animals and to create the illusion that infantry awaited the Confederates and not dismounted cavalry.[43] Dismounting the cavalrymen to fight on foot, however, reduced Gamble's effective strength by 25 percent, as one out of every four troopers drew the unwelcome but necessary task of holding his horse and those of three of his comrades so the mounts were nearby and could be quickly brought up if they were needed.

A blacksmith named Ephraim Wisler owned the property where Union Lieutenant Jones fired the first shot of the battle. His curiosity piqued, Wisler stepped out of his house to see what the commotion was all about. He foolishly stood in the middle of the Chambersburg Pike atop Knoxlyn Ridge to watch the Confederates advancing from the west. A well-aimed shot by one of Pegram's gunners hit the road near Wisler's feet, showering him with gravel and dirt. The terrified Wisler fled back inside his home and was apparently so mortified by this experience that he died of heart failure shortly after the end of the battle.[44]

---

40 Abner Doubleday, *Chancellorsville and Gettysburg* (New York, 1882), 126.

41 Theophilus F. Rodenbough, *The Bravest Five Hundred of '61* (New York, 1891), 41.

42 Asa Sleath Hardman, "As a Union Prisoner Saw the Battle of Gettysburg," *Civil War Times Illustrated* (July 1962), 47.

43 Wilson, "Dedication Oration," 186.

44 "Some Stories of the Great Battle," *Gettysburg Compiler*, January 14, 1903.

The Virginia artillerists limbered up and proceeded on for another mile or so before taking position "in the edge of a beautiful oak grove on the left of the pike." Pegram deployed the rest of his battalion perpendicular to the road on either side facing east toward Willoughby Run. "Steady and well aimed" fire from Calef's guns ranged in, "though none of our battery was struck in this position." When Heth shouted for Pegram to "Whale away!" his gunners returned the fire, triggering a heavy counter-battery duel. "The enemy . . . showered us warmly," admitted Colonel Chapman of the 3rd Indiana Cavalry. Lieutenant John Morris, "a gallant young gentleman" who served as the Confederate artillery battalion's ordnance officer, "was mortally wounded here, while riding in rear of our guns across the line of fire." Calef's accurate artillery fire finally convinced Heth that he was facing units from the Army of the Potomac, and not home guard militia.[45]

"After a dozen shots had been fired into the grove by the Fredericksburg battery, General Heth directed Archer's Tennessee brigade against it [the grove] realizing that, once in their possession, the Federal line from the Fairfield Road to Oak Hill was theirs," correctly observed a veteran of the Army of the Potomac's Cavalry Corps after the battle and with the benefit of hindsight. "But his experience with Buford's videttes, and with a squadron of skirmishers mounted and dismounted, compelled him to great caution without cavalry when he was strong enough to have marched to the crest of McPherson's Ridge, with loss of course, but could not have been stopped by the small force that opposed him. There was something in the air about him that he did not understand."[46] Heth ordered up his infantry for battle, which took some time and was precisely what Buford needed.

James Archer followed his orders to deploy, but was unhappy about the entire arrangement. His Tennesseans and Alabama troops fell into line south of the Chambersburg Pike, with Fry's 13th Alabama on the far right and the 1st, 14th, and 7th Tennessee regiments extending the line northward toward the roadway. Major A. S. Van de Graff's 5th Alabama Battalion spread across Archer's front as skirmishers. Joe Davis' men, meanwhile, deployed north of the pike, with the 42nd Mississippi closest to the road, and the 2nd Mississippi

---

45 J. David Petruzzi, "John Buford by the Book," *America's Civil War* (July 2005), 28; Chapman Diary, July 1, 1863; Krick, *The Fredericksburg Artillery*, 58-59; Chamberlaine, *Memoirs of the Civil War*, 67.

46 James K. P. Scott, *The Story of the Battles at Gettysburg* (Harrisburg, PA, 1927), 136-137.

and 55th North Carolina extending the line north. Clouds of skirmishers from the 55th North Carolina took position well in advance of the main line. When all was ready Heth ordered his brigadiers "to advance, the object being to feel the enemy, to make a forced reconnaissance, and determine in what force the enemy were—whether or not he was massing his forces on Gettysburg." Archer protested. His combat-depleted command, he explained, was too "light to risk so far in advance of support." Heth rejected this wise advice and repeated the order to move forward. The long line stepped forward.[47]

Following behind Archer and Davis were Heth's two remaining brigades, Col. John M. Brockenbrough's Virginians and Johnston Pettigrew's Tar Heels.[48] Both halted to deploy into line of battle. The Virginians went into line of battle just south of the pike, with 55th's left near the road, and the 47th, 40th, and 22nd Virginia Battalion extending the line south. Pettigrew organized a line on Brockenbrough's right, with the 26th, 11th, 47th, and 52nd North Carolina regiments running farther south. Heth's entire division resumed its slow advance toward Gettysburg, with Davis and Archer well to the front. Taking the time to organize his entire division into lines of battle and then moving east committed Heth to a large fight he had been ordered not to bring on. If he met with stout resistance, however—and he knew at this time that he was facing some elements of the Army of the Potomac—Heth would be hard-pressed to disengage.

"As soon as skirmishers deployed, firing commenced all along the line," recalled Major Beveridge of the 8th Illinois Cavalry. "Our pickets mounted, firing, fell back slowly upon the reserve, when dismounting, sent their horses to the rear and fighting on foot, bravely resisted and retarded the advance of the

---

47 OR 27, pt. 2, 637; J. B. Turney, "The First Tennessee at Gettysburg," Confederate Veteran (December 1900), vol. 8, 535.

48 Colonel John Mercer Brockenbrough was the weakest link in a division that had a number of weak links, beginning at the top with Heth himself. A 33-year-old farmer trained at the Virginia Military Institute, Brockenbrough was made colonel of the 40th Virginia Infantry in 1861. He led his regiment in combat throughout the 1862 Peninsula campaign and succeeded to brigade command at the September 1, 1862 battle of Chantilly when brigade commander Brig. Gen. Charles Field fell wounded. His brigade, previously one of the best in the Army of Northern Virginia, lost much of its effectiveness under Brockenbrough's distinctly uninspired command. He was not competent to command anything larger than a regiment, and he failed miserably on both July 1 and July 3 at Gettysburg. Tagg, *The Generals of Gettysburg*, 346-347. For a detailed discussion of Brockenbrough's poor performance at Gettysburg, see Bradley M. Gottfried, "To Fail Twice: Brockenbrough's Brigade at Gettysburg," *Gettysburg Magazine: Articles of Lasting Historical Interest* (July 2000), No. 23, 66-75.

A post-war image of Col. John M. Brockenbrough, commander, Brockenbrough's Brigade, Heth's Division. Brockenbrough performed very poorly at the Battle of Gettysburg, was passed over for promotion to general, and resigned his commission. *USAHEC*

enemy."[49] A mounted and unidentified Union trooper riding a white horse—perhaps trooper David Diffen-baugh of Co. G, 8th Illinois Cavalry—strayed in front of the advance of the reinforcements and was immediately shot from the saddle.[50] A few minutes later, Pvt. John E. Weaver of Co. A, 3rd Indiana Cavalry, was badly wounded in the left thigh by Confederate artillery fire. His leg was later amputated, but Weaver did not survive the wound and died a month later.[51] Major Van de Graff, whose 5th Alabama Battalion provided Archer's skirmishers on this day, "lost only 7 men wounded although we drove the Calvary Pickets & Skirmishers of the Enemy over three miles," he wrote his wife a few days after the fight. "[D]uring the battle a shell exploded at my feet covering me with dirt and filling my eyes."[52]

A small dog trotting along with Van de Graff's 5th Alabama was its first fatality: "He was the first fellow shot in the ranks in the first day's battle," recalled one of the Alabama men. "He was an innocent bystander, a harmless onlooker, so to speak, with no concern either way as to which side should win, yet he was first struck in the shower of lead and his life surrendered in the good cause of States Rights and Home Rule." With their mascot down, the Alabamans pressed forward. To their great amusement, a local farmer appeared

49 Beveridge, "Address," 19.

50 William T. Ivry, "At Gettysburg—Who was the Lone Cavalryman Killed Between the Lines?," *The National Tribune*, July 11, 1901.

51 Augustus C. Weaver, *Third Indiana Cavalry* (Greenwood, IN, 1919), 4-5.

52 A. S. Van de Graff to his wife, July 8, 1863, http://historysites.com/civilwar/units/5albn/Vandegraaffltr.htm.

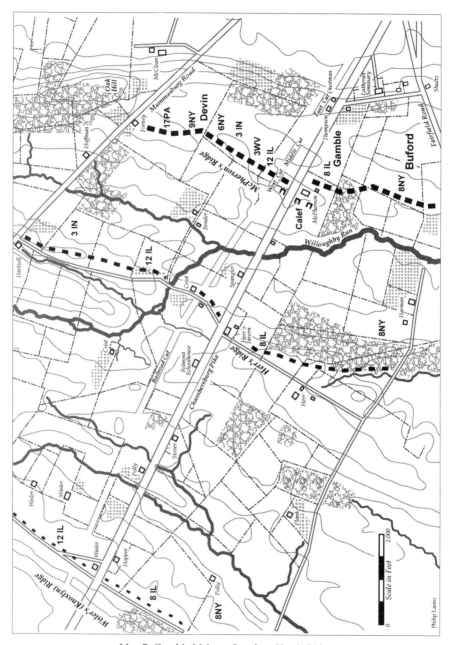

Map 7: Gamble Makes a Stand on Herr's Ridge

and called out, "Tell Lee to hold on just a little until I get my cow out the pasture!" Colonel Fry of the 13th Alabama contended Buford's troopers "did us no damage" and that their resistance was "inconsiderable," but the evidence does not support Fry's claim. "The enemy fell back slowly, resisting our approach," countered a soldier of the 7th Tennessee.[53]

The first Confederate casualties fell during this phase of the fighting, both on the skirmish line. Private C. L. F. Worley of Co. A, 5th Alabama Battalion, suffered a severe wound to this thigh and was carried from the battlefield. He refused chloroform, declaring, "cut off the leg, Doc, but leave off the chloroform, if you can stand it, I can."[54] Henry Raison of Co. B of the 7th Tennessee was killed.[55]

Gamble sent some 900 skirmishers of his First Brigade forward to Herr's and Belmont Schoolhouse Ridges to "keep back the enemy as long as possible till our infantry came up to support."[56] Gamble also ordered Calef's six three-inch rifles into action along the Chambersburg Pike. The Irishman permitted Calef to select the positions for his three sections. The artilleryman chose the center of Gamble's line, on either side of the road "on a crest on top of the one he had occupied during the night." After his men leveled fences and his guns were posted, Calef sought out Buford and found the general with his staff in the road. On Buford's orders, Calef changed his deployment, moving one of his two-gun sections 600 yards away "to cover as large a front as possible with my battery . . . for the purpose of deceiving the enemy as to [our] strength."[57] Buford also ordered farmer Slentz to get his family out of the line of fire; the battle was coming right at them.[58]

Buford's deployment of Calef's guns 600 yards apart was in compliance with army doctrine. Buford's friend, John Gibbon, was a career artillerist and the author of *The Artillerists' Manual*, the "bible" for U.S. army gunners. According to Gibbon's manual, "the contour of the ground is of the first importance, and if properly taken advantage of, may be made to double the force and importance of artillery." Gibbon's doctrine also stated, "A rifled battery when in support of a battle line, opposed by superior numbers of

53 Fulton, *War Reminiscences*, 76; Petruzzi and Stanley, *The Complete Gettysburg Guide*, 26; Birkett D. Fry to John B. Bachelder, February 10, 1878, *Bachelder Papers*, 3:1932; Venner, *7th Tennessee Infantry*, 85.

54 Fulton, *War Reminiscences*, 79-80.

55 Swallow, "The First Day at Gettysburg," 441.

56 Gamble to Church, March 10, 1864.

57 Calef, "The Opening Gun," 47.

58 Slentz reparations claims file, copy in files at Gettysburg National Military Park.

A post-war view looking west from McPherson's Ridge toward Herr's Ridge. This would have been the view Buford had on the morning of July 1, 1863. Note the tollhouse in the center of the photograph and the Herr Tavern at the top of the photo on the south side of the Chambersburg Pike. Willoughby Run cuts through the valley between the two ridges.

Gettysburg National Military Park

infantry (and artillery), will be split up and placed by the governing general to strengthen the line. These pieces will concentrate their fire toward the enemy's strongest point and display as much fire power as to convince the enemy there are more guns."[59] As a result, Calef deployed Lt. John Roder's section of two guns on the right side of the Chambersburg Pike, and Sgt. Joseph Newman's section left of the road. The third two-gun section under Sgt. Charles Pergel unlimbered just beyond McPherson's Woods between the 8th New York Cavalry and the 8th Illinois Cavalry.

Once his guns were in place, Calef spotted a "double line of battle gray, and not over a thousand yards distant." The sight impressed the gunner, who thought "their battle flags looked redder and bloodier in the strong July sun than I had ever seen them before."[60] Calef carefully trained his pieces on the double line of gray and opened on them with accurate fire that tore holes in their ranks. A member of the 8th Illinois Cavalry later recalled that, "as our artillery was getting into position a golden feathered chanticleer mounted the

59 John Gibbon, *The Artillerists' Manual, Compiled from Various Sources, and Adapted to the Service of the United States* (Washington, DC, 1860), 354-356.

60 Calef, "The Opening Gun," 48.

top rail of the fence nearby, and looked to the front of the advancing column of rebels; at this moment, our battery opened and chanticleer crowed, and the ball was opened from both sides."[61]

One of Calef's shots knocked down Sgt. George Lamberson of Co. A of the 7th Tennessee. The 28-year-old sergeant shook the cobwebs away and glanced at his rifle. Disgusted, he tossed the weapon aside. "They commenced shooting . . . at us and one [piece of shrapnel] hit the [breech] of my gun and tore it off and turned me around." Unarmed, Lamberson stood and slowly resumed the march east in an effort to catch up with his comrades, who were now advancing at the double-quick "attempting to run from under the shells."[62]

Amelia Harmon's family owned a farm between Willoughby Run and Herr's Ridge. About nine that morning, Amelia and her aunt, who were the only ones at home, heard the boom of Marye's single gun. "We rushed to the window to behold hundreds of galloping horses coming up the road, through the fields and even past our very door," she remembered. "Boom! Again spoke the cannon, more and more galloping horses, their excited riders shouting and yelling to each other and pushing westward in hot haste, past the house and barn, seeing the shelter of a strip of woods on the ridge beyond. But the ridge was alive with the enemy! A few warning shots from its cover sent them flying back to find shelter behind the barn, outbuildings, trees, and even the pump, seeking to hold the enemy in check." The Harmon farm soon became the center of the whirling fight.

"Horses and men were falling under our eyes by shots from an unseen foe, and the confusion became greater every minute," continued Amelia, who with her aunt watched as the Confederates picked off men and horses. A Union officer happened by. "'Look'—we fairly shrieked to him, 'the field is full of Rebels.' 'Leave the window,' he shouted in return, 'or you'll be killed!' We needed no second warning and rushed to the cupola," where the women watched the drama unfold in front of them as Buford's troopers resisted the weight of the Confederate advance.[63]

---

61 Unidentified member, 8th Illinois Cavalry to Editor Beacon, July 31, 1863, in *Aurora Beacon*, August 20, 1863.

62 Venner, *The 7th Tennessee Infantry*, 86.

63 Andrew I. Dalton, *Beyond the Run: The Emanuel Harmon Farm at Gettysburg* (Gettysburg, PA, 2013), 14.

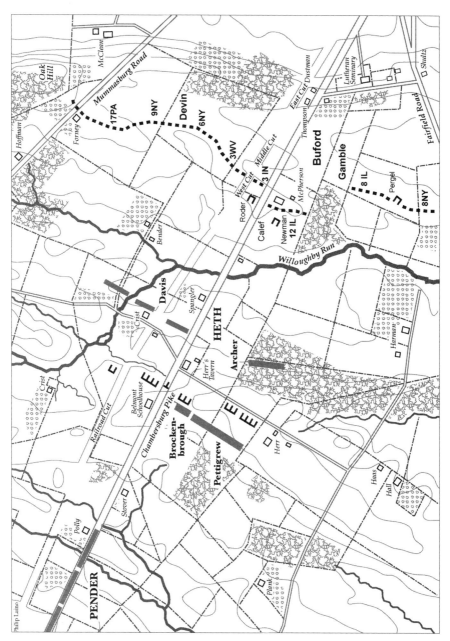

Map 8: Heth Drives Gamble from Herr's Ridge and Advances on McPherson's Ridge

The unexpected, effective, and rapid fire of the dismounted troopers, combined with the well-aimed shots of Calef's guns, slowed the Confederate advance to a crawl. "Buford was there to stay, and stay he did," recalled a trooper of the 8th Illinois Cavalry. "We could hold any skirmish line the rebels could put against us in check."[64] Colonel William L. Markell of the 8th New York observed, "The fighting soon became general and sharp along the whole line, our skirmishers stubbornly resisting every inch of the enemy's advance although the Confederates were there in overpowering numbers. In a short time the line was compelled to fall back to the next ridge, less than a quarter of a mile in the rear."[65]

Buford's command suffered several casualties during the fight for Belmont Schoolhouse Ridge and Herr's Ridge. One of Marye's shells burst near 18-year-old Pvt. Ferdinand Ushuer of Co. C of the 12th Illinois Cavalry. The spraying shrapnel struck and instantly killed Ushuer, who was on the western slope of Herr's Ridge when he fell. Captain William H. Redman of the 12th Illinois remembered Ushuer as "a manly boy, a true patriot, and as brave a hero as ever unsheathed a sword." He was "the first man to lay his life on the altar of his country at Gettysburg."[66]

Heth had not expected such stiff resistance. After the war he candidly admitted as much and, thinking he faced militia and not the Army of the Potomac, wrote that he was careless with the disposition of his troops that morning. Buford's dismounted cavalry maintained a sharp fire that slowly but surely took a toll on Heth's men.[67] The advance took nearly 90 minutes to cover the single mile between Knoxlyn Ridge and Herr Ridge. Just by opening fire on

---

64 J. M. Gardner, "Union vs. Rebel Cavalry: The Superiority of the Former Proved on Many Bloody Fields," *The National Tribune*, May 24, 1888.

65 Col. William L. Markell, "Historical Sketch of the 8th New York Cavalry," in *New York at Gettysburg*, 3 vols. (Albany, NY, 1902), 3:1145.

66 "Address of W. H. Redman at the Dedication of the Monument to the 12th Illinois Cavalry," *Illinois Monuments at Gettysburg* (Springfield, IL, 1892), 33. Redman believed Ushuer's remains were never identified and that he likely rests in the "unknown" section of the Gettysburg National Cemetery. It is important to note Redman was not correct in his claim that Ushuer was the first Union soldier to fall at Gettysburg. That sad honor went to Pvt. George Sandoe, a member of a local militia cavalry company, Bell's Cavalry, when Jubal Early's Confederate division advanced on Gettysburg on June 26. For a detailed discussion of the circumstances of Sandoe's death, see J. David Petruzzi and Steven Stanley, *The Complete Gettysburg Guide: Walking and Driving Tours of the Battlefield, Town, Cemeteries, Field Hospital Sites, and other Topics of Historical Interest* (El Dorado Hills, CA, 2009), 16-17.

67 Kempster, "The Cavalry at Gettysburg," 402-403. In fact, Heth's after-action report of the battle states, "It may not be improper to remark at this time—9 o'clock on the morning of July 1—I was ignorant of what force was at or near Gettysburg, and I supposed that it consisted of cavalry, most probably supported by a brigade or two of infantry." *OR* 27, pt. 2, 637.

Heth's unsuspecting men, Buford gained two hours of precious time for the Union infantry to come up, and his command was still in good fighting trim.

Pegram, meanwhile, ordered up his entire battalion of 21 guns, which unlimbered and focused their fire on Calef's six dispersed pieces. The gunners traded fire at some 1,300 yards for more than an hour, with both sides landing well-aimed shots that inflicted casualties on the crews and horses of both sides.[68] "At one time the enemy had a concentric fire on this battery [Calef] from twelve guns, all at short range," noted Buford.[69]

Gamble's troopers held Herr Ridge for about half an hour until the overwhelming force of the Southern infantry, coupled with the severe and accurate fire of Marye's artillery, drove their thin single-rank skirmish line off the ridge about 8:00.[70] Gamble's troopers withdrew in orderly skirmish lines .

During this phase of the fighting, Gamble deployed the rest of his men into line farther east atop McPherson's Ridge as his pickets retired to their prepared positions, taking heavy fire from Marye's guns as they fell back. Trooper Flavius Bellamy of the 3rd Indiana Cavalry noted in his journal, "Our regt. stood the shelling from three Rebel batteries for more than an hour."[71] Major William H. Medill of the 8th Illinois recorded, "We held our position . . . we actually compelled them to change their line of battle several times."[72] Marcellus Jones, who had fired the first round that morning with a Sharps carbine, recalled, "The smoke from our carbines was visible along the entire line. . . . Now we were determined to hold Herr Ridge. At last we yielded to superior numbers and slowly retired down the hill, keeping up a hot fire," he continued. "Now as the enemy's skirmishers came in full view of them [Calef's] four guns echoed along the hills, to show the enemy we had support at hand. Soon however the enemy ran up to their skirmish line sixteen pieces of artillery and opened fire."[73]

68 Carmichael, *Lee's Young Artillerist*, 100.

69 OR 27, pt. 1, 927.

70 Bean, "Who Fired the First Shot!"

71 Flavius J. Bellamy, Diary, July 1, 1863, F.J. Bellamy Papers, Robert Brake Collection, USAHEC.

72 Letter of William H. Medill, *The Chicago Tribune*, November 22, 1863.

73 Journal of Marcellus E. Jones, July 1, 1863.

Col. William Sackett, commander of the 9th New York Cavalry of Devin's Brigade. Sackett was killed in action on June 11, 1864 on the first day of the Battle of Trevilian Station.
Library of Congress

Given the heavy odds he faced west of Gettysburg, Buford's carefully constructed plan had thus worked to perfection. Whether it would continue to do so remained to be seen.

*   *   *

Colonel William Sackett of the 9th New York Cavalry commanded Tom Devin's picket line, which extended from the Chambersburg Pike north and east in a wide arc to the York Road on the eastern side of Gettysburg. The broad swath of Union videttes covered four different important roads. Sackett placed a squadron of his regiment on high ground astride the Harrisburg Road. Three miles north of Gettysburg, a battalion of the 17th Pennsylvania Cavalry under the command of Maj. James Q. Anderson covered the Carlisle Road. Several troopers of the 9th New York Cavalry picketed the Hunterstown Road. Early that morning, some time between 5:00 and 6:00 a.m., a small party of the Confederates attacked these videttes.[74] As Capt. Edwin E. Bouldin of the 14th Virginia Cavalry, part of Albert Jenkins' brigade, recalled, "some of Jenkins' brigade were in the extreme advance, the 1st day, and brought on the first fighting at Gettysburg."[75] These troopers likely led the advance of Ewell's Second Corps as it made its way toward Gettysburg. It is well possible that either one of Bouldin's men—or possibly one of Major Anderson's men—fired the first shot of the battle, and not Marcellus Jones, for Bouldin's Rebel troopers moved toward Gettysburg

74 Wilber G. Bentley, "Dedication of Monument. 9th Regiment Cavalry—'Westfield Cavalry,'" in *New York at Gettysburg*, 3 vols. (Albany, NY, 1902), 3:1153.

75 E. E. Bouldin to Benjamin F. Eakle, March 31, 1886, *Bachelder Papers*, 2:1271-1272.

Brig. Gen. Albert G. Jenkins, commander, Jenkin's Brigade. One of Jenkins' cavalrymen may have fired the first shot of the Battle of Gettysburg. *Library of Congress*

along the Hunterstown Road well before Heth's advance along the Chambersburg Pike.[76]

It was about daybreak when one of Major Anderson's videttes spotted a contingent of Confederate skirmishers advancing toward their position on the Carlisle Road. Anderson ordered his men to fall back, called for reinforcements, and reported the advance of the lead elements of Ewell's Second Corps. His dismounted troopers took position behind a stone wall on the Samuel Cobean farm, where the reserves arrived to reinforce them. They sent their horses to the rear and waited for the Southerners—probably Brig. Gen. Albert G. Jenkins' cavalrymen—to move within range of their carbines. Once they did, the Union horse soldiers opened fire on them, and a brisk little exchange erupted.[77]

Corporal Cyrus James served in Co. G of the 9th New York Cavalry. That morning, he told his friend John Baker, "John, if I am killed or wounded in this battle, you see that I am cared for or buried, and if you are killed or wounded, I will do the same for you," to which Baker readily agreed. The two horse soldiers rode out to the northern end of Devin's vidette line to a knoll on the Samuel Cobean farm to get a better look. "There is a lot of the Graybacks now," observed James right before one of them shot and killed him. His horse reared and galloped away, dragging the dead man into the town, with Baker following

76 It is unknown precisely who fired the first shots in Devin's sector of the battlefield. The fact that the first shot was probably fired in Devin's sector does not in any way detract from or diminish the significance of the actions of Lieutenant Jones and his brave little band of videttes. In the end, their action had a much greater impact on the course and outcome of the battle than did this forgotten little exchange of shots along the Carlisle Road.

77 Richard S. Shue, *Morning on Willoughby Run, July 1, 1863* (Gettysburg, PA, 1995), 54.

Maj. James Q. Anderson, who commanded a battalion of the 17th Pennsylvania Cavalry on July 1. Anderson was the final colonel of the 17th Pennsylvania.
Moyer, History of the Seventeenth Regiment, Pennsylvania Volunteer Cavalry

after his friend. James' right leg remained tangled in the stirrup of his saddle until septuagenarian, town constable, and War of 1812 veteran John Burns calmed the panicked horse and cut the unfortunate corporal loose. "After exacting a promise from John Burns that he would bury the body, with a very heavy heart I returned to my company," recalled Baker. James was the first Union soldier to die on the northern end of the vidette line.[78]

Tom Devin cobbled together a skirmish line north of Gamble's position. According to Capt. William L. Heermance of the 6th New York Cavalry, "I commanded the skirmish line and advanced over [McPherson's] ridge before the infantry came up." The enemy "They were well on my right flank, and it was supposed we were gobbled up; and with the usual forethought, our horses were called back and we were left to care for ourselves as best we could."[79]

Hearing the firefight blazing at the Cobean farm, Sackett ordered all 6th and 9th New York troopers not otherwise engaged to reinforce Anderson's little command. The men of Capt. Timothy Hanley's squadron of the 9th New York were watering their horses when the order came to mount up. "As soon as each squadron returned it was ordered out on the Mummasburg Road to support the pickets," recounted the regimental historian. "Frapier, the bugler, blew the calls 'Boots and Saddles,' 'Double Quick,' 'Prepare to Mount' in quick

78 John Baker, "The First Man Killed at Gettysburg," *The National Tribune*, September 12, 1901; Cheney, *History of the Ninth Regiment*, 108. Burns became a legendary figure when he grabbed his squirrel rifle and joined the ranks of the Pennsylvanians of Col. Roy Stone's First Corps brigade along McPherson's Ridge after Buford was relieved by Reynolds' arriving infantry.

79 William L. Heermance, "Oration at the Dedication of the Monument to the 6th New York Cavalry," *New York at Gettysburg*, 3:1134.

The Samuel Cobean farmhouse. The first shots of the Battle of Gettysburg were probably fired near here, not at the Wisler blacksmith shop. *Adams County Historical Society*

succession, the men promptly responding, companies F and K having watered their horses were the first to saddle up and reach the picket line."[80]

Captain Hanley ordered 20 men to determine the enemy's position and strength on the 112-acre John Forney farm, prompting the family, who had a six-month-old daughter, to flee to the safety of Mary Forney's father's farm farther west on the Mummasburg Road.[81] These troopers snuck up on some Confederate infantrymen, surprised them, and drove them off. Private Daniel Cornish spotted a fleeing Rebel and squeezed off a perfectly aimed shot that dropped the Southerner. Private Perry Nichols of Co. F of the 9th New York grabbed a winded Confederate—the first prisoner taken during the battle.

80 Cheney, *History of the Ninth Regiment*, 107.

81 Timothy H. Smith, *Farms at Gettysburg: The Fields of Battle* (Gettysburg, PA, 2007), 9. When the Forneys returned home after the Confederates withdrew from Gettysburg, "everything about the place was completely destroyed by the battle except the house and barn, and they were well riddled by shot and shell." Many of the dead men of Brig. Gen. Alfred Iverson's brigade of North Carolinians were buried on the Forney farm property. The Forney house itself was torn down in 1938 prior to the dedication of the Eternal Peace Light Memorial atop Oak Hill. Ibid.

Maj. William E. Beardsley, the commander of
the 6th New York Cavalry at Gettysburg.
USAHEC

Private W. A. Scranton of Co. F, 9th
New York Cavalry, was wounded
during this intensifying skirmishing.[82]

Back closer to the Chambersburg
Pike, meanwhile, Joe Davis' brigade,
arrayed in a long sweeping line of
battle, pressed forward, the left portion
of his front heading straight for some
of Devin's troopers. These Rebels,
recalled one writer, "realizing the
magnitude of resistance . . . nerved themselves for the arduous task, and with
that inimitable 'rebel yell' rushed forward."[83] This was the first combat for many
of Davis' men, and they were about to experience what, for most of them,
would be the hardest day of fighting they would ever experience. Major Alfred
H. Belo, the commander of Davis' 55th North Carolina, held the far left of
brigade's line of battle. "Buford's cavalry were on the extreme right of the
Union lines and were the attacking party opposed to our own left," recalled
Belo, "so I deployed a line of skirmishers from the two extreme left companies
to protect us at that end, and at the same time pick off the cavalrymen, which
move was successful."[84] The 55th North Carolina drove Devin's men beyond

---

82 Cheney, *History of the Ninth Regiment,* 107.

83 William Love, "Mississippi at Gettysburg," *Publications of the Mississippi Historical Society*
(1906), 9:30.

84 Alfred H. Belo, *Memoirs of Alfred Horatio Belo: Reminiscences of a North Carolina Volunteer, Stuart
Wright,* ed. (Gaithersburg, MD, 1992), 20. In an article published in *Confederate Veteran,* Belo
wrote, "The Fifty-Fifth North Carolina was to the left of the line, and as the cavalry was
threatening them, a company was thrown out to protect our left flank." Alfred H. Belo, "The
Battle of Gettysburg: Reminiscences of the Sanguinary Conflict Related by Col. A. H. Belo, of
the Fifty-Fifth North Carolina Infantry, Before the Sterling Price camp, of Dallas, Tex., January
20, 1900," *Confederate Veteran* (April 1900), 8:165. It seems clear that both Pettigrew and Belo
were concerned about the possibility of Buford's cavalry making a mounted charge into their
exposed flanks.

Maj. Alfred H. Belo, 55th North Carolina
Infantry. Belo's troops made some of the
earliest attacks on July 1.
North Carolina Dept. of Archives and History

the Forney farm buildings until some of the New Yorkers rallied and shoved the Tar Heels back to the protection of the Forney Woods.[85]

It was about 9:00 a.m. when Devin, with pressure mounting across his front, pulled his troopers back from the front slope of McPherson's Ridge to take advantage of woods and stone walls to his rear on Seminary Ridge. "I was ordered to retire gradually, as they (the enemy) succeeded in getting the range of my position," he reported. "This I affected in successive formations in line to the rear by regiment."[86] Captain Hanley's battalion of the 9th New York Cavalry "formed dismounted behind a stone wall along the crest of the ridge supported by the other companies of the regiment mounted."[87] The rest of this line extended south toward the Chambersburg Pike, with the 17th Pennsylvania holding the right end of that line, which was positioned on the Mummasburg Road and on Oak Hill.

About the same time Devin was pulling his troopers back to Seminary Ridge, Buford rode up, pointed to the area north of the railroad cut, and said, "Devin, this is the key to the army's position. We must hold this if it costs every man in your command."[88]

The moment of crisis was at hand. Would Buford be able to hold against the mounting pressure long enough for the army's infantry to arrive?

85 Jeffrey M. Girvan, *The 55th North Carolina in the Civil War: A History and Roster* (Jefferson, NC, 2006), 48.

86 OR 27, pt. 1, 939.

87 Cheney, *History of the Ninth Regiment*, 108.

88 *New York at Gettysburg*, 3:1153.

The John Forney farm buildings along the Mummasburg Road. This farm was heavily fought over on July 1. None of these buildings exist today. The house was torn down before the dedication of the Peace Light Memorial in 1938. This photograph was taken from the cupola of Schmucker Hall at the Lutheran Seminary. *Adams County Historical Society*

Chapter 6

The Devil's to Pay: Buford Holds On

The cavalry general conspicuously rode the lines, almost daring the Confederates to fire at him. "Buford was almost omnipresent," observed one cavalry historian, "personally encouraging the men, strengthening a weak spot or anxiously scanning the Emmitsburg Road for signs of re-inforcement."[1] At one point during the fighting a staff courier found him mounted on Grey Eagle while calmly puffing his pipe. When the courier asked him if he should go back into town to see if he could locate a telegraph operator so word of the battle could be sent, Buford laconically replied, "All right; we will all be back there soon."[2]

"From 8 to 10 o'clock the unequal conflict was maintained," recorded Lt. Henry Dana of the 8th Illinois Cavalry, "yielding ground to the enemy step by step, suffering severe loss in officers and men, with many of our led horses, which from time to time came within range of the enemy's guns." The troopers laid down a steady fire, and ammunition stocks were running low.[3] "It was a grand spectacle, that of this little band of troopers disputing foot by foot the advance of a larger force of infantry—steadily, unflinchingly, and for hours holding them back," recalled Capt. William C. Hazelton of the 8th Illinois Cavalry.[4]

---

1 Theophilus F. Rodenbough, "Cavalry War Lessons," *Journal of the United States Cavalry Association* (1889), 2:113. Rodenbough commanded Buford's old regiment, the 2nd U.S. Cavalry, at Gettysburg.

2 "A Day With Buford," *The National Tribune*, July 5, 1888.

3 Bean, "Who Fired the First Shots!"

4 Hazelton, "An Address Made at a Regimental Reunion."

"With consummate generalship, [Buford] led the enemy to believe that they were contending with infantry, and that it was a large force. They were therefore cautious, and felt their way with deliberation," observed an admiring infantry officer who would soon arrive to continue the fighting west of town to advantage because of the cavalry's good work. "Buford himself knew, as well as any one, the prize for which he was making the gallant fight. It lay behind him in the natural fortifications on the other side of Gettysburg, and Buford meant to save it for his comrades, rushing to his support."[5]

While traveling from one section of his guns to another, Calef encountered Buford riding his lines companied by one lone bugler. "The demoniac 'whir-r-r' of the rifled shot, the 'ping' of the bursting shell and the wicked 'zip' of the bullet, as it hurried by, filled the air," remembered the artilleryman. The general turned to Calef and said, "Our men are in a pretty hot pocket, but, my boy, we must hold this position until the infantry comes up; then you withdraw your guns in each section by piece, fill up your limber chests from the caissons and await my orders." Just as Buford finished speaking, a Rebel shell exploded nearby, causing their horses to rear in fright.[6]

While Buford rode his line and encouraged his men, Harry Heth on the other side of the battlefield ordered his brigade commanders to press the attack, determined to fully develop the nature and extent of the Federal force confronting him. Heth's Confederate skirmishers drove aggressively eastward with heavy lines of gray infantry advancing behind them, pushing Gamble's men off Herr Ridge and back toward the banks of Willoughby Run. The stout Union resistance had to be broken apart if Heth was going to discover what, if anything, waited behind the cavalry. It was time for the infantry to take up the fight.[7]

"Presently the boys of the 8th Illinois with the led horses were seen coming over [Herr's Ridge], in our immediate front: then a line of smoke along and beyond the crest of the hill: then our pickets: then another line of smoke: then the skirmishers: then twelve guns wheeled into line, unlimbered and opened fire," recalled Major Beveridge. "As the pickets retired slowly down the slope, followed by the skirmishers, Archer's brigade in line of battle, rose above the

---

5   Theodore B. Gates, *The "Ulster Guard" and the War of the Rebellion* (New York, 1879), 424

6   Calef, "The Opening Gun," 48.

7   OR 27, pt. 2, 637.

A previously unpublished image of Maj. George M. Van Buren of the 6th New York Cavalry. Van Buren, a great-nephew of Pres. Martin Van Buren, was captured during the Battle of Williamsport, MD on July 6, 1863.

Joseph Stahl

hill, marched up to and past the guns." The guns stopped firing long enough for Archer's infantry to pass by, and then they opened again.[8]

Archer, a veteran of some of the hardest fighting of the war and opposed to the deep drive forward ordered by Heth, was worried about his dispositions. He ordered a quick halt to redress his lines and evaluate the situation. J. B. Turney of the 1st Tennessee of Archer's brigade thought the halt "about one mile of the town." He remembered, "for thirty minutes the firing was severe, and the smoke of battle hovered near the ground, shutting out from view the movements of the federal forces."[9] "We were not over 40 or 50 yards from the enemy when we opened fire," recalled Lt. Col. Samuel G. Shepard of the 7th Tennessee. "Our men fired with great coolness and deliberation, and with terrible effect."[10] The Tennesseans "were lying down, loading while on their backs and rolling to their bellies to aim and fire."[11]

The stubborn stand by Buford's troopers and the accurate fire of Calef's gunners impressed Adjutant John Robinson of the 52nd North Carolina of Pettigrew's Brigade. "The cavalry, pressing Archer very hard, and skillfully using their artillery, checked his advance," he wrote, "when Pettigrew's Brigade, the Fifty-Second [North Carolina] holding the right of his line, was rapidly

---

8   Beveridge, "Address," 19.

9   Turney, "The First Tennessee at Gettysburg," 535.

10 *OR* 27, pt. 2, 646.

11 Pfanz, *Gettysburg: The First Day*, 66.

advanced to his support."[12] At that point, Heth rode up and ordered Archer to advance to determine the "strength and battle line of the enemy." Heth also ordered up Col. John Brockenbrough's brigade, meaning that he had now committed his entire division to the fray.[13]

Captain Albert Mills of the 8th New York Cavalry worried that he and his men would "hear the rebels yell and see the swift charge of their superior numbers which would sweep us from our position. We held our line down there along Willoughby Run as best we could, hoping that reinforcements would come, fearing that they would not."[14] Colonel William Markell of the same 8th regiment credited "the skirmishers fighting stubbornly . . . behind fences and trees, and our artillery doing good execution, the advance of the enemy was retarded."[15] Another captain of the 8th New York Cavalry, Henry D. Follett, fell mortally wounded during this phase of the fighting. Follett and an enlisted man were shot almost simultaneously, with the captain dying of his wound on July 4.[16]

Although their rapid-firing breech-loading carbines gave them a distinct advantage over the Rebel infantry, Buford's men pushed down into the valley along the banks of Willoughby Run, caught in the low ground between Herr's Ridge and the main line of battle on McPherson's Ridge. Archer's pursuing Rebels advanced down the eastern slope of Herr's Ridge, pressing Gamble's dismounted troopers hard.

The horse soldiers of the 8th Illinois, who had been averaging eight shots per minute with their Sharps carbines, paused to dip the barrels of their weapons in the waters of Willoughby Run to cool them. They then retreated up the western slope of McPherson's Ridge.[17] "The moment was critical, two guns to one, three men to one," wrote Beveridge. "We could easily fall back and elude pursuit, but we were not here to retreat, nor was it our habit to retreat."[18]

---

12 Clark, *Histories*, 3:236.

13 Turney, "The First Tennessee at Gettysburg," 535.

14 Albert M. Mills, "Oration of Captain Albert M. Mills, U.S.V.," *In Memoriam James Samuel Wadsworth 1807-1864* (Albany, NY, 1916), 53.

15 Markell, *New York at Gettysburg*, 3:1145.

16 Norton, *Deeds of Daring*, 69, 172.

17 "Opened the Fight at Gettysburg."

18 Gilpin, "Address."

As Jerome pointed out, "The general held on with as stubborn a fight as ever faced an enemy."[19]

Gamble's troopers fell back about 300 yards from the western part of McPherson's Ridge to the eastern crest of the ridge near Herbst's Woods. As the 8th Illinois pulled out of the line, a trooper who had been lying concealed in the wheat field until Archer's infantrymen were almost on top of him sprang to his feet and shouted loudly, "Forward, forward—now we have them!" Uncertain of what surprise awaited them, Archer's men hesitated. Impressed by the man's courage, Buford later commented that he had never seen such a daring and successful thing.[20]

Private Willet S. Haight of the 12th Illinois Cavalry acted as a courier that morning, carrying messages back and forth from Buford to his subordinates. As Haight rode along the line of battle, a Confederate artillery shell exploded, killing his horse and pitching the unfortunate trooper to the ground. A shell fragment "which struck him in the face, breaking his left jaw badly and tearing a hole under his chin and next to his throat in such a manner that his nourishment would escape by the wound." Haight survived this horrific wound, and received a medical discharge later that year. The damage done by that shell fragment haunted him for the rest of his life. He could not open his mouth more than an inch or so, and chewing was a very painful experience. The impact of the shell fragment also damaged his spine, meaning that he could not stand up without assistance for the rest of his life.[21]

"Just before reaching Willoughby Run," recalled E. T. Boland of the 13th Alabama, part of General Archer's brigade, "the cavalry began to get stubborn and our [main battle] line passed the skirmish line."[22] Archer pushed his Tennessee and Alabama infantry toward the creek, his lines advancing at a steady walk, loading and firing as they moved. Once at the bottom of the valley, which was protected by the steep slope of McPherson's Ridge that loomed overhead, Archer's Confederates paused to "reform, reload, catch our breath and cool off a little," one Rebel would recall decades later. "It was about nine

---

19 Aaron B. Jerome to Winfield S. Hancock, October 18, 1865, *The Bachelder Papers*, 1:201.

20 Hard, *Eighth Cavalry*, 256-257.

21 Samuel M. Blackwell, Jr., *In the First Line of Battle: The 12th Illinois Cavalry in the Civil War* (DeKalb, IL, 2002), 106.

22 Boland, "Beginning the Battle of Gettysburg," 308.

o'clock in the morning and hot, hotter, hottest!"[23] The morning mist had burned off, the sun was out, and the temperature was soaring.

Buford calmly rode up and down his lines, puffing his pipe, and yelling words of encouragement to his beleaguered troopers. "Boys, we must hold this position until Reynolds comes up or die in the attempt!" he cried.[24] By now it was nearly 10 a.m., and Gamble's men had been engaged with the Confederate infantry for nearly three hours. Buford "held on with as stubborn a front as ever faced an enemy, for half an hour," recalled an admiring Lt. Aaron B. Jerome, Buford's signal officer, "unaided, against a whole corps of rebels."[25]

The sheer weight of Confederate numbers began driving Gamble's men from McPherson's Ridge. Calef's battery limbered up and fell back, and Gamble's men were in danger of being flanked to the south of the Chambersburg Pike. "A portion of our regiment was dismounted to fight the rebels that were coming down through a strip of woods to our left; our battery had to give way with considerable loss," recalled a member of the 8th Illinois. "We all moved onward to the left of the strip of woods, and there drew up to meet the rebels; as they were advancing but four hundred yards distant, one section of our battery opened on them with good effect, but had to move as their musket balls were too many."[26] Gamble later observed, "we had to fight the whole army corps of Genl. A. P. Hill, 25,000 strong, for three and one-half hours, from 7 am till 10 ½ am to hold the original line of battle selected by me according to previous hours."[27] Gamble's hard-pressed troopers were taking casualties—more than 60 men and 70 horses had already gone down—but they were also inflicting losses on Heth's men.[28] "Oh, if Reynolds would only come," wished the blue-clad troopers as they scanned for the approach of the First Corps.[29]

---

23 H. W. Moon, "Beginning the Battle of Gettysburg," *Confederate Veteran* (December 1925), 23:449.

24 J. McGardner, "Fighting Them Over," *The National Tribune*, May 24, 1885.

25 Jerome to Hancock, October 18, 1865, *The Bachelder Papers*, 1201.

26 *Aurora Beacon*, August 20, 1863.

27 Gamble to Church, March 10, 1864.

28 Ibid.

29 Gardner, "Union vs. Rebel Cavalry."

Two spent balls struck Cpl. Edward Marriott of Co. K, 8th New York Cavalry, knocking him from his horse and stunning him. He was captured, paroled, and then sent to a field hospital located in Westminster, Maryland. Early accounts reported that Marriott had been killed in action, leaving his parents inconsolable over the reported loss of their son. However, a letter from Marriott changed that quickly, prompting his local newspaper to chide, "Too much reliance should not be placed on the first reports from the battlefield—they are frequently erroneous, and people who have friends in the army would do well to await an official list of casualties."[30]

While the action raged along the Chambersburg Pike, Buford received word of Confederates advancing from the north. Major General Robert E. Rodes' division of Ewell's Second Corps was coming from the direction of Heidlersburg. Faced with this new threat, Buford worried about his ability to hold on. He sent Jerome up into the cupola of the Seminary with instructions to look for Reynolds' advance guard. Jerome recalled, "The engagement was desperate, as we were opposed to the whole of Hill's corps. We held them in check fully two hours, and were nearly overpowered when, in looking about the country, I saw the corps-flag of General Reynolds (First Corps)." Alone in the cupola, Jerome called for one of his men to locate Buford and relate the good news. Buford rode over, climbed up into the cupola, and borrowed Jerome's spyglass. Spotting the advancing blue column, Buford, with great relief, said, "Now we can hold the place."[31]

To hasten Reynolds' approach, Buford detailed two of his staff officers to find and escort him to the front. One of them found Reynolds about three miles from the town, advancing along the Emmitsburg Road. Hearing of Buford's plight, the 42-year-old career Regular put his spurs to his horse and surged forward toward his date with destiny.[32] In order to guide the wing commander, Buford posted additional aides along the route, including one whom Reynolds met in front of the Blue Eagle Hotel.

---

30 *Rochester Daily Union and Advertiser*, July 10, 1863.

31 Jerome, in *Decisive Conflicts of the Civil War*, 152.

32 In May 1863, after the battle of Chancellorsville, Lincoln apparently offered the well-regarded Reynolds command of the Army of the Potomac, but the Pennsylvanian demurred, not wanting to be ensnared in the maelstrom of army politics that accompanied that position. Ironically, he found himself in command—and having to make those critical decisions—on the morning of July 1, 1863.

Reynolds' orderly, Sgt. Charles Veil, remembered, "When we got into town we saw there was considerable excitement, so the Genl rode to the front at once."[33] Reynolds and his staff "saw the Confederate batteries going into position...the lines of battle forming and skirmishers being thrown out. Opposed to them were our cavalry skirmishers, spread out like the fingers of the hand, falling back and firing, and, as I remember it, occasionally firing from a field battery."[34] Major Joseph G. Rosengarten of Reynolds' staff noted that when Reynolds received Buford's request for infantry support, Reynolds "with characteristic energy . . . went forward, . . . [and] accepted at once the responsibility" for continuing the fight at Gettysburg.[35]

Buford evidently entertained thoughts of retreat before the good news of Reynolds' approach arrived. Jerome noted, "I am confident that he intended to retire to Cemetery Hill, and endeavor to hold on longer, but seeing Reynolds coming (some one and one-half miles off) at the double-quick to his support, held on."[36] Jerome saw Reynolds and his staff spur ahead of the infantry column, and signaled to Buford, "Reynolds, himself, will be here in five minutes, his corps is about a mile behind." Buford returned to the cupola to observe Reynolds' approach, "watching anxiously" through his telescope. When Reynolds finally arrived shortly after 10 a.m., he spotted Buford in the cupola, and called out, "What's the matter, John?"

Buford responded, "The devil's to pay!" and started down the ladder toward his old friend John Reynolds.

Reynolds asked Buford if he could "hold out until his corps came up." The laconic Kentuckian responded briefly. "With characteristic brevity Buford said, 'I reckon I can.'"

---

33 Charles H. Veil to David McConaughy, April 7, 1864, copy in files at Gettysburg National Military Park.

34 Stephen Minot Weld, *War Diary and Letters of Stephen Minot Weld, 1861-1865* (Boston, 1912), 230.

35 Maj. Joseph G. Rosengarten, "General Reynolds' Last Battle," in The Annals of the War, originally published in *The Philadelphia Weekly Times* (Dayton, OH, 1988), 61.

36 Jerome, Decisive Conflicts of the Civil War, 152-153. The location and specifics of the meeting between Reynolds and Buford has been the subject of much controversy over the years. For a detailed analysis of this controversy, see Eric J. Wittenberg, "An Analysis of the Buford Manuscripts," Gettysburg: Articles of Lasting Historical Interest (July 1996), Issue 15, 7-24.

Maj. Gen. John F. Reynolds, commander of the Army of the Potomac's Left Wing. Reynolds validated Buford's decision to stand and fight at Gettysburg, and was killed in action while placing the Iron Brigade of the 1st Corps line of battle on the morning of July 1, 1863.
USAHEC

Reynolds remarked, "Let's ride out and see all about it." The officers mounted and rode out to observe the situation first-hand. Under fire from both Confederate artillery and infantry, Buford turned to Reynolds and asked him "not to expose himself so much," as Jerome recalled, "but Reynolds laughed and moved closer still."[37] Reynolds was known as "remarkably brave and intelligent, an honest true gentleman."[38] However, his bravery cost him his life that warm July morning.

The two officers briefly conferred along the Chambersburg Pike, discussing "the lay of the land and other military points of pressing interest."[39] During this discussion, Buford turned and pointed out Cemetery Ridge as the proper defensive position for the Army of the Potomac.[40] Reynolds instructed Buford "to keep the enemy in check as long as possible to keep them from getting into the town," and that he would hurry his men forward to Buford's aid.[41] Reynolds then turned to his aide, Capt. Stephen Minot Weld, and gave him a verbal message to deliver to Meade, with instructions for Weld to run his horse to death, if necessary. Weld spurred off, carrying the following message to the army commander: "The enemy are advancing in strong force . . . I fear they will get into the heights beyond the town before I can. I will fight them inch by inch, and if driven into the town, I will barricade the streets and hold them back as long as possible." Weld made the 14-mile ride to Emmitsburg in record time and related the message to Meade, who exclaimed, "Good! That is just like Reynolds, he will hold on to the bitter end!"[42]

---

37 Ibid.

38 George B. McClellan, *McClellan's Own Story* (New York, 1887), 140.

39 Calef, "The Opening Gun," 47.

40 Letter of General Frank Wheaton, January 16, 1894, in *Proceedings of the Buford Memorial Association*.

41 Veil to McConaughy, April 7, 1864.

42 Weld, *War Diary*, 230. Before receiving this information (as well as a note from Buford written at 10:10 a.m.), Meade apparently intended to abandon Gettysburg as a position for the Army of the Potomac. Previously, he had put together a plan for the army to take up a position between Westminster and Manchester, Maryland, on commanding high ground along Big Pipe Creek, known to posterity as the "Pipe Creek Line." Early on the morning of July 1, Meade circulated a general order, known as the Pipe Creek Circular, which ordered his army to concentrate on Pipe Creek Line, with Meade's headquarters to be situated at Taneytown. See *OR* 27, pt. 3, 416. However, the intelligence delivered by Buford and Weld that morning evidently changed Meade's mind. When he learned of Reynolds' death, he sent Maj. Gen. Winfield Scott Hancock, a trusted subordinate, to go to Gettysburg to evaluate it as a place for the Army of the Potomac to make a stand. Late that afternoon, Hancock reported that the terrain at Gettysburg—that chosen by Buford—was favorable. *OR* 27, pt. 1, 366. Hancock then rode to Taneytown to report to Meade in person. After hearing Hancock's report, Meade ordered the Army of the Potomac to concentrate at Gettysburg.

The morning began as a normal day's marching for the men of the First Corps. "I remember the march was very leisurely," recalled one of Reynolds' foot soldiers, "officers and men comforting themselves with the cherries which grew in abundance by the wayside."[43] However, as they made their way north, rumors flew up and down their column. One common one held that the enormously popular Maj. Gen. George B. McClellan had been restored to command of the Army of the Potomac, a thought that greatly heartened the marching soldiers. "Cannonading could be faintly heard to the right," recalled a sergeant of the Iron Brigade, "and word passed through the ranks that Buford had heard the Johnnies over at York and Hanover."[44] However, as the men of Brig. Gen. James Wadsworth's First Corps division, at the van of Reynolds' column, got closer to Gettysburg, they could hear the guns booming and could see Buford's stubborn troopers being driven back in front of them. "Forward, double quick!" yelled their officers as their bands struck up rousing marching tunes. Directed by staff officers, they turned off the road and went cross-country, trampling farm fields as they went, hurrying to Buford's assistance.[45]

Meanwhile, Reynolds found Wadsworth's division, "took it in hand, brought it to the front, put it in position, renewed his orders for the rest of the corps, assigned the positions for the other divisions, sent for his other corps, urged their coming with the greatest speed, directed the point to be held by the reserve . . . then calmly and coolly hurried some fresh troops forward to fill a gap in his lengthening lines, and as he returned to find fresh divisions, fell at the first onset."[46] He also sent a courier to Maj. Gen. O. O. Howard, commander of the Eleventh Corps, with instructions to hasten his command to Gettysburg. He also told Maj. Gen. Abner Doubleday, who commanded the next division of the First Corps to arrive on the field, that he would hold the Confederates on

43 James Beale, *From Marsh Run to Seminary Ridge* (n.p., 1891), 4.

44 William J. K. Beaudot and Lance J. Herdegen, eds., *An Irishman in the Iron Brigade: The Civil War Memoirs of James P. Sullivan, Sergt., Company K, 6th Wisconsin Volunteers* (New York, 1993), 93.

45 Rufus R. Dawes to Bachelder, March 18, 1868, *Bachelder Papers*, 1:323; William H. Harries, "The Iron Brigade in the First Day's Battle at Gettysburg," *Glimpses of the Nation's Struggle*, Military Order of the Loyal Legion of the United States, Wisconsin Commandery (St. Paul, MN, 1898), 4:339.

46 Rosengarten, "General Reynolds' Last Battle," 63.

Brig. Gen. James Wadsworth, commander, 1st Division, First Corps. Wadsworth's infantrymen were the first to reach the battlefield on July 1. *Library of Congress*

the Chambersburg Pike while Doubleday would hold them on the Mummasburg Road.

And with that, Reynolds "assumed the task for the whole army that Buford had already performed for the First Corps—to check the enemy's advance until the main body of the army should arrive and take position on the heights in rear of Gettysburg."[47] Reynolds, "who was known as an officer of superior merit," validated Buford's decision to stand and fight on the ridges to the north and west of Gettysburg in order to buy time for the rest of the Army of the Potomac to reach the battlefield.[48] The only question was whether they could hang on long enough.

"The rebels opened on us furiously with artillery; at this instance Gen. Reynolds rode up, as his infantry had just arrived," said a member of the 8th Illinois, "a portion of our regiment was dismounted to fight the rebels that were coming down through a strip of woods on our left; our battery had to give way with considerable loss; we all moved onward to the left of the strip of woods, and there drew up to meet the rebels; as they were advancing but four hundred yards distant, one section of our battery opened on them with good effect, but had to move as their musket balls were too many."[49]

"From 8 to 10 o'clock, the unequal conflict was maintained, yielding ground to the enemy step by step, suffering severe loss in officers and men, with many of our led horses, which from time to time came within range of the

47 Gates, "*The Ulster Guard,*" 427.

48 Carl Schurz, *The Reminiscences of Carl Schurz*, 3 vols. (New York, 1907-1908), 3:6. Schurz also stated, "in the opinion of many it was that [Reynolds] that ought to have been put at the head of the Army of the Potomac," and not Meade. Ibid.

49 *Aurora Beacon*, August 20, 1863.

enemy's guns," remembered Lt. Col. Theodore W. Bean of the 17th Pennsylvania Cavalry. "Our ammunition was almost exhausted, and it was becoming painfully evident that the Seminary Ridge, on which this fierce struggle was raging, would have to be abandoned unless additional support speedily reached us."[50] As Reynolds approached the front, Gamble galloped up, excitedly crying, "Hurry up, General, hurry up! They are breaking our line! They are breaking our line!" Reynolds calmly rode on, smiling at Buford's weary troopers and praising their performance.[51]

Davis' Brigade, attacking north of the railroad cut, pressed Devin's men hard. Only a small portion of his brigade—the 6th New York and two squadrons of the 9th New York, supported by a section of Calef's battery—resisted the Confederate approach on McPherson's Ridge; the rest of Devin's command was deployed on Oak Hill and on the plain below to the east. Davis' 42nd Mississippi advanced toward McPherson's Ridge, drawing fire along the way. The Mississippians heard "the peculiar hiss of the minnie ball," but pressed on anyway. The 42nd and the two right companies of the 2nd Mississippi became heavily engaged with Devin's dismounted troopers. Colonel John M. Stone of the 42nd Mississippi tried to reach the right of his line but dismounted because a stout fence near the Forney farm buildings blocked his way. As he climbed the fence, one of Devin's men shot him, meaning that the first regimental commander of the battle of Gettysburg had fallen. Davis ordered his men to charge, and the cavalrymen began giving way.[52]

"Suffice it to say that the enemy poured their veteran columns against our line of dismounted men, who stood like a wall of fire and repulsed their repeated charges for two mortal hours," proudly declared Lt. Col. Wilber Bentley of the 9th New York Cavalry.[53] "The cavalrymen responded with a rapid carbine fire from behind the trees, rocks and stone walls, their sturdy resistance giving the enemy the impression that he had infantry before him, and

---

50 Bean, "Who Fired the First Shots!"

51 Albert Huntington, *8th New York Cavalry: Historical Paper* (Palmyra, NY, 1902), 14; *The National Tribune*, May 24, 1885.

52 *OR* 27, pt. 2, 549; John M. Stone to Joseph R. Davis, undated letter, *Bachelder Papers*, 3:328-330.

53 Wilber G. Bentley, "Dedication of Monument. 9th Regiment Cavalry—'Westfield Cavalry,'" included in *New York at Gettysburg*, 3 vols. (Albany, 1902), 3:1153-54.

causing him to advance slowly and cautiously."[54] So far, the New Yorkers had conducted a textbook delaying action, but by 10:15 a.m. the sheer weight of Confederate numbers were driving them from McPherson's Ridge.

On the morning of July 1st the pickets of the First Brigade, on the road to Cashtown, were driven in by a force advancing from that direction. The Second Brigade was ordered to prepare for action. The 6th New York was placed on the right of the brigade, on the road to Mummasburg, where it deployed on foot. "At one time the Sixth New York Cavalry was thought to have been captured, so fierce were the attacks," recorded an early historian of the 6th New York.[55] Since the New Yorkers were rapidly running out of ammunition, it appeared that they would have to withdraw, exposing Gamble's flank to attack. The situation had now grown desperate. "They wer to much for us and drove us back," remembered a member of the 9th New York Cavalry.[56]

Just when things appeared bleakest for Buford's troopers, Brig. Gen. Lynsander Cutler's brigade, the lead elements of Wadsworth's division, arrived at the double-quick, with the winded soldiers puffing from the exertion. The sight of the advancing foot soldiers gave Buford's beleaguered troopers a boost. Major John L. Beveridge, commanding the 8th Illinois Cavalry, heaved a sigh of relief at the sight of the Union infantry, "led by Reynolds and Wadsworth in person, coming across the meadow on the double-quick."[57] An officer of the 8th New York said simply, "How grateful and glad we battered troopers were then."[58] Another trooper of the 8th New York named Joel Swett recalled, "There was a sense of relief on my own part which I shall never forget when we saw the grand old 1st corps coming."[59]

Reynolds deployed the winded infantry into line directly behind Gamble's tired troopers, and the infantry opened ranks to permit the dismounted

---

54 Hall, *History of the Sixth New York Cavalry*, 138.

55 Augustus P. Clarke, "Historical Sketch of the Sixth Cavalry Regiment, New York," *Final Report on the Battlefield of Gettysburg (New York at Gettysburg)* by the New York Monuments Commission for the Battlefields of Gettysburg and Chattanooga (Albany, NY, 1902), 3:1138.

56 Dr. Gray Nelson Taylor, ed., *Saddle and Saber: The Letters of Civil War Cavalryman Corporal Nelson Taylor* (Bowie, MD, 1993), 96.

57 Beveridge, "The First Gun at Gettysburg," 9.

58 Mills, "Oration," 54.

59 Joel Swett, "The Eighth New York Cavalry at Gettyburg," *The National Tribune*, April 3, 1884.

Brig. Gen. Lysander Cutler, commander of the 1st Brigade, 1st Division, the first Union infantry to arrive on the battlefield at Gettysburg. *Library of Congress*

cavalrymen to retire. "As we were forming, our cavalry came rushing out of the woods on our left," recalled Col. Edward B. Fowler of the 14th Brooklyn, "crying 'they are coming, give it to them.'"[60] As Gamble's men withdrew, they urged on the men of the First Corps, yelling, "Go in and give them hell!"[61] Jerome described the scene: "The first division of [Reynolds's] corps moved up on a run, wheeled into line apparently without command, as solid as a stone wall, and were in action instantly, the cavalry holding the flanks."[62] Buford ordered Gamble's troopers to withdraw from the field in front of the Seminary to "the south side of town."[63] Trooper Flavius J. Bellamy of the 3rd Indiana recalled, "As we fell back in the morning a band of ladies in the Cupola of the . . . College sang 'Rally around the flag boys' amid the shrieking of shells."[64]

The arrival of the infantrymen energized the weary troopers: "the advanced infantry was seen going into position. Then we felt assured and our carbines were willing to fire their last bullet and many of them did before leaving the line to their equally courageous comrades, fresh and eager for the fray."[65]

60 C. V. Tevis, *The History of the Fighting Fourteenth: Published in Commemoration of the Fiftieth Anniversary of the Must of the Regiment into the United States Service, May 23, 1861* (Brooklyn, NY, 1911), 132.

61 Huntington, *8th New York Cavalry*, 14.

62 Jerome, in *Decisive Conflicts of the Civil War*, 153.

63 Martin, *Gettysburg, July 1*, 170.

64 Bellamy, Diary, July 1, 1863.

65 Bean, "Who Fired the Opening Shots?"

As the First Corps approached, Buford scribbled a dispatch to Meade:

The enemy's force (A. P. Hill's) are advancing on me at this point, and driving my pickets and skirmishers very rapidly. There is also a large force at Heidlersburg that is driving my pickets at that point from that direction. General Reynolds is advancing, and is within three miles of this point with his leading division. I am positive that the whole of A. P. Hill's force is advancing.[66]

The two small brigades had accomplished their mission—they had held off the Confederate advance until the infantry could arrive and assume the defense. Once forced to withdraw, the videttes fell in beside the main body.

After positioning the 2nd Wisconsin of Col. Solomon Meredith's famed Iron Brigade to meet an attack by Archer's brigade, and while awaiting the arrival of the next regiment in the column, a bullet struck Reynolds in the back of the head, mortally wounding him. Shortly after Reynolds fell, a staff courier "found Gen. Buford sitting quietly on his horse, accompanied by one or two of his staff. He did not seem to have a happy or satisfied look, and I judged at once from his quiet, uneasy manner that something was wrong. I soon found out. Gen. Reynolds was lying by the two little elms alongside the fence, dying or dead. This was what put so serious and sorrowful an expression on the faces of the officers just then."[67] Command of the Federal forces devolved to Maj. Gen. Abner Doubleday, the senior divisional commander of the First Corps. Reynolds validated Buford's choice of the ground to the north and west of the town and continued the delaying action strategy by choosing to stand and fight on McPherson's Ridge, leaving the high ground to the south of the town to be occupied by the rest of the Army of the Potomac.

Although officially relieved by the arrival of the Iron Brigade, some of the men of the 3rd Indiana of Gamble's brigade stayed to fight alongside the infantry, helping to repulse Archer's attack. In his after-action report of the battle, Buford noted proudly, "The First Brigade ... most reluctantly ... gave up its front."[68] One member of the 3rd Indiana recalled that he and his mates "fought like wild cats all day."[69]

---

66 *OR* 27, pt. 1, 924.

67 "A Day with Buford," *The National Tribune*, July 5, 1888.

68 W.N. Pickerill, *History of the Third Indiana Cavalry* (Indianapolis, 1906), 82; *OR* 27, pt. 1, 927.

69 Augustus C. Weaver, Co. A, 3rd Indiana Cavalry, Diary, July 1, 1863, USAHEC.

Col. Solomon Meredith, commander of the legendary Iron Brigade. Reynolds
was placing the Iron Brigade into position when he was killed.
Library of Congress

As Wadsworth's division deployed, he ordered up Capt. James A. Hall's
Battery B, 2nd Maine Light Artillery, which took position along the
Chambersburg Pike. Brigadier General James J. Archer's brigade soon swept
Wadsworth's right back to Seminary Ridge. Most of Hall's horses were shot
down, meaning that Hall had to abandon one of his guns. A determined
counterattack drove the Confederate infantry back toward Willoughby Run and
Archer and much of his brigade were captured. As Wadsworth's men regained
McPherson's Ridge, Buford sent Calef's battery to support the infantry. Calef's

gunners, who had already had a long morning under fire, took position on the same ground formerly occupied by Hall's battery.

There, Calef's gunners drew heavy fire from three different Confederate batteries, suffering heavily in losses among men and horses. "As I was giving the order to Sergeant [Joseph] Newman, commanding the centre section, a shell burst under the horses of one of the pieces, killing or disabling four out of six," recalled Calef, "but by strenuous exertions the brave old soldier managed to get the piece off with the remaining team." Buford also ordered Calef to detail one of Roder's guns to enfilade Davis' infantry as it advanced along the unfinished railroad cut to the north of the Chambersburg Pike. "As the piece was being unlimbered its chief, Cpl. Robert Watrous, appreciating the necessity for instant action, secured a double round of canister, but as he was running with it to the gun he was shot down. Private [Thomas] Slattery, the No. 2, with commendable presence of mind, snatched the ammunition from the hands of his fallen comrade and got it into the gun just as the enemy were rushing to capture it. Some of them were so close that when the piece was fired they were literally blown away from the muzzle."[70]

About 10:45 a.m., Jerome received a message from one of his signalmen that another corps of infantry was approaching, probably Maj. Gen. Oliver O. Howard's Eleventh Corps. Jerome verified this welcome news, and reported the news to Buford, who ordered Jerome "to ride as fast as my horse could carry me and ask Howard to come up at the double-quick." Jerome relayed the message to Howard, and Howard sent his batteries ahead to Gettysburg while his infantry struggled along behind.[71]

Howard spurred his horse and headed to the battlefield. He wanted to get a good look at the lay of the land and of the dispositions of the Union troops, and unsuccessfully tried to ascend to the belfry of the Adams County courthouse. Instead, he found another steeple where he could see: "The roads, now so familiar, from [Hanover], York, Harrisburg, Carlisle, Shippensburg, Chambersburg, and Hagerstown; roads emerging from Gettysburg like the spokes from the hub of a wheel; roads which are exceedingly important for the solider in command to have engraven on his memory. I saw Buford's division of cavalry perhaps two miles off toward the northwest, seeming, in the distance and in the largeness of the field beyond the college, but a handful." He could

---

70 Calef, "The First Gun at Gettysburg," 28.

71 Jerome, in *Decisive Conflicts of the Civil War*, 153.

Maj. Gen. Oliver O. Howard, commander of the 11th Corps. Howard assumed command of the field upon his arrival at Gettysburg. *Library of Congress*

also see the long lines of the First Corps infantry as they went into battle. As Howard surveyed the scene, a young officer reported to him that Reynolds had

Brig. Gen. John C. Robinson, commander, 2nd Division, First Corps. Robinson's troops were the second Union infantry command to arrive on the battlefield at Gettysburg.
Library of Congress

been wounded and that he now had command of the field. The general sent his brother, Maj. Charles H. Howard, to consult with Buford and to ascertain the status of things.[72]

At 11:00, Doubleday's division—now commanded by its senior brigade commander, Brig. Gen. Thomas A. Rowley—arrived on the field and extended Wadsworth's line to the left. Brigadier General John C. Robinson's division also arrived, extending the right of the Union line of battle north onto Oak Hill. The arrival of Rowley's and Robinson's divisions meant that all of the First Corps was now on the battlefield and was fully engaged.

Once Rowley's infantry deployed, the rest of Gamble's brigade fell back out of range of the Confederate batteries and retired to the south side of the Fairfield Road, to guard the left flank of Rowley's division.[73] As they withdrew, the men of the 8th New York Cavalry passed Reynolds' body, which still lay at the spot where he fell.[74] Major William Medill of the 8th Illinois observed, "we gave [the enemy] great annoyance and materially retarded his advance by making frequent bold charges on him, obliging him to halt and change front to

---

72 Oliver Otis Howard, "The Campaign and Battle of Gettysburg," included in Peter Cozzens, ed., *Battles and Leaders of the Civil War* (Chicago, 2002), 5:325, 328.

73 *OR* 27, pt. 1, 927. Rowley was apparently intoxicated that day, and he was ultimately court-martialed for drunkenness and insubordination as a result. He was found guilty and was sent to a backwater of the war. He resigned his commission in December 1864. For a detailed discussion of this sad episode, see John F. Krumwiede, *Disgrace at Gettysburg: The Arrest and Court Martial of Brigadier General Thomas A. Rowley* (Jefferson, NC, 2006).

74 William H. Benjamin to John B. Bachelder, February 4, 1891, *Bachelder Papers*, 3:1792.

Maj. Gen. Robert Rodes, who commanded a division of Ewell's Second Corps. Rodes was still new to division command at Gettysburg. This fine soldier was killed in action at the October 19, 1864 Battle of Cedar Creek. *Valentine Museum*

keep us from sabering his back and rear."[75] Gamble's small brigade successfully held off an entire division of veteran infantry for nearly four hours. Once relieved, Gamble's hungry men—who had been constantly working since manning the vidette lines the night before—took a few minutes to have a quick

75 *The Chicago Tribune*, November 22, 1863.

Col. Charles S. Wainwright, the capable chief of artillery for the Army of the Potomac's First Corps. *USAHEC*

breakfast on Seminary Ridge before moving to their next position, guarding the flank of the First Corps.[76]

After Rowley's and Robinson's divisions formed line of battle, Col. Charles S. Wainwright, the chief of artillery for the First Corps, argued with Wadsworth, who was not a professional soldier, about the proper deployment of artillery. Wainwright refused to place a battery where Wadsworth wanted it, not liking the position's exposed flank. "Wadsworth was much provoked at my not allowing Hall to bring his battery back at once," Wainwright noted in his diary, "and finding Tidball's Horse Battery near by had ordered it into position. Lieutenant Calef . . . refused to go on the grounds it was not a proper place for a battery."

Buford asked Wadsworth to relieve Calef's battery. Wadsworth passed this request on to Wainwright, who promptly "ordered [Capt. Gilbert] Reynolds' [Battery L, 1st New York Artillery] out there." Wainwright also "requested that Reynolds' battery must not be required to support Wadsworth; this was granted, on condition that Wainwright stayed with the Battery." Wainwright called the assigned position for the two batteries "an ugly place," but he nevertheless moved off with Reynolds' guns, leaving their caissons behind for safety.[77]

Wainwright found Calef's guns on a knoll across a road to the front near the position that Hall's guns had held, and saw that Calef was engaged "with a Rebel battery on the high ridge to the west." A dozen Confederate guns opened on

---

76 Benjamin to Bachelder, *Bachelder Papers*, 3:1792.

77 For a detailed discussion of the ordeal faced by Gilbert Reynolds and his gunners that morning, see R. L. Murray, "Reynolds' 1st New York, Battery L, at Gettysburg," *Gettysburg Magazine: Articles of Lasting Historical Interest* (July 2012), No. 47, 21-34.

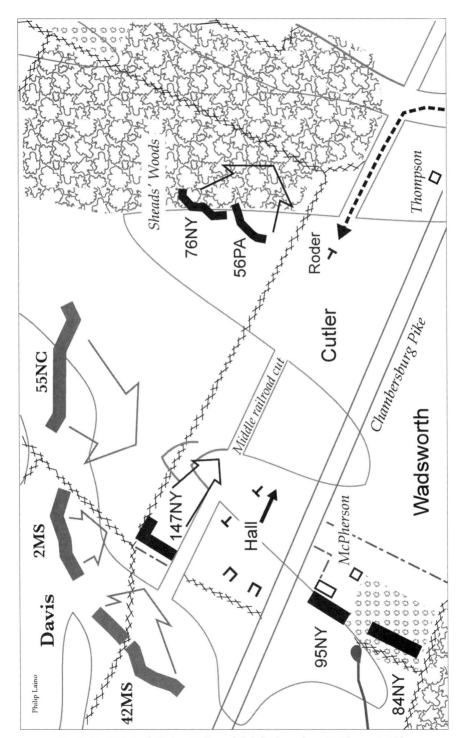

Map 9: Davis' Brigade Drives Hall's and Calef's Guns from McPherson's Ridge

Calef's four rifles. Reynolds' battery deployed to the rear of Calef's guns, so that Battery A could be withdrawn. However, Pegram opened another battery from the left at close range, sweeping the position with enfilade fire. This severe fire cost Captain Reynolds an eye and nearly cost Wainwright his leg. Taking such severe cross-fire, Wainwright realized that he had to pull both batteries out of their exposed position, regardless of what Wadsworth might say about it.

Wainwright relocated both batteries across the Chambersburg Pike to a position approximately 200 yards to the south, "where they would be sheltered by the wood from the Rebel battery up the road, and [could safely] engaged the new one." Shortly thereafter, Wainwright relieved Calef pursuant to Buford's previous request.[78] After taking heavy losses, Calef gladly limbered up his guns and resumed his position on the flank with Buford's cavalry after his brave stand.[79]

Devin Hangs On

Trooper A. R. Mix of the 6th New York, whom Buford had told to be ready to fight that morning, had a close call. Riding on Oak Hill to the north of the Mummasburg Road, Mix realized that the woods were "full of Johnnies." A heavy volley by Confederate infantry of Maj. Gen. Robert E. Rodes' division of Ewell's corps alerted him to their presence. He ducked down as low on the saddle as he could to minimize his profile and to ensure that as much of his body as possible was shielded by his horse, and galloped back to his company to report the advance of Rodes' division from the northwest. After reporting this important intelligence, he realized that two balls had clipped his horse's mane but had somehow missed him. He decided that it was a miracle that he escaped unfazed by the heavy volley.[80]

Rodes' division broke its bivouac near Heidlersburg, seven miles north of Gettysburg, at 6:00 that morning. He as originally headed toward the concentration point at Cashtown, but instead went to the sound of the guns at Gettysburg. Brigadier General Alfred Iverson's North Carolina brigade led the

---

78 Charles S. Wainwright, Diary, July 1, 1863, copy in files at GNMP; OR 27, pt. 1, 1031-1032, 344-45.

79 Tidball, *The Artillery Service in the War of the Rebellion*, 169.

80 Mix, "Experiences at Gettysburg."

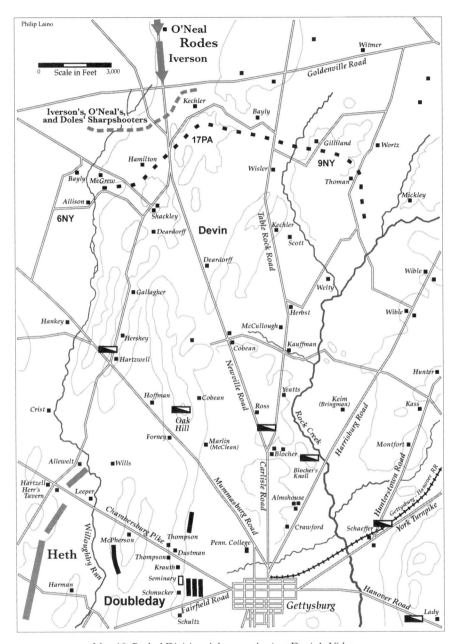

Map 10: Rodes' Division Advances Against Devin's Videttes

Col. Josiah H. Kellogg, commander of the
17th Pennsylvania Cavalry of Devin's Brigade.
*Moyer, History of the Seventeenth Regiment,
Pennsylvania Volunteer Cavalry*

way.[81] Iverson's Tar Heels were
shocked to hear artillery booming in
their front. About 10:00 that morning,
the North Carolinians encountered
videttes of the 17th Pennsylvania
Cavalry of Devin's brigade near
Keckler's Hill, to the north of Oak Hill.
Rodes deployed Iverson's Tar Heels in
response to the desultory fire of the
federal videttes. Captain Benjamin
Robinson of the 5th North Carolina
commanded Iverson's sharpshooter detachment, which rapidly went to the
head of Iverson's column. "The Yankee cavalry threatening our left, we threw
out skirmishers on our left front, and watched them fight the Yankee cavalry for
perhaps an hour," recalled one of Iverson's officers.[82] Rodes also called the
sharpshooter detachments of his other two brigades forward to drive off
Devin's videttes, meaning that about 400 men led Rodes' advance.

Major Eugene Blackford of the 5th Alabama, who commanded the
detachment of sharpshooters assigned to the brigade of Col. Edward A.
O'Neal, reported that his men "moved steadily forward upon the town, driving
in the cavalry videttes, posted on the road and on commanding hills." Devin's

---

81 Alfred Iverson was not a professional soldier. His father, a Georgian, was a vehement
proponent of secession. Iverson was a lawyer and contractor by profession, but he served
admirably in the Mexican War, and his experience as an officer in the Mexican War earned him
a commission in the 1st U.S. Cavalry in 1855. Not surprisingly, he cast his lot with the
Confederacy. Iverson performed poorly at Gettysburg on July 1, 1863, nearly leading to the
destruction of his command, and his taking a great deal of the blame for the Confederate defeat
at Gettysburg. For a detailed discussion of the ordeal of Alfred Iverson and his Tar Heels at
Gettysburg, see Robert J. Wynstra, *The Rashness of That Hour: Politics, Gettysburg, and the Downfall of
Confederate Brigadier General Alfred Iverson* (El Dorado Hills, CA, 2010).

82 *Raleigh Daily Progress*, July 24, 1863; J. B. Oliver, "My Recollections of the Battle of
Gettysburg," Military History Collection, North Carolina Department of Archives and History,
Raleigh, North Carolina.

stubborn videttes "repeatedly charged, but my men rallying coolly & promptly sent them back every time with more empty saddles."

As if Devin's little band hadn't faced a stern enough test contending with Davis' brigade, the arrival of Rodes' men stretched their thin skirmish line to its limits. Rodes' men could see Devin's pickets being driven back, which only hastened them to come up and join the fight. After skirmishing heavily for about an hour, Rodes' sharpshooters drove the videttes back to their main skirmish line on the southern end of the Cobean farm, about 1,000 yards from the town of Gettysburg. "About half a mile from the suburbs, a large force of cavalry was observed in line, with a heavy line of men dismounted as skirmishers," recalled Blackford. "The former charged us twice, but were easily repulsed."[83]

Devin "immediately placed the Ninth New York in support and dismounting the rest of my available force, succeeded in holding the rebel line in check."[84] Rodes responded by deploying his division into line of battle and ordered it to advance. He also brought up and deployed his artillery battalion to support the infantry. Soon, they were heavily pressing Devin's beleaguered cavalrymen. Things were truly growing desperate, and it did not appear that Buford's stubborn troopers would be able to hang on much longer.[85]

With the arrival of Rodes's division on Oak Hill, Devin withdrew to a defensive position on a low ridge to the northeast of the Samuel Cobean farm buildings.[86] He sent an officer of the 9th New York to Doubleday with the news that Devin could not hold on much longer. Doubleday responded by dispatching Brig. Gen. Henry Baxter's brigade of Brig. Gen. John C. Robinson's division to relieve Devin's hard-pressed troopers on Oak Ridge.

---

83 Eugene Blackford memoirs, 239, Civil War Miscellaneous Collection, USAHEC. Each Confederate brigade included a battalion of sharpshooters drawn from each of the regiments that made up that brigade. The sharpshooters were typically the best marksmen of each command. For a history of the Army of Northern Virginia's sharpshooter battalions, see Fred L. Ray, *Shock Troops of the Confederacy: The Sharpshooter Battalions of the Army of Northern Virginia* (Asheville, NC, 2006).

84 *OR* 27, pt. 1, 939.

85 William B. Styple, ed., *Writing & Fighting from the Army of Northern Virginia: A Collection of Confederate Soldier Correspondence* (Kearny, NJ, 2003), 247.

86 Some people incorrectly call this low ridge Keckler's Hill, and others indicate that it is part of Oak Ridge. It is neither. This low ridge has no specific name, so the author has dubbed it Devin's Ridge.

The arrival of the First Corps infantry gave Devin's troopers a well-deserved respite, which they used to redeploy to the support of those elements of the 9th New York and 17th Pennsylvania engaged in the fields to the north of the town. They also used the time to take a new position stretching from the Carlisle Road to the bridge where the Harrisburg Pike crossed Rock Creek. Devin's pickets maintained a thin skirmish line over two miles long, and thus watched three main roads—the Harrisburg, Carlisle, and York roads. A noontime lull of approximately two hours fell over the battlefield as both sides regrouped and prepared to resume fighting.

Spotting the approach of Maj. Gen. Jubal A. Early's division from the direction of Heidlersburg, Devin deployed into line in the fields to the north of the town. Realizing that he had to delay Early's advance to buy time for the approaching Eleventh Corps, Devin sent the 9th New York forward to reinforce his picket line.[87] There, the blue-clad troopers awaited the Confederate onslaught, and his men fought a strong delaying action, with orders to retire "to the rear by successive formations in line by regiment," until Howard could arrive. By conducting a delaying action to the north of the town, Devin "succeeded in holding the rebel line in check for two hours, until relieved by the arrival of the Eleventh Corps."[88]

Between 12 p.m. and 12:30 p.m., Jerome sent a signal to Howard: "Over a division of rebels is making a flank movement on our right; the line extends over a mile, and is advancing, skirmishing. There is nothing but cavalry to oppose them."[89] This ominous news meant that the already overextended Federal line faced a major new threat from the right. Unless Howard could arrive in time, the First Corps was doomed. When the Eleventh Corps finally relieved Devin, the New Yorker moved his small brigade to the east of the York Pike along the banks of Rock Creek, to cover the Federal right flank.

In spite of terrible odds, Buford had hung on just long enough. Reynolds then validated Buford's strategy by ordering his First Corps and Howard's Eleventh Corps to come up to take position on the battlefield selected by the Kentuckian. Only Buford's stubborn stand gave the Union high command the option to do so. Buford's tired troopers had already performed yeoman service

87 Cheney, *Ninth New York*, 109-110.

88 Ibid.; *OR* 27, pt. 1, 939.

89 *OR* 27, pt. 3, 488.

that warm July morning. However, another heavy task lay ahead of them. There was plenty of hard work yet to be done before they could rest.

In a speech to veterans of the 3rd Indiana Cavalry years after the war, Sgt. Samuel Gilpin left a vivid description of the stout stand made by Gamble's command that morning:

> How from hill top to hill top they fought the division back to the outskirts of the town, when at eleven o'clock Reynolds and his infantry came and Reynolds was killed in your immediate front, and how when relieved by the infantry on that part of the line, you supported batteries on the left till evening came and the infantry fell back through Gettysburg and the division was thrown in dismounted behind the stone wall on the Seminary Ridge, while across the plain came the three lines of Confederate infantry, with flying flags and measured steps, seemingly heedless of the shower of balls from your breech-loading carbines and navy revolvers, filling their gaps and moving forward like living walls, their steady pace neither quickened nor retarded until they stood on the other side of your barricade, you had never seen anything grander, you could not withhold admiration for such magnificent courage, so you said, "those damned Rebels are glorious Americans."

Clearly, the years did not dim the vivid memories of that terrible morning.[90]

---

90 Samuel J. Gilpin, "Address," *The Daily Courier*, October 16, 1885.

Chapter 7

Gamble Saves the First Corps

Leaving the fighting to John Reynolds' First Corps, William Gamble's troopers fell back southwest of Gettysburg at noon. About 1:00 p.m., a strong force of Confederates threatened the First Corps' left flank near the southern end of modern-day Reynolds Avenue. Because Reynolds was dead, Maj. Gen. Abner Doubleday was in command of the corps.

Colonel Chapman Biddle's brigade held the left end of Doubleday's line. Biddle's men were in grave danger of being flanked by Col. James K. Marshall's 52nd North Carolina Infantry of Pettigrew's brigade near the Herbst farm buildings and orchard. A deep swale on the Herbst farm property hid their advance and allowed the Tar Heels to approach Biddle's flank unseen. From his vantage point, however, Gamble could see the threat and determined to do something about it. The aggressive trooper ordered the commander of the 8th Illinois Cavalry, Maj. John Beveridge, to take his regiment southwest along the Hagerstown Road. Beveridge did as ordered, positioning his horsemen in an orchard south of the road near a stand of woods.[1]

---

1 John L. Beveridge is an interesting character. He was born in Washington County, New York, in 1824 and moved to DeKalb County, Illinois, in 1842. He practiced law there until 1856, when he relocated to Chicago, where he became a prominent attorney. In the fall of 1861, Beveridge was commissioned major of the 8th Illinois Cavalry. In the winter of 1863-1864, he was sent to Chicago to organize the 17th Illinois Cavalry and was commissioned colonel of the new regiment. The 17th Illinois served in the Department of Missouri, where Beveridge served once again under Alfred Pleasonton, who was assigned to command the cavalry forces there after he was relieved of command with the Army of the Potomac during the winter of 1864. Beveridge was eventually brevetted to brigadier general of volunteers in 1865. After the war, he served as sheriff of Cook County, as a state senator, did a single term in Congress, and served as the 15th governor of Illinois. At Gettysburg, he proved to be the right man in the right place at

Maj. John L. Beveridge, commander of the 8th Illinois Cavalry at Gettysburg. Beveridge performed admirably, particularly during the afternoon phase of the fighting on July 1.

USAHEC

"About this time [Pettigrew's] brigade . . . which had formed under cover of the woods, emerged from the timber *in echelon*, from left to right, his last regiment coming out of the woods near the orchard by the [Fairfield] Road, with the 8th Illinois squadron on picket, hanging upon his flank," recalled Beveridge. The major could see Doubleday's distant right flank retreating, and his center beginning to follow suit. After decimating Archer's brigade, the Iron Brigade was also pulling back from its position in McPherson's Woods. He also spotted the threat to Biddle's exposed flank, and decided to act to protect it. "I ordered the 8th Illinois, in column of squadrons, forward, increased its gait to a trot, as if about to make a charge upon [Marshall's] right," explained Beveridge. "His right regiment halted, changed front, and fired a volley; Biddle's brigade rose to their feet, saw the enemy, fired, and retired across the field toward Seminary Ridge ."[2]

The appearance of enemy cavalry on its flank stopped Marshall's 52nd North Carolina dead in its tracks. In one of the most unusual (and least known) moves of the battle, Marshall employed a Napoleonic tactic: the formation of a hollow square. The move was designed specifically to defend against a mounted charge. Adjutant John Robinson of the 52nd recalled advancing "through the open field our right flank was menaced by a body of the enemy's cavalry, seeking an opportunity to charge our lines." According to Robinson, the regiment was still advancing and suffering under a "heavy fire" (from Biddle to

the right time. "Gen. John L. Beveridge. The Republican Candidate in Illinois for Congressman at Large," *New York Times*, September 24, 1871; Jeriah Bonham, *Fifty Years' Recollections with Observations and Reflections on Historical Events Giving Sketches of Eminent Citizens—Their Lives and Public Services* (Peoria, IL, 1883), 134-145.

2 Beveridge, "Address," 21.

The VMI cadet standing to the left in the back row of this group of cadets is Col. James K. Marshall, commander of the 52nd North Carolina Infantry. Marshall was a cousin of Pattie Buford. He was killed in action on July 3, 1863. *Virginia Military Institute*

its front) when "Col. Marshall formed his regiment in square to guard against attack from this body, and at the same time deployed Company B . . . to protect his flank. [They] succeeded in holding the cavalry in check and finally drove them from our flank. This maneuver was executed by the regiment as promptly and accurately as if it had been upon its drill grounds."[3]

Major William Medill of the 8th Illinois Cavalry knew what he and his comrades had achieved and their maneuver made him proud. My regiment, he explained, "saved a whole brigade of our infantry and a battery from being captured and cut to pieces. The rebels had them nearly surrounded and hemmed in, perceiving which, we made a detour to our left, gained their flank, and charged right on the rear of one of the living walls that was moving to crush our infantry." According to Medill, their advance brought the North Carolinians to a halt, when they "faced about, formed to receive us, and fired a

---

3 Clark, *Histories of the Several Regiments*, 3:326-327.

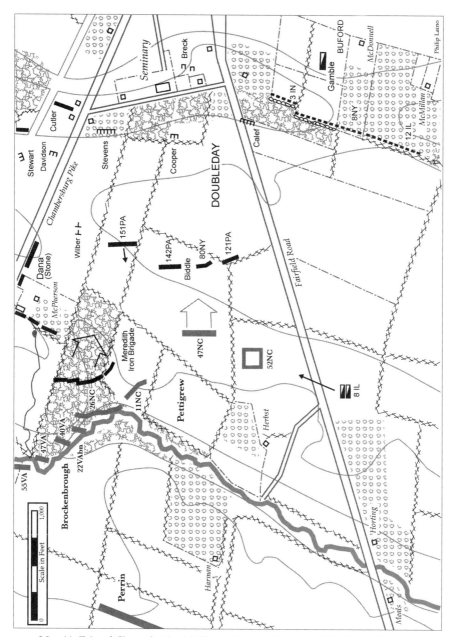

Map 11: Feinted Charge by the 8th Illinois Cavalry Causes the 52nd North Carolina
Infantry to Halt and Form a Square.

Maj. Gen. William Dorsey Pender, commander of Pender's Division, Hill's Corps. Pender was mortally wounded on July 1, 1863. *Library of Congress*

volley that mostly went over our heads. We returned fire with our carbines and galloped away. But during the time they were delayed, the infantry escaped."[4]

Major Alexander Biddle commanded the 121st Pennsylvania Infantry in his cousin Chapman's brigade. The rapid advance of Pettigrew's Rebels needed to be repelled and he had ordered his regiment to change front to meet this threat. It was too little, too late. "As the contest continued . . . the enemy could be plainly seen developing their lines further to the south, and as there were no

4   *The Chicago Tribune*, November 22, 1863.

troops there to receive them, it became painfully evident that the line would be forced to fall back."[5] After a brief stand, Col. Chapman Biddle ordered his brigade to retire. After firing a final heavy volley, his command retreated from its position on McPherson's Ridge about a quarter of a mile eastward to Seminary Ridge. The hard-pressed infantry made the move in a slow and orderly manner under heavy Rebel fire.[6] Only the diligence, bold response and initiative by Gamble and Beveridge, coupled with their own bravery, made their ordered escape possible. With their mission accomplished, the 8th Illinois troopers fell back to rejoin the rest of Gamble's brigade.

It was about this time that a brief lull in the fighting fell over the battlefield. The Confederates were not only reorganizing their lines, but aligning another division under Dorsey Pender to storm the Union position on Seminary Ridge. Buford took the opportunity to scrawl another message to Pleasonton. "I am satisfied that Longstreet and Hill have made a junction," concluded the cavalryman in his 3:20 p.m. dispatch. "A tremendous battle has been raging since 9:30 a.m., with varying success. At the present moment, the battle is raging on the road to Cashtown [Chambersburg Pike], and within short cannon range of this town. The enemy's line is a semicircle on the height, from north to west," Buford continued. "General Reynolds was killed early this morning. In my opinion, there seems to be no directing person. We need help now."[7]

According to Buford's signal officer, Lieutenant Jerome, Buford also sent a note to General Meade that does not appear in the *Official Records* volumes: "For God's sake send up Hancock. Everything at odds. Reynolds is killed, and we need a controlling spirit."[8] Buford fully recognized the crisis confronting the Union army and knew the right man for such desperate times. When Meade learned of Buford's concern about the lack of a directing hand, he ordered Maj. Gen. Winfield S. Hancock, the commander of the Second Corps, to ride to Gettysburg, assess the situation, and assume command of the battlefield.[9]

---

5   *History of the 121st Regiment Pennsylvania Volunteers by the Survivors' Association* (Philadelphia, 1893), 47.

6   Seward R. Osborne, *Holding the Left at Gettysburg: The 20th New York State Militia on July 1, 1863* (Hightstown, NJ, 1990), 13-14.

7   OR 27, pt. 1, 924-25.

8   Jerome, 153.

9   OR 27, pt. 3, 461. This order created some friction between Hancock and Howard. Howard outranked Hancock, and per army protocol, was not required to obey the orders of an officer

Col. Abner Perrin, commander, Perrin's Brigade, Pender's Division. Perrin's troops took heavy fire from Gamble's dismounted troopers during the afternoon phase of the July 1 fighting. *Civil War Museum and Library*

A strong guiding hand and more reinforcements were desperately needed. Early that morning, Maj. Gen. William Dorsey Pender's division departed Fayetteville several hours after Heth's had marched toward Gettysburg. He did so with three of his four brigades under Brig. Gens. James Lane and Alfred Scales, and Col. Abner Perrin. Pender's fourth brigade, under Brig. Gen. Edward Thomas, remained behind with Confederate artillery. Before Pender's men had covered four miles, the sound of artillery fire rumbling in the distance reached their ears: Heth had run into trouble. Pender's troops caught up with Heth while his brigades were battling Gamble's dogged horse soldiers.[10] Pender deployed his three brigades into lines of battle south of the Chambersburg Pike about a mile west of Herr's Ridge, with Lane on the left near the pike, followed on his right by Scales and Perrin. Concern about his right flank resulted in Pender shifting Lane south, where he became the right-flank element. Although he was ready to engage much earlier, Pender did not advance to attack Seminary Ridge until about 4:00 p.m. Robert E. Lee had reached the front and, unsure what he was facing and unwilling to bring on a major engagement, kept the Confederates west of town in check. It was not until he fully understood that Ewell's Second Corps was in

---

junior to him. Hancock, on the other hand, had direct orders from the commander of the Army of the Potomac to assume command of the field. Ultimately, Howard agreed to cooperate with Hancock, and the two officers did a fine job cobbling together the army's ultimate defensive position on Cemetery Hill.

10 Frances H. Casstevens, *The 28th North Carolina Infantry: A Civil War History and Roster* (Jefferson, NC, 2008), 93.

position north of town and heavily engaged to advantage that he ordered Pender to resume the offensive.[11]

As Pender understood it, General Heth's men were in his front and attacking Seminary Ridge, where a motley but powerful collection of Union commands had gathered in a last-ditch attempt to defend Gettysburg. His division would support Heth in the assault. Pender advised Col. Abner Perrin as much, and that he was to guide his advance with Scales (who was more experienced) on his left. As Perrin later explained it, "if we came upon Heath's Division at a halt to move on and engage the enemy closely and manage my brigade according to my own judgment."[12] Once Pender's men reached and advanced past Mcpherson's Ridge into the swale beyond, recalled one of Perrin's South Carolinians, "The field was thick with wounded hurrying to the rear, and the ground was grey with dead and disabled."[13] The long heavy lines of

11 At 29, William Dorsey Pender was one of the rising stars of the Army of Northern Virginia. He was the youngest of Lee's major generals, and was in command of A. P. Hill's Light Division at Gettysburg. He graduated 16th in the West Point Class of 1854 and served in the artillery and the dragoons prior to the Civil War. Pender became colonel of the 3rd North Carolina Infantry in August 1861 and was the recipient of a battlefield promotion from Jefferson Davis at the battle of Seven Pines on June 1, 1862, after which he assumed command of a brigade in the Light Division. When Hill was wounded by the same friendly fire that mortally wounded Stonewall Jackson at Chancellorsville, Pender assumed command of the division and was promoted to major general on May 27, 1863. Hill wrote of him, "Gen. Pender has fought with the Division in every battle, has been four times wounded and never left the field, has risen by death and wounds from fifth brigadier to be its senior, has the best drilled and disciplined Brigade in the Division, and more than all, possesses the unbounded confidence of the Division." General Lee agreed: "Pender is an excellent officer, attentive, industrious, and brave; has been conspicuous in every battle." He was probably the most promising young officer in the Army of Northern Virginia and likely would have enjoyed an outstanding career as head of his division had he not received a mortal wound late on the afternoon of July 2. Tagg, *The Generals of Gettysburg*, 325-326.

12 Abner Perrin to Gov. Milledge L. Bonham, July 29, 1863, ed. by Milledge L. Bonham, *Mississippi Valley Historical Review* (March 1938), 522. Abner Perrin was 36 years old on July 1, 1863. He had served during the Mexican War, but was not a professional soldier. After the Mexican War he studied law and was admitted to the bar in 1854. In 1861, he became captain of a company of the 14th South Carolina and rose to command the regiment in January of 1863. Perrin led the 14th South Carolina in combat as its colonel for the first time at Chancellorsville, and succeeded to brigade command in the absence of Brig. Gen. Samuel McGowan, who was recuperating from a leg wound suffered during the fighting at Chancellorsville that May. Perrin led one of the most storied brigades of the Army of Northern Virginia and acquitted himself well. Perrin would fall mortally wounded at Spotsylvania on May 12, 1864, when a musket ball severed his femoral artery. Tagg, *The Generals of Gettysburg*, 330-331.

13 J. F. J. Caldwell, *The History of a Brigade of South Carolinians, Known First as "Gregg's" and Subsequently as "McGowan's Brigade"* (Philadelphia, 1866), 97.

Rebel soldiers, perfectly aligned with parade-like precision, impressed the Union men awaiting them on the next ridge. "Their bearing was magnificent," remembered an admiring officer of the Iron Brigade. "They maintained their alignment with great precision."[14]

Buford knew a fresh attack against Seminary Ridge was only a matter of time. About 2:30 p.m., an hour and one-half before Pender stepped off, Buford led Gamble's brigade forward to a strong defensive position behind a low stone wall ending on the southwest side of the Fairfield Road just south of the Seminary grounds in Shultz's Woods. The line of troopers extended 500-600 yards south to the McMillan house. About half of Gamble's troopers dismounted to fight on foot while the other half remained mounted in the declivity behind the ridge. A retreating First Corps artillerist passed a squadron of these cavalrymen mounted on gray horses in line of battle facing Shultz's Woods, "as stolid as the stones under their horses' noses."[15]

"We rushed up to a stone wall in the center of the ridge," recalled Pvt. Thomas Day of the 3rd Indiana Cavalry. Major Charles Lemmon led these Hoosier troopers into the fresh combat yelling, "Come on, boys!" Because the battle flag of the advancing Confederates was either hidden or simply not in view, the Indiana men could not tell whether the approaching line of infantry was friend or foe. By the time they realized the Rebels were approaching, heavy volleys flooded the field. Lemmon was "among the first to fall," shot through the head and mortally wounded. The popular major was remembered as being "every inch a soldier, both wise in counsel and brave in action," wrote the regimental historian, "and, while he was a strict disciplinarian, the men well knew he never asked of them other than what he deemed just and what he conceded could justly be exacted of him by his superiors."[16] He died the next day.[17]

Supported by Calef's battery, the Federals laid down a galling fire described as "perfectly terrific" by Buford.[18] Gamble's concentrated fire was so severe

14 Rufus R. Dawes, *Service with the Sixth Wisconsin Volunteers* (Marietta, OH, 1890), 175.

15 William Henry Shelton Autobiography, Archives, New York Historical Society, New York, New York.

16 Pickerill, *History of the Third Indiana Cavalry*, 94.

17 Day, "Opening the Battle."

18 *OR* 27, pt. 1, 927.

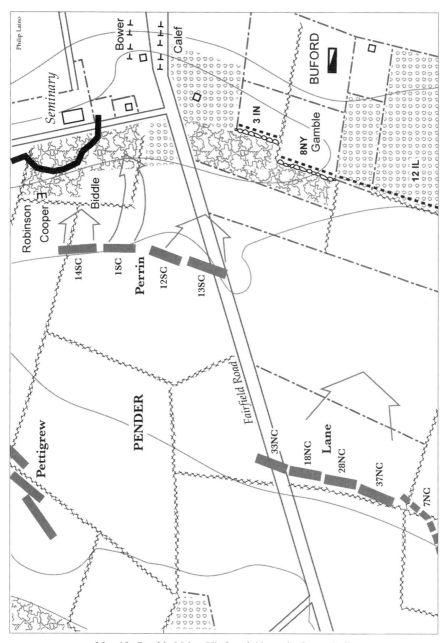

Map 12: Gamble Makes His Stand Along the Stone Wall.

Pender's men thought they were facing infantry instead of a relatively small force of dismounted cavalry.[19] "We fired into them as fast as we could, until we were face to face at the wall; then we had to go, as we were flanked also," recalled a Hoosier. "Here we lost more men than in all the rest of the day; but we had done what we were sent to do."[20] Some of Gamble's horse holders gave their mounts to retreating infantry and went forward to join the fighting.[21]

"In the afternoon the Rebels advanced for half a mile to where the other portion of our cavalry brigade dismounted, and repulsed them from behind a stone wall," reported a trooper of the 8th Illinois Cavalry, whose regiment held a position near the Shultz house.[22] Colonel William Markell of the 8th New York Cavalry, who fought here just below the Fairfield Road, observed, "The enemy being close upon us we opened an effective, rapid fire with our breech-loading carbines, which killed and wounded so many of their first line, that after a short heroic struggle to continue the advance, they could stand it no longer and fell back on the second line."[23] Daniel Pulis, also of the 8th New York, recalled much the same thing: "We went to popping at them. . . . They fell like rain. The ground soon got covered with them. The front column broke and started to run but their rear column pressed on."[24]

The "front column" may well have been a reference to the last effort by Heth's men (Pettigrew), and the "rear column" the fresh troops under Pender stepping into the attack. Colonel Joseph Brown of the 14th South Carolina of Perrin's brigade was attacking the infantry above the Fairfield Road. "By this time the Brigade had attained a point which exposed it to a raking fire from the cavalry," recalled Brown, which was "behind a stone wall on our right."[25]

19 Ibid., pt. 2, 657.

20 Day, "Opening the Battle."

21 Gen. Charles H. Morgan, "Narrative of the Operations of the Second Army Corps, from the time General Hancock assumed command, June 9, 1863, Until the Close of the Battle of Gettysburg," in Almira Hancock, *Reminiscences of General Hancock by His Wife* (New York, 1887), 189.

22 *Aurora Beacon*, August 20, 1863.

23 Markell, "Address," 3:1145.

24 Daniel W. Pulis to his parents, July 6, 1863, Daniel W. Pulis correspondence, Rochester Public Library, Rochester, New York.

25 Varina Davis Brown, ed., *A Colonel at Gettysburg and Spotsylvania* (Columbia, SC, 1931), 80.

Unfortunately for the Union defenders, although Scales' troops were decimated just south of the Chambersburg Pike, Perrin's South Carolinians managed to turn Biddle's left flank just north of the Fairfield Road. Although he had sustained heavy losses, Perrin pressed his attack as ordered, part of which focused upon a yawning gap of some 150 yards in the Union line between the Fairfield Road and the left flank of Biddle's command. "I now directed the [1st South Carolina] . . . to oblique to the right," wrote Perrin in his after-action report, "to avoid a breastwork of rails behind where I discovered the enemy was posted, and then to change front to the left and attack his flank."[26] Perrin's men struck the gap, flanking the infantry in a way that unraveled the Federal position one unit at a time like row of tumbling dominoes. The Union soldiers, exhausted, bloodied, and defeated, fled east toward the town and perceived safety of Cemetery Hill. "Their second line was advancing too near their support," recalled a member of the 8th Illinois Cavalry, "this time the rebels drove our boys from their position, which gave them possession of this part of the town."[27]

The defeat of the infantry farther north exposed Gamble's right flank, and Lane's North Carolina brigade farther south was advancing to threaten Gamble's left. How much of this the troopers could see or determine at the time is anyone's guess. Flavius Bellamy of the 3rd Indiana Cavalry fought that last stand in the center of Gamble's embattled line. Bellamy observed the Confederates fight their way to "within less than 10 paces" of Gamble's position before the Yankee troopers finally had to withdraw.[28] "At last our whole left wing was routed," recalled another Hoosier named Edward C. Reid. "We held it for a time against a whole rebel brigade of infantry—but at last were forced to fall back."[29] Another trooper, Colonel Markell, recalled, "Our men kept up the fire until the enemy, in overwhelming numbers, approached so near that in order to save our men and horses we were obliged to mount and fall rapidly to the next ridge, carrying our wounded with us. The stand we there

26 *OR* 27, pt. 2, 662.

27 *Aurora Beacon*, August 20, 1863.

28 Flavius Bellamy to his parents, July 3, 1863, Diary and Correspondence, Indiana State Library, Indianapolis, Indiana.

29 Edward C. Reid, Diary, July 1, 1863.

Col. George H. Chapman, commander of the 3rd Indiana Cavalry. Although he had no formal military training, Chapman became a very capable cavalry commander. *Library of Congress*

made against the enemy prevented our left flank from being turned, and saved [Rowley's] division of our infantry."[30]

The stand made by Gamble's troopers indeed helped hold Seminary Ridge much longer than would otherwise have been possible, and it came with a high cost. "[M]ost of our losses occurred here in a fight with infantry at short range," admitted Maj. Edwin M. Pope of the 8th New York. "The regiment held the position against a rebel brigade until the division had been got into position, and received the thanks of General Buford 'for the gallant manner in which we withstood the attack, thereby saving an entire division from destruction.'"[31]

Lieutenant Calef, the artillerist who had done his own good work that day, recalled finding "Gamble's brigade dismounted behind a stone wall, contending against [Lane's] Brigade of [Pender's] division, which was stealing a march on our left flank to seize the Emmitsburg Road. Gamble's carbines," recalled Calef in describing an earlier stage of the fighting, "drove the first line of [Pettigrew] back on the second, and put an end, for the time being, to the flanking operation." Ultimately, concluded Calef, "Gamble lost heavily, but the importance of the gallant stand made by this handful of dismounted troopers has never been properly recognized, for had Lane reached the Emmitsburg road his position on the flank and rear of the First Corps would have seriously compromised the retrograde movement of that corps, being executed, toward

30 Markell, 3:1145.

31 "List of Casualties in the Eighth New York Cavalry," *Rochester Daily Union and Advertiser*, July 11, 1863.

Cemetery Hill."[32] Once flanked and nearly overrun, Gamble mounted his men and pulled back to Cemetery Ridge, the spine of ground running south from Cemetery Hill.

"[T]he rebels outflanked our left," explained Gamble in a letter dated March 10, 1864. "[T]his Brigade of Cavalry was again ordered to the front, dismounted and fought the Rebels on the Seminary Ridge and saved a whole Division of our Infantry from being surrounded and captured."[33] Colonel George H. Chapman of the 3rd Indiana Cavalry agreed with Gamble and wrote as much just three weeks after the general's letter. The troopers, he argued, had been outflanked and not defeated outright. "Although but a short time in that position, we so checked the advance of the enemy, as to enable a division of the 1st Corps to pass safely through the town, to the new position which was then being taken up," wrote Chapman.[34] "They never came any farther," boasted Pvt. Thomas G. Day of the same regiment, "and if we had not stopped that column of Gen. Lee's they would have swept our disorganized infantry from the Cemetery, where they were breaking for. This, I think, was of much more importance than who fired the first shot."[35]

Throughout this part of the fighting, Calef's gunners once again performed excellent service, as they had throughout the long and trying day. My pieces "made some excellent shots," thought the gunner, "but my ammunition being nearly exhausted, the firing was very deliberate." When the line began to crumble, Calef withdrew toward the left of the army just east of the Emmitsburg Road, where his guns remained until the next morning.[36]

While Gamble's men made their stand along the stone wall near the Seminary, Tom Devin's troopers were holding their position along the banks of Rock Creek farther north and east. About 3:00 p.m., artillery rounds rained into their position. Unfortunately, the fire originated from Capt. Michael Wiedrich's Battery I of the 1st New York Light Artillery positioned atop Cemetery Hill. Wiedrich's gunners had spotted Jubal Early's approaching Rebel infantry and, under orders from General Howard, opened fire on them. The shells from

---

32 Calef, "The Opening Gun," 51.

33 Gamble to Church, March 10, 1864.

34 Col. George H. Chapman to John B. Bachelder, March 30, 1864, *Bachelder Papers*, 1:130-31.

35 Day, "Opening the Battle."

36 Calef, "Gettysburg Notes," 51-52.

Wiedrich's six rifled guns fell short, wounding several horses in Devin's brigade. When Weidrich spotted a cavalry guidon in the landing zone of his shells, he ordered his men to cease firing. Fortunately for the Union troopers the iron had not killed or wounded any men, though it lasted much longer than anyone on the receiving end desired.

"A battery of the Eleventh Corps, placed in the cemetery, shelled us so persistently that after sending them word that we were not the enemy, with no cessation of their firing at us, we were forced to fall back from our position to the town, being shelled all the way back," remembered a frustrated officer of the 6th New York Cavalry.[37] "The excuse given by the officer in command of the battery was that he supposed Devin's brigade to be a force of the enemy's cavalry," reported another New Yorker. "It was quite evident that this officer's military ardor had been too much stimulated."[38] Demonstrating once again the confusion of combat, at least one of Devin's men, however, believed the artillery fire came from the Confederates. "The enemy shelled us out of our position," he noted in his diary.[39]

As the above New York account mentioned, Devin abandoned his position under this shelling and pulled his troopers back into Gettysburg. He did so because he believed the enemy had somehow gotten behind him. His retreat, however, left the Federal flank uncovered. A few minutes later, Early's troops slammed into the exposed flank of Howard's Eleventh Corps and after some sharp fighting drove it from the field in a wild rout. When Howard ordered Buford to send some of his cavalry to help slow down Early's infantry,[40] Devin deployed his brigade into line along the Emmitsburg Road with his right flank resting in the streets of the town. This alignment allowed the cavalry to protect the retreating Eleventh Corps batteries.[41]

"The enemy, having possession of the road we had left, advanced their sharpshooters attacking our flank; they were driven back by dismounted men of the 9th New York Cavalry," recalled Maj. William Heermance of the 6th New

---

37 Heermance, "The Cavalry at Gettysburg," 200.

38 Cheney, *Ninth Regiment*, 111.

39 John Inglis, Diary, July 1, 1863, John Inglis Papers, Archives, New York State Library, Albany, New York.

40 *OR* 27, pt. 1, 939.

41 Ibid.

York Cavalry.[42] "The broken lines of battle were forced in hastily formed columns through narrow streets with artillery, mounted troops and trains," recalled the historian of the 17th Pennsylvania. "The regiment preserved its formation throughout this trying ordeal, and with the brigade in division went into position on Cemetery Hill, holding the extreme left of the new line." The Pennsylvanians took position on Cemetery Hill where they could support Calef's weary artillerists.[43]

Onrushing Confederates attacked Devin's men in the streets of the town. Devin dismounted a squadron of the 9th New York Cavalry, who turned on their pursuers and, by maintaining a steady, rapid fire with their carbines, drove them back through the town some distance, "punishing them severely" while temporarily securing the flank.[44] Troopers of the 17th Pennsylvania delayed Early's pursuit along the York Road by massing the fire of their carbines and answering the Rebel yell with "a ringing loyal cheer."[45] With these delaying tactics, Devin slowed the Confederate advance and bought time for the routed infantry of the Eleventh Corps to reach safety atop Cemetery Hill. When the weight of Confederate numbers became too great, and the risk of remaining in place too lethal, Devin ordered his men to pull back to the hill where, protected by the batteries of the First and Eleventh corps, they formed a line on the high ground south of town.

With the evening approaching, perhaps many of the troopers believed their long and bloody day was finally at an end. What they were about to learn, however, was that a new threat was approaching—one final challenge for Buford's weary troopers to deal with in a day full of them.

---

42 Heermance, "The Cavalry at Gettysburg," 200.

43 Bean, "Address at the Dedication," 2:878.

44 Cheney, *Ninth Regiment*, 109.

45 Moyer, *Seventeenth Pennsylvania*, 53-65.

Chapter 8
Unshaken and Undaunted

About 4:00 p.m., with the Seminary Ridge line being pressed and in danger of collapsing, General Doubleday sent his staff officer Capt. Eminel P. Halstead in search of the Eleventh Corps' General Howard. When Halstead reported the Confederate threat and asked for reinforcements. Howard admitted he had no troops to spare, and suggested Halstead "go to General Buford, give him my compliments, and tell him to go to Doubleday's support." When Halstead inquired as to Buford's whereabouts, Howard could only offer a general reply: the cavalry general, he said, was somewhere east of Cemetery Hill. Halstead set off in search of the Kentuckian. In fact, John Buford had remained with the remnants of Reynolds' First Corps on its final line of resistance atop Seminary Ridge until Dorsey Pender's hammer strokes finally broke the Union line.[1]

After Abner Perrin's South Carolinians finally drove them from the stone wall, Buford ordered Gamble's weary troopers to fall into line on the Emmitsburg Road near the cemetery. Tom Devin's brigade joined them there after their fight north of town, extending the line almost to the small white clapboard Bryan farmhouse. Captain Halstead found Buford there, mounted on Grey Eagle while overseeing the disposition of his line of cavalry. When Halstead delivered Howard's order, an agitated Buford, who had experienced as long and trying of a day as anyone on the field, "rose in his stirrups upon his tiptoes and exclaimed, 'What in hell and damnation does he think I can do against those long lines of the enemy out there!'"

1   E. P. Halstead, "The First Day of the Battle of Gettysburg," War Papers, District of Columbia Commandery, Military Order of the Loyal Legion of the United States, Read March 2, 1887, 6.

Maj. Gen. Winfield S. Hancock, commander of the Army of the Potomac's 2nd Corps. Meade
sent Hancock to assess and stabilize the situation at Gettysburg after Reynolds fell.

Library of Congress

"I don't know anything about that, General, those are General Howard's
orders," Halstead responded.

Brig. Gen. James H. "Little Jim" Lane, commander, Lane's Brigade, Pender's Division. The advance of Lane's brigade was halted by the sight of Buford's two brigades drawn up in a mounted line of battle late on the afternoon of July 1. *Valentine Museum*

"Very well," replied the exasperated Buford, "I will see what I can do." About 5:00 p.m., Buford ordered his mounted command to move out into the fields in front of Cemetery Hill, in plain view of the enemy.[2] The sight impressed Second Corps commander Hancock, who had been sent by Meade to take command of the field. The corps historian, Francis Walker, described Hancock's impression thusly: "[O]ne of the most inspiring sights of [Hancock's] military career was the splendid spectacle of that gallant cavalry, as it stood there unshaken and undaunted, in the face of the advancing Confederate infantry."[3] Hancock observed in his after-action report that when he arrived on the battlefield, the First and Eleventh Corps were already retiring through the town of Gettysburg, closely pursued by the enemy. "The cavalry of General Buford," he continued, "was occupying a firm position on the plain to the left of Gettysburg, covering the rear of the repeating corps."[4]

As the Rebel lines advanced, Gamble ordered his 8th Illinois Cavalry to retire toward Cemetery Hill, "making as much show as possible." Major Beveridge, who commanded the Illinois regiment, recalled the squadron of his regiment doing picket duty to the west of the woods. "I moved the regiment into the open fields to the southeast, threw down the fences, and formed the regiment in column of squadrons," preparing to charge.[5]

2   Ibid., 8.

3   Maj. Gen. Francis A. Walker, *History of the Second Army Corps* (New York, 1886), 266.

4   *OR* 27, pt. 1, 368.

5   Beveridge, "Address," 21.

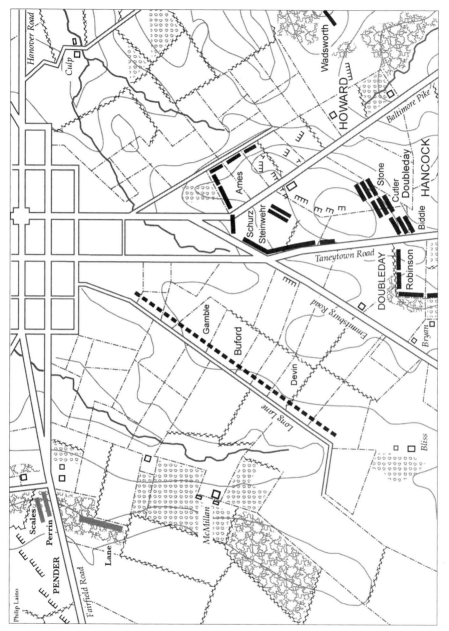

Map 13: "Unshaken and Undaunted": Buford's Feint Halts Lane's Advance

Drawn up in line of battle, Buford's exhausted troopers stood their ground, daring the infantry of General Lane's brigade to close and attack.[6] "We moved to the south edge of Gettysburg and formed a line there," recalled a member of the 9th New York Cavalry. "The Confederates were already getting rather thick in the town. We fired a few shots at them."[7] In some instances, Buford's horse holders handed off their mounts to retreating infantrymen so the troopers given the unwelcome task of horse holding could instead go to the front and wield their carbines against the looming Confederate threat.[8]

Elements of the 8th Illinois Cavalry tried to outflank the right of Lane's advancing brigade near Willoughby Run. Lane ordered Capt. Daniel L. Hudson and the 40 men of Co. G of the 37th North Carolina to disperse the Illinois horsemen. The Tar Heels dislodged Beveridge's troopers, and Lane ordered his brigade the resume its advance. Lane's "men gave a yell, and rushed forward at the double-quick, the whole of the enemy's force beating a hasty retreat to Cemetery Hill."[9]

That night, Doubleday noted in his diary, "Having thus strengthened his right, General Hancock extended his line by posting Buford's Cavalry . . . on the left. This gave us an appearance of strength we did not possess and the enemy did not press the attack, preferring to wait for reinforcements."[10] Brigadier General Gouverneur K. Warren, the Army of the Potomac's chief engineer, later recorded, "General Buford's cavalry was all in line of battle between our position [on Cemetery Hill] and the enemy. Our cavalry presented a very

6 James "Little Jim" Lane was an 1854 graduate of the Virginia Military Institute, where he taught mathematics and tactics after graduating from the University of Virginia with a second degree in 1857. When the Civil War broke out, he was a professor of natural philosophy and instructor in tactics at the North Carolina Military Institute. He became major of the 1st North Carolina Infantry and in September 1861 he was commissioned colonel of the 28th North Carolina, part of A. P. Hill's Light Division. He was promoted to brigadier general on November 1, 1862. Lane led his brigade at Fredericksburg and Chancellorsville, where some of his men fired the fateful volley that mortally wounded Stonewall Jackson. Tagg, *The Generals of Gettysburg*, 333-34.

7 Mix, "Veteran of the 9th N.Y. Cav."

8 Winfield S. Hancock, "Gettysburg: A Reply to General Howard," in Peter Cozzens, ed., *Battles and Leaders of the Civil War* (Chicago, 2002), 5:363.

9 Michael C. Hardy, *The Thirty-seventh North Carolina Troops: Tar Heels in the Army of Northern Virginia* (Jefferson, NC, 2003), 98.

10 Maj. Gen. Abner Doubleday, Diary, July 1, 1863, The National Archives, Washington, DC.

handsome front, and I think probably checked the advance of the enemy."[11] Doubleday's aide Captain Halstead recounted, "the enemy, seeing the movement, formed squares in echelon, which delayed them and materially aided in the escape of the First Corps if it did not save a large portion of the remnant from capture."[12] Doubleday later claimed that with the feinted charge, Buford "rendered essential service . . . and prevented them from cutting us off from our line of retreat to Cemetery Hill."[13]

As Lane's brigade advanced, he ordered Maj. J. McLeod Turner, the commander of the 7th North Carolina Infantry, "to watch the movements of the enemy's cavalry, with instructions to move by the left flank 'as skirmishers,' so as to cover the right of the brigade in its advance." The entire brigade advanced about 4:00, helping to drive the remaining First Corps infantry back into the town. "On account of the threatening attitude of the cavalry, the [7th North Carolina] was detained, but subsequently rejoined the brigade on Seminary Ridge, near McMillan's house," recalled a member of the regiment. Buford's dispositions caused Lane to pause, which undoubtedly permitted the remaining remnants of the First Corps to make it to safety on Cemetery Hill without active pursuit by the Confederates.[14]

Major General William Dorsey Pender, Lane's division commander, ordered Lane "not to advance farther [beyond Seminary Ridge] unless there was another general forward movement." After quickly checking to see what the units around him were doing, Lane "could see nothing at that time to indicate

11 Moyer, *Seventeenth Regiment*, 64.

12 Halstead, 8. The question of whether Lane's men actually formed a square has been the subject of much debate over the years. The Halstead account is the only known account to state specifically that the Confederates formed a square. Confederate soldier John Purifoy, for example, wrote an article in a 1925 issue of *Confederate Veteran* that unequivocally stated that all of the Federal cavalry fighting that day was dismounted and that Lane's men did not stop to form square. John Purifoy, "The Myth of the Confederate Hollow Square," *Confederate Veteran* (February, 1925), 33:53-55.

13 Doubleday, *Chancellorsville and Gettysburg*, 147-148. According to Maj. William Medill of the 8th Illinois Cavalry, Gamble's men did charge: "Our brigade then formed columns of attack, and charged after the screaming devils. When close on their heels we gave them a volley that sent scores of them headlong into the ground. Their lines halted, changed front, and delivered a volley after us as we fell back. By this time our infantry had time to take up another and stronger position, and succeeded in checking the furthest advance of the enemy." *The Chicago Tribune*, November 22, 1863. This account is unsubstantiated. None of the reports filed by Buford, Gamble, or the Confederates mention an actual mounted charge that afternoon.

14 "The Record of the Seventh," *Charlotte Observer*, May 12, 1895.

Brig. Gen. John W. Geary, commander, 2nd Division, 12th Corps. Buford's two brigades relieved Geary's division of the duty of picketing the area around Little Round Top on the night of July 1, 1863. *Library of Congress*

such a movement," so he ordered his brigade to retire to the stone fence on Seminary Ridge previously held by Gamble's troopers so that the wall could provide some shelter from Union batteries on Cemetery Hill, which were "doing us some damage."[15] Thus, even though his line extended almost one-quarter of a mile beyond the Union left, Lane failed to capitalize upon that opportunity. There was nothing to prevent him from turning that flank and then advancing on Cemetery Hill—there were no other Union troops available to stop him from attacking the Union position atop the hill—meaning that the Army of Northern Virginia lost a great opportunity there.

Lane's report of the action fails to address the feinted charge by Buford's mounted troopers. He stated that the fire of a body of the enemy's cavalry and some infantry opened on them from the cover of woods. He did not say anything about forming squares in echelon in response to that feinted charge, and he also did not say anything about his advance being hindered or halted by the presence of the Union cavalry, in direct contradiction of the accounts of the Union officers quoted above.[16]

Seeing the Rebels halt, and satisfied that the situation was now in hand, Buford rode off to find Howard on Cemetery Hill. Shortly thereafter, Hancock rode up, "and in a very few minutes he made superb dispositions to resist any

---

15 *OR* 27, pt. 2, 665.

16 Ibid. The question of whether Lane's brigade formed squares in echelon late on the afternoon of July 1, 1863, is the subject of Appendix D to this book.

attack that might be made."[17] There, Buford, Howard, Hancock, and Warren joined forces to forge a strong defensive position on East Cemetery Hill, now bristling with the survivors of two corps and the batteries of both commands. As Hancock reported, "In forming the lines, I received material assistance from Brigadier-General Buford."[18] Buford's two tired brigades fell into line on the Emmitsburg Road, covering the Army of the Potomac's otherwise exposed left flank.

Perhaps intimidated by the formidable defensive position and by the feint of the mounted charge by Buford's troopers, and certainly tired and disorganized as a result of the hard day's fighting, the Confederates did not press the attack or their advantage, and the day's fighting petered out.[19] Gamble's men had borne the brunt of the fighting in Buford's division—they had been engaged for almost 12 solid hours. "As our army was heavily engaged two miles to the right, we fell back, but as they did not advance any further we picketed here during the night in which time our main army arrived."[20]

As more Federal infantry arrived, the weary troopers withdrew down the Emmitsburg Road toward a peach orchard owned by a local farmer named Joseph Sherfy, where they camped for the night. Pursuant to Hancock's orders to occupy the hills visible south of Gettysburg, Brig. Gen. John W. Geary's Twelfth Corps division had already formed nearby, while Maj. Gen. Dan Sickles' Third Corps spent the night coming up to take its place in the line that would eventually be formed along the high ground spotted by John Buford the day before. By adopting the strong defensive position ranging from Culp's Hill and East Cemetery Hill on the northern end of the line and Little Round Top at the southern end of the line, the army's high command validated Buford's decision to defend this strong position by making his stand to the north and west of the town of Gettysburg.[21]

17 Ibid., pt 1, 927.

18 Gen. Charles H. Morgan, "Narrative," 189; *OR* 27, pt. 1, 368.

19 A detailed discussion of the controversy surrounding whether Lt. Gen. Richard S. Ewell obeyed Lee's orders to "take [Culp's Hill] if practicable," and whether Ewell's Second Corps could have or should have taken Culp's Hill on July 1 strays far beyond the scope of this book. For readers interested in a detailed discussion of this never-ending controversy, see Pfanz, *Gettysburg—The First Day*, 342-49.

20 *Aurora Beacon*, August 20, 1863.

21 Calef, "The Opening Gun," 52.

As Buford rode south along the road toward the peach orchard, he stopped by Calef's camp, where he found the exhausted artillerists resting on the ground near their guns. "Men, you have done splendidly," announced the cavalry general. "I never saw a battery served so well in my life." As a prideful Calef confirmed, "This recognition of their services by their general was ample compensation to these brave men for the hardships of the day and nerved them for the trials which the morrow's sun would surely bring."[22]

It was the end of a very long day. John Buford and his weary command had opened and closed the long day of fighting, and in doing so endured more than a dozen hours of nearly continuous combat. They had done their duty well, buying sufficient time for the infantry to come to the battlefield and secure its defensible terrain. Buford had every reason to be proud of these men.

---

22 Ibid. This same orchard gained notoriety as the infamous Peach Orchard the next day, July 2, 1863.

Chapter 9

The Night of July 1-2, 1863

Buford's troopers spent the night strung out in a picket formation, much like the one used the night before. Even though the long day of fighting was over, Buford's exhausted men remained the eyes and ears of the Army of the Potomac, a critical duty no one performed better than they did.

His line stretched from near the Evergreen Cemetery atop Cemetery Hill all the way south to Little Round Top, about two miles distant. Their exact positions are not documented, but on the southern front it appears the vidette line extended from the Joseph Sherfy peach orchard on the Emmitsburg Road to Little Round Top. "We . . . went into camp down on [Plum Run], covering the left flank of the army," recalled Maj. John L. Beveridge, the commander of the 8th Illinois Cavalry.[1] The regimental historian of the 6th New York, part of Tom Devin's brigade, recorded, "Buford . . . formed his division in front of Cemetery Ridge, southwest of the town, near the low ground east of Stevens' Run, where he occupied an advanced but firm position."[2] Important work remained to be done, but the men were completely exhausted after their bloody day-long ordeal. The Army of the Potomac's high command knew little of General Lee's intentions or dispositions, and the army's flanks still needed to be protected. This critical task, one of the traditional functions of cavalry, necessarily fell to Buford's weary troopers.

1 Beveridge, "Address," 21.

2 Hall, *Sixth New York Cavalry*, 141.

Buford's men had orders to stand to horse through the hours of darkness and to be ready for action at any time.[3] "We went into camp and were assigned to various tasks to prepare for the night," recalled a member of the 9th New York after the battle. "The enemy, who had taken Gettysburg that day, began to feel quite confident that they could capture the whole business on the morrow. As we learned later from some of the captives, they were having quite a celebration in town in commemoration of their accomplishments."[4]

The men were uncertain about what would face them in the morning. "At the close of the first day's fight I felt discouraged. It was a hard fight all day against superior numbers," admitted Pvt. Henry F. Long of the 17th Pennsylvania Cavalry. "But as one [infantry] corps after the other came on the field during the night, I felt more hopeful."[5] Another private, Thomas B. Kelley of the 8th Illinois Cavalry, recalled, "It was a gloomy night for us, I can tell you, with picket duty, knowing that at daylight the battle would be resumed. A man thinks pretty hard at such times."[6]

Elements of the 6th New York Cavalry spent the night on picket duty in the Sherfy peach orchard, "watching for the enemy and directing the different commands where to go."[7] A full moon graced the night sky, its shimmering light hiding some of the horrors of the day's bloodletting.[8] "Bivouacked last night near the battlefield on the left," wrote Col. George Chapman, the commander of the 3rd Indiana, who went on to describe their situation as "Slim fare & slight cover."[9] Theodore W. Bean, of the 17th Pennsylvania Cavalry boasted of the service he and his men undertook that night: "The Seventeenth Pennsylvania Cavalry fully performed its share of service on the night of July 1, and cheerfully labored without rest or sleep in preventing the advance of the enemy on every road it occupied, and in preparing the field in its rear for the

---

3   Ibid., 66.

4   Day, "Veteran of the 9th N.Y. Cav."

5   Moyer, *Seventeenth Regiment*, 284-285.

6   "Opened the Battle at Gettysburg."

7   Hall, *Sixth New York Cavalry*, 142.

8   http://aa.usno.navy.mil/data/docs/RS_OneDay.php

9   Chapman, Diary, July 2, 1863.

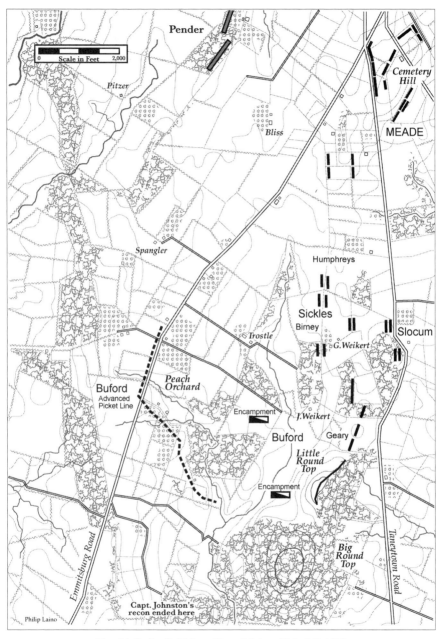

Map 14: Buford's Vidette Lines, Night of July 1-2, 1863

operations of those then marching out to relief."[10] Lieutenant John Hoffman of
the 3rd West Virginia Cavalry told his diary that it drizzled all night, which of
course made him and his comrades miserable.[11] Some of their misery was
alleviated when Buford's wagon train came up during the night with
well-earned rations and ammunition.[12]

That night, Henry J. Wakerly, the bugler for Company G of the 6th New
York Cavalry, captured three Confederates. The musician-trooper took the
three unfortunates to Buford's headquarters so the Kentuckian could
interrogate them. Buford complimented Wakerly warmly and later promoted
him to sergeant.[13] Captain William H. Redman of the 12th Illinois Cavalry
recognized the extent of the ordeal he and his comrades had passed through
that day. "I thank God for His kind protection," he declared in a letter home.
My company, he explained, "lost three men—one killed instantly with a piece of
a shell—one wounded in the hip (he is now in hospital all right)—John
Burrows—(quite badly), and one wounded and taken prisoner. One Company
just beside us, of the 3rd Indiana Regt., lost 15 men and one [Company] 12 and
we had a great many killed and wounded in our Regiment. We dismounted and
fought on foot," he continued. "I shot 10 or 12 times and I did not hit the
enemy every time, I give them close calls." With the bulk of the Army of the
Potomac now at Gettysburg, Redman confidently concluded, "I think that we
will be able to annihilate all of General Lee's Army in Pa. . . . God grant that we
may. I am willing to kill my part of the DEVILS."[14]

During the night, General Lee ordered one of his engineering officers,
Capt. Samuel Johnston, to take a small detail of men and scout beyond the
Confederate right in the hope of finding the left flank of the Union line. They
set off on their reconnaissance about 4:00 a.m., while the full moon still hung
over the battlefield.[15] Johnston later claimed he reached the area of the Round
Tops without resistance about 5:30 a.m. If this was true, however, he almost

10 Moyer, *Seventeenth Regiment*, 66.

11 Lt. John E. Hoffman, Diary, July 2, 1863, Robert L. Brake Collection, USAHEC.

12 *Aurora Beacon*, August 20, 1863.

13 Foster, *Reminiscences and Record*, 136.

14 Redman to his mother, July 1, 1863.

15 http://aa.usno.navy.mil/data/docs/RS_oneday.php. The moon did not set until 5:08 a.m.,
during Johnston's reconnaissance.

certainly would have run into Buford's videttes, which were positioned between the Sherfy peach orchard and Little Round Top at that hour. Johnston and his party, together with the Union troopers, would have been clearly visible under the full moon. While their picket line that night was likely as thinly manned as their picket line was the night before, the diligence of these troopers in detecting enemy threats had already been amply demonstrated. Johnston never mentioned seeing any of Buford's videttes, and there are no accounts of the videttes spotting any Confederate activity. The only reasonable conclusion is that in the darkness Johnston mistook nearby Bushman's Hill for Little Round Top, which lay farther north and east. Regardless of where he scouted or what he did or did not see, Johnston's report that the Union left did not extend as far as the Round Tops had far-reaching implications for the manner in which Lee conducted the battle on July 2. Johnston's reconnaissance was both incomplete and inaccurate, which meant that Lee did not understand where the Union left was located when he planned the second day's attack.[16]

While his men rested and pondered what would transpire when the sun rose, John Buford fretted about the state of his command. His horse soldiers had been in the saddle nearly nonstop since the beginning of George Stoneman's raid on April 30 during the Chancellorsville campaign. Along the way, they had participated in an extended raid and had waged more than a dozen engagements, including large-scale clashes at Brandy Station and Upperville and their epic defensive stand on July 1. His troopers were beyond exhausted, and their mounts were in even worse shape from overuse, poor nutrition, and a lack of preventive medical care. He knew that if his men and animals did not get a break from their constant campaigning—and soon—his entire division would be *hors de combat*. As it was, his command had already lost nearly 20 percent of its effective strength since Brandy Station on June 9, and it

16 David A. Powell, "A Reconnaissance Gone Awry: Capt. Samuel R. Johnston's Fateful Trip to Little Round Top," *Gettysburg Magazine: Articles of Lasting Historical Interest* (July 2000), Issue 23, 88-99. For a contrary view suggesting Johnston passed through Buford's vidette line undetected, see Bill Hyde, "Did You Get There? Capt. Samuel Johnston's Reconnaissance at Gettysburg," *Gettysburg Magazine: Articles of Lasting Historical Interest* (July 2003), Issue 29, 86-93. It seems unlikely that Johnston and his mounted contingent could have passed through Buford's vidette line without being seen or heard by any of Buford's troopers, and it seems almost as unlikely that the experienced engineering officer did not know where he was that early morning. Perhaps the timing of Johnston's account is off, which would explain the discrepancy.

looked as though there would be plenty of hard work as long as the Army of Northern Virginia remained north of the Potomac River.[17]

17 J. David Petruzzi, "A Bloody Summer for Horsemen," *Civil War Times* (June 2013), 37.

Chapter 10

Devin's Brigade Skirmishes
in Pitzer's Woods

The sun began peeking above the horizon not long after 4:00 a.m. on July 2. "The morning of July 2d broke upon the two armies lying as quiet as though they were friends," remembered the historian of the 8th Illinois Cavalry.[1] As the dawn would soon reveal, the Union line extended from Culp's Hill on Meade's far right westward to East Cemetery Hill, where it made a turn south and ran down Cemetery Ridge toward two neighboring hills called Big Round Top and Little Round Top. There was a gap in the line between Culp's Hill and where Rock Creek split the Baltimore Pike. Brigadier General Alpheus Williams' division of the 12th Corps was beyond Wolf's Hill to the east of Rock Creek. Reinforcements would be needed to strengthen the right. Another Twelfth Corps division under Brig. Gen. John W. Geary had spent the night in the area of Little Round Top and was pulled out of line early that morning to march north and take position near Culp's Hill. Geary's withdrawal left only John Buford's two brigades to cover the area between the Sherfy peach orchard on a plateau on the Emmitsburg Road and Little Round Top. His men spent most of their time patrolling to the west along the Millerstown Road, which runs perpendicular to the Emmitsburg Road and intersects with it at the Sherfy peach orchard.

"Almost immediately after daylight we were exchanging compliments with the enemy and held them in check until relieved by the Third Corps, commanded by General Sickles," recalled a member of the 17th Pennsylvania Cavalry.[2] Some of Devin's men were engaged as early as 5:00 a.m. At daylight, Capt. Benjamin J. Coffin led his Company E of the 9th New York Cavalry on a

---

1 Hard, *History of the Eighth Cavalry*, 258.

2 Moyer, *Seventeenth Regiment*, 398.

patrol into a narrow stand of woods to the west, netting a prisoner who may have been a manservant to one of Lt. Gen. James Longstreet's staff officers. The prisoner provided valuable information concerning the disposition of Longstreet's Corps, which the Union high command had not yet identified as having reached the field. Later that morning, Sgt. William T. Bradshaw led a patrol of half a dozen troopers of the same 9th New York west of Pitzer's Schoolhouse, where Bradshaw spotted Confederate infantry of Brig. Gen. Cadmus M. Wilcox's Third Corps brigade moving into position across from the Union left flank.[3] Captain Coffin heard the firing and sent 20 men to reinforce the effort. Devin's men engaged the Rebel pickets and, supported by Calef's battery in the Sherfy peach orchard, waged a firefight with the enemy infantry.[4] "We had some pretty warm work," reported a New York private named Daniel Peck.[5] One of Peck's comrades, another trooper in the same New York command, predicted there would be "some bloody work done today."[6]

Trooper A. R. Mix of the 9th New York Cavalry was assigned to a scouting job that day. He was sent alone to watch for the enemy on a road along the east side of Culp's Hill. He was riding slowly along when the door of a small shack opened and a woman's voice drifted out, warning him to be careful because Confederates were just down the road. Mix thanked her and continued along more cautiously than before. At the top of a hill he spotted an untended Confederate cannon planted in the distance with its crew sprawled upon the ground drinking coffee. Mix wisely withdrew and reported the presence of Confederate artillery on the Army of the Potomac's right flank.[7]

Private Samuel W. Brown served in Company F of the 9th New York Cavalry. "In the morning our company and Co. K were sent to look after our wagon train and turn it back to the division," recalled Brown, "and on our

---

3 Harry W. Pfanz, *Gettysburg: The Second Day* (Chapel Hill, NC, 1988), 88-89.

4 Calef remembered that the position along the Emmitsburg Road had an excellent field of fire. The Confederate artillerists would learn this the next day, as their grand cannonade preceded the Pickett-Pettigrew-Trimble charge that was the climax of the battle of Gettysburg. *OR* 27, pt. 1, 1,032.

5 Martha Gerber Stanford, *Dear Rachel: The Civil War Letters of Daniel Peck* (Ashville, NY, 1993), 50.

6 Inglis, Diary, July 2, 1863.

7 Mix, "Veteran of the 9th N.Y.Cav."

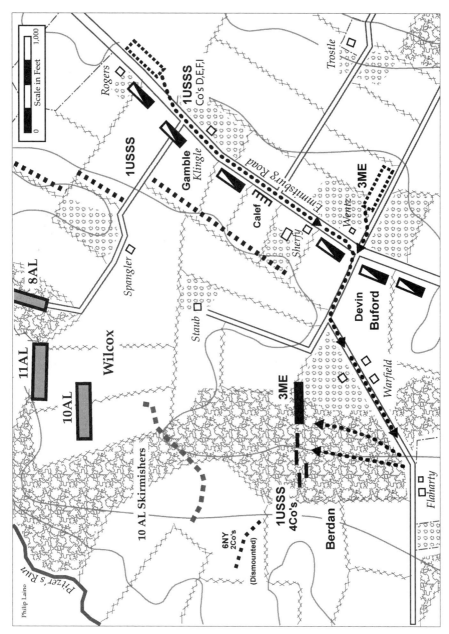

Map 15: Buford's Men Skirmish on July 2, 1863

Maj. Gen. Daniel E. Sickles, commander of the 3rd Corps. Sickles gave the fateful orders to move his corps forward to the Emmitsburg Road in violation of his orders from Meade. He and his command both paid for that decision.

Library of Congress

return found the division had gone to Westminster for supplies, where we overtook them about 11 o'clock that night."[8]

While Mix scouted, troopers of the 6th New York Cavalry deployed to support Col. Hiram Berdan's 1st United States Sharpshooters in the area around Pitzer's Woods. Six companies of the Sharpshooters had deployed in a skirmish line that morning to help cover the army's left flank in front of Sickles' Third Corps. The Sharpshooters detected what they thought was a large force of Southern infantry massing inside Pitzer's Woods. They were right, for that was exactly where General Cadmus M. Wilcox's Alabama brigade, part of A. P. Hill's Corps, had taken up position to protect the Confederate right flank.[9]

About 10 that morning, William Gamble told Calef to deploy his battery to support the 6th New York men and Berdan's Sharpshooters. Calef unlimbered his guns to the right of the two brigades at the Sherfy peach orchard. "The Confederates appeared to secret themselves in every available position not directly exposed to the Union lines," observed one New Yorker. "Whenever the effects of their deadly aim uncovered their hiding places, the Sixth New York, with the other regiments, was employed in dislodging them from their strongholds."[10] Troopers from the 17th Pennsylvania advanced through the

---

8   Samuel W. Brown, "One Who Was There," *The National Tribune*, January 27, 1910.

9   Charles A. Stevens, *Berdan's United States Sharpshooters in the Army of the Potomac 1861-1865* (St. Paul, MN, 1892), 302-303. The advance of Devin's men and the detachment of Berdan's Sharpshooters to Pitzer's Woods constituted the farthest western advance by Union troops on the second or third day of the battle of Gettysburg.

10 Hall, *Sixth New York Cavalry*, 143.

peach orchard, crossed the Emmitsburg Road, and engaged Wilcox's infantry. "The regiment made several charges but was repulsed each time," claimed the regimental historian.[11] Buford proudly reported that his division "held its own until relieved by General Sickles' corps."[12]

When Captain Coffin returned from his scout, he found General Sickles, commander of the Third Corps, and reported what he had seen. Coffin also reported to Buford, who reinforced his line, placed Calef's battery in position, and formed his men to charge, if necessary.[13] The heavy skirmishing in Pitzer's Woods proved the Confederate line extended at least that far south. This crucial intelligence rightly worried Sickles, whose troops had responsibility for this sector. The plateau running along the Emmitsburg Road was higher than the position farther east along lower Cemetery Ridge he was tasked to hold. The higher crest, Sickles believed, was a better defensive position for his troops. Sickles determined to occupy it, a decision that would have far-reaching implications for the day's fighting.[14]

Gamble's men enjoyed an easier morning overall, standing picket duty and relaxing in their bivouacs, than Devin's troopers. According to Colonel Chapman of the 3rd Indiana Cavalry, "The morning has been comparatively quiet, a little work between the skirmishers & an occasional shot from the artillery is all." However, he went on to note with some prescience, "The Enemy seems to be making dispositions to attack our left where the 3rd Corps has taken position."[15]

Some of Gamble's men recalled the morning of July 2 quite differently. Jasper Cheney of the 8th New York Cavalry told his diary that his regiment engaged in "heavy skirmishing in the morning."[16] Another member of the same regiment recalled that, "while we were drawn up in line to support skirmishers,

11 Moyer, *Seventeenth Regiment*, 51. The historian of the 17th Pennsylvania is almost certainly referring to dismounted attacks.

12 *OR* 27, pt. 1, 927-928.

13 Cheney, *History of the Ninth New York*, 115.

14 A detailed discussion of the implications of Sickles' conduct on July 2, 1863, strays beyond the scope of this book. For the best treatment of these events, see James A. Hessler, *Sickles at Gettysburg: The Controversial Civil War General Who Committed Murder, Abandoned Little Round Top, and Declared Himself the Hero of Gettysburg* (El Dorado Hills, CA, 2009).

15 Chapman, Diary, July 2, 1863.

16 Jasper Cheney, Diary, July 2, 1863, *Civil War Times Illustrated Collection*, USAHEC.

Brig. Gen. Henry J. Hunt, the Army of the Potomac's chief of artillery. Hunt played a role in the movement forward of Sickles' 3rd Corps on July 2.
Library of Congress

our company lost one of its faithful and trusty soldiers, Jonathan Macomber, of Livingston County, who was nearly directly behind myself, being struck full in the forehead by a bullet, killing him instantly without a word or a groan. May a just God have more mercy upon him, than erring mortals bestow upon each other."[17]

Later that morning, Sickles moved some of his infantry farther west as support for the skirmishing taking place in the woods beyond. Buford withdrew his troopers to the Emmitsburg Road area and took up a position along the flank of the Third Corps, extending Sickles' line in the area of the Wheatfield and Little Round Top.[18] About noon, Sickles (on the advice of the Army of the Potomac's chief of artillery, Brig. Gen. Henry J. Hunt) ordered four companies of Berdan's Sharpshooters and 210 men of the 3rd Maine Infantry back into Pitzer's Woods to reconnoiter for enemy movements. They clashed with Wilcox's infantry who, after a spirited fight, drove Berdan's Federals back and began pressing farther east toward the Union left. All but a squadron of the 9th New York

---

17 "Genesee," "From the 8th Cavalry."

18 In a postwar speech, Sickles claimed that when Buford's cavalry withdrew without other cavalry forces being sent to cover his flank, it forced him to send Berdan's Sharpshooters forward on a reconnaissance in force which, in turn, uncovered the enemy plan to turn the Army of the Potomac's flank. See "Gettysburg. Great Speech of General Sickles on the Battlefield July 2," *The National Tribune,* July 15 and July 22, 1886. This contention, however, is demonstrably wrong. Buford's two brigades were still on the battlefield when Sickles ordered the reconnaissance by Berdan's Sharpshooters and the 3rd Maine Infantry, and his troopers supported that reconnaissance into Pitzer's Woods.

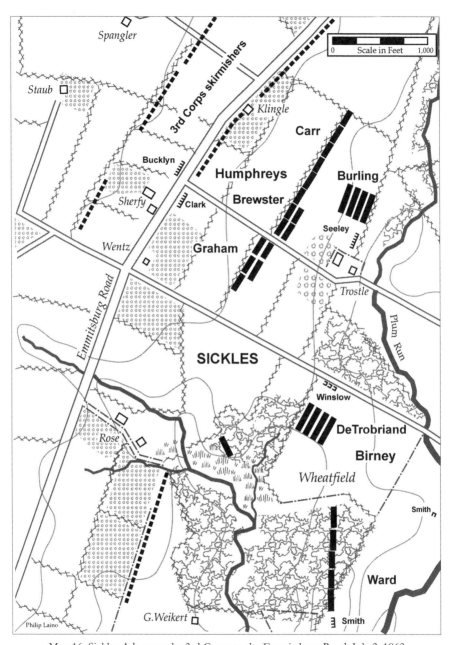

Map 16: Sickles Advances the 3rd Corps to the Emmitsburg Road, July 2, 1863

Cavalry withdrew to the main line along Cemetery Ridge, rejoining the rest of Buford's division there. Only that single squadron of the 9th New York remained in position to guard Sickles' flank.[19]

"I had strengthened and supported my outposts in order to give me timely notice of the attack," claimed Sickles when he testified before the Joint Committee on the Conduct of the War during the winter of 1864. "Buford's cavalry, which had been on the left, had been withdrawn," he said. "I remonstrated against that, and expressed the hope that the cavalry, or some portion of it, at all events, might be allowed to remain there. I was informed that it was not the intention to remove the whole of the cavalry, and that a portion of it would be returned. It did not return, however."[20]

The withdrawal of Buford's troopers, coupled with the unknown but sizeable numbers of Confederate infantry in the woods across the way, made Sickles very nervous. Taking great liberties with General Meade's orders, Sickles decided to move his entire corps forward, determined to possess the higher ground along the Emmitsburg Road, anchored there by a prominent knoll in the Sherfy peach orchard. Once formed, Sickles corps stretched from Houck's Ridge on his left westward over rough terrain to the rise along the road and the peach orchard, where his line turned north and ran along the road before simply petering out with nothing on his immediate right. He later claimed he took up his new position to deprive the Confederates of the benefit of holding the higher ground around the Sherfy orchard. "It was either a good line or a bad one," he observed, "and whichever it was, I took it on my own responsibility."[21] This movement, however, created a large salient in the Union line. It also left a yawning gap between the right flank of Sickles corps and the left flank of Hancock's Second Corps, which was behind him and farther north along Cemetery Ridge.[22] When Sickles advanced his entire corps to occupy the higher

---

19 OR 27, pt. 1, 939. The Baltimore Pike is a direct route from Gettysburg to Westminster on the way to Baltimore. Buford's troopers took this direct route, meaning that, to reach the pike from their positions along the Emmitsburg Road, they had to fall back across Cemetery Ridge to get to the Baltimore Pike.

20 Bill Hyde, ed., *The Union Generals Speak: The Meade Hearings on the Battle of Gettysburg* (Baton Rouge, LA, 2003), 42. The withdrawal of Buford's troopers is addressed in detail in the next chapter.

21 Ibid.

22 Sickles' movement forward triggered years of bitter recriminations. Sickles defended his actions as necessary to save the Army of the Potomac. Sickles apparently also took up his acid

ground, some of it along the Emmitsburg Road, the remaining squadron of the 9th New York fell back to Cemetery Ridge, having suffered six casualties.[23]

Thus ended Buford's role in the fighting at Gettysburg. He and his other troopers had other work to do.

---

pen to defend his apparent insubordination and criticize Meade's conduct of the battle, and he did so in a number of newspaper articles under the pseudonym "Historicus." These heated debates triggered a series of Congressional hearings before the Joint Committee on the Conduct of the War in the winter of 1864 regarding the Union high command's conduct of the battle and the pursuit of Lee's beaten army afterward—much to the disgust of George Gordon Meade. For a detailed discussion of the roots and consequences of the Meade-Sickles arguments, see Richard A. Sauers, *Gettysburg: The Meade-Sickles Controversy* (Washington, DC, 2003).

23 Cheney, *History of the Ninth New York*, 115.

Chapter 11

Buford Departs the Battlefield

John Buford knew he had performed a long and good day's work, but it had also been a bloody endeavor. His command had suffered heavily since the campaign began in earnest at Brandy Station on June 9. His horses were in poor condition and had received little in the way of rations during their several weeks of hard riding and fighting. As one of General Meade's staff officers noted, the lack of forage and "loss of shoes from continuously hard work" had conspired to make large numbers of horses completely "unserviceable."[1] "Our supplies have been out for two days," observed Col. George Chapman of the 3rd Indiana Cavalry in his diary on July 2, "and horses are growing lank."[2]

Buford's mounts needed rest and new shoes, and they needed both soon. Rumors of a significant Confederate threat to the Army of the Potomac's supply trains, still advancing through Maryland toward Gettysburg, reached Meade's headquarters. If true, Buford and his men would be thrown back into active operations for which their mounts were unprepared.[3] Further, although part of his army had fought on July 1, Meade had not yet decided whether to concentrate and fight the campaign's primary battle at Gettysburg. His competent engineering staff had identified a strong defensive position in Maryland known as the Pipe Creek line, named for Big Pipe Creek, which meandered along the front of the formidable ridgeline that anchored the position. Meade was still considering whether to fall back and assume a

---

1   G.G. Meade, ed., *The Life and Letters of George Gordon Meade*, 2 vols. (New York, 1913), 2:71.

2   Chapman, Diary, July 2, 1863.

3   Hard, *Eighth Regiment*, 259.

Maj. Gen. George G. Meade, who was ordered to assume command of the Army of the
Potomac on June 28, 1863. *Library of Congress*

Maj. Gen. Daniel Butterfield, who was
Meade's chief of staff on July 2, 1863.
Butterfield wrote the order for Buford's
command to leave the battlefield.

Library of Congress

defensive position there when the sun
rose on what would be the morning of
the second day of the battle.

New orders reached Buford on the
morning of July 2, when Meade's chief
of staff, Maj. Gen. Daniel Butterfield,
notified Maj. Gen. Alfred Pleasonton
that more work awaited his troopers:
"The major-general commanding
directs that General Buford collect all
the trains in the area of Taneytown and
take them down to Westminster."[4] That simple order triggered controversy that
remains to this day. The execution of this order uncovered the Federal left
flank, which is exactly where General Lee planned to land sledgehammer blows
in the form of James Longstreet's two divisions just a few hours later that same
afternoon. When he received the orders, Pleasonton instructed Buford to move
his division the 30 miles to Westminster, Maryland, as directed, and guard the
army's wagon trains. The precise language of Pleasonton's order to Buford has
never been ascertained, but presumably it tracked the language contained in
Meade's order. Westminster was the terminus of the Western Maryland
Railroad, a major artery of supply for the Army of the Potomac. A careful
review of Meade's order to Buford indicates that this was a peremptory
directive from the army commander, and thus not subject to dispute,
discussion, or much discretion.

Several men who made the movement to Westminster described it.
According to Lieutenant Calef, Buford's division went "to Westminster,
whither it was . . . to guard our communications, as well as to supply itself with

---

4 OR vol. 27, pt. 3, 1086. This order is buried in an appendix to volume 27 of the *Official
Records*, and is not in the proper chronological sequence. Consequently, historians overlooked it
for years.

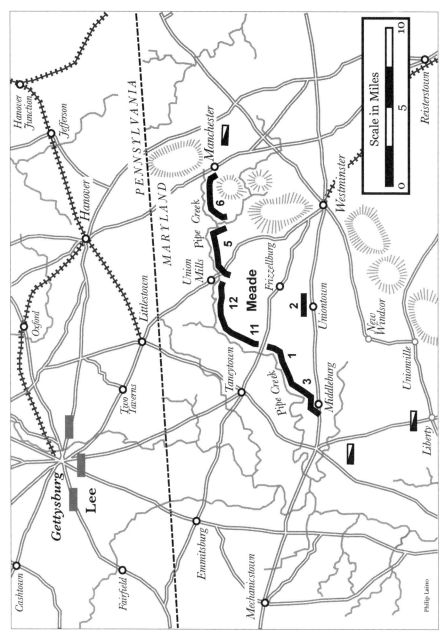

Map 17: The Pipe Creek Line

forage, rations, and ammunition, from which it had been separated many days."[5] An officer of the 8th Illinois noted, "Gen. Meade . . . ordered our cavalry division to fall back to . . . Westminster, and take position on the railroad to guard our left against an apprehended flank movement of the enemy to cut off our communications and supply trains."[6]

Although it led to controversy, the order for Buford to ride to Westminster makes a great deal of sense. Meade did not make a final decision to stay and fight at Gettysburg on July 3 until he held a counsel of war at his headquarters on the night of July 2; he was willing to still consider falling back to Pipe Creek if seriously threatened. Two writings by Meade support his contention. At 3:00 p.m. on July 2, just before Longstreet opened his attack against the Union left, Meade sent a dispatch to general in chief, Maj. Gen. Henry W. Halleck, "If I find it hazardous to do so, or am satisfied the enemy is endeavoring to move to my rear, and interpose between me and Washington, I shall fall back to my supplies at Westminster," suggesting that if there was a threat to his flank or rear, he intended to abandon his position at Gettysburg.[7] Meade elaborated on his thought process in an 1870 letter. "Longstreet's advice to Lee was sound military sense; it was the step I feared Lee would take, and to meet which, and be prepared for which was the object of my instructions," he explained. "But suppose Ewell with 20,000 men had occupied Culp's Hill and our brave soldiers had been compelled to evacuate Cemetery Ridge and withdraw . . . would the Pipe Clay Creek (the real military feature is Parr Ridge which extends through Westminster) order have been so very much out of place?"[8] Meade was justifiably worried about his lines of communication and supply, and in that sense knew Buford was the right man to protect them. The cavalry general had fought precisely the same sort of delaying action the day before, and understood what would be required if forced into the same situation a second time.

After the war, when the controversy about sending away Buford's cavalry was a hot topic, medical orderly Walter Kempster, who served with the Cavalry Corps, took up his pen to explain. "Buford's men and horses were in no worse

5 Calef, "The Opening Gun", 52.

6 *The Chicago Tribune*, November 22, 1863.

7 *OR* vol. 27, pt. 1, 72.

8 George G. Meade to G.G. Benedict, March 16, 1870, included in *The Life and Letters of George Gordon Meade*, 2:351.

condition than Gregg's or Kilpatrick's," he wrote, "but assuming that they were—to send a large body of veteran troops from the firing line during an engagement, in which those troops were taking an active part, is proof that the commanding general considered the position thirty miles in the rear of more importance than the battle line; this conclusion cannot be successfully disproved," he correctly observed.[9]

The order for Buford's withdrawal was not given until Brig. Gen. Henry J. Hunt, Meade's chief of artillery, personally inspected the area and approved the removal of Buford's troopers from the line. Once Hunt approved that order, Buford's two brigades mounted up from their positions screening what was essentially Dan Sickles Third Corps front, and rode south out the Baltimore Pike, which was the direct route to Westminster. The first regiments from William Gamble's brigade departed about 11:00 a.m., and the final regiments of Tom Devin's brigade about two hours later. Other Federal cavalry was supposed to assume Buford's role of covering the army's exposed left flank, but only one regiment, the 4th Pennsylvania Cavalry, was sent to do so. This small regiment could not cover the entire left flank of the Union army. It is unclear where the direct responsibility for the failure to replace Buford's brigades rests, but it ultimately must fall upon the cavalry corps commander. Pleasonton knew the order had come down, was involved in directing it to Buford, and for reasons that remain unexplained, failed to recognize the need to protect the army's position with a sufficient cavalry screen. His failure to act exposed that portion of the army to the heavy infantry and artillery attack that came later that afternoon.

The fact that a mistake was made was not lost on anyone, at least after the fact, "About eleven o'clock was committed a blunder on the left which had a serious effect on the immediately ensuing movements on that part of the field," explained General Meade's son George, who served on his father's staff. "With only partial information afforded him by Generals Pleasonton and Butterfield, chief of staff, the commanding general [Meade] became a party to an action the bearings of which, when he soon thereafter learned of them, he repudiated as wholly beside his intention."[10]

---

9   Walter Kempster, "The Cavalry at Gettysburg," *War Papers*, Military Order of the Loyal Legion of the United States, Wisconsin Commandery (Milwaukee, WI, 1905), 4:423.

10 George G. Meade, *The Battle of Gettysburg* (Ambler, PA, 1924), 68.

Young Meade, who held a captain's commission in the 6th Pennsylvania Cavalry of Merritt's Reserve Brigade, and understood the travails faced by the cavalry, went on to point out that the Federal horses had been badly used up and were short on forage, which is one of the primary reasons why Buford was sent to Westminster in the first place—to refit his command. "General Meade, having previously been informed that all of the cavalry was up and taking it for granted that Pleasonton would substitute other cavalry for Buford's, gave permission to relieve him, directing that he should collect the trains of the army and guard them to Westminster where he could refit," he continued. "Without replacing Buford's with other cavalry, Pleasonton relieved him from duty, and thus the whole left flank of the army was destitute of cavalry. General Meade did not learn of this state of affairs until shortly before one o'clock. He was exceedingly annoyed," continued the captain, "stating emphatically that he had had no intention of denuding his left wing by stripping it of cavalry."[11] By this time, however it was too late to recall Buford, who received unfair and unwarranted criticism for leaving the battlefield for decades as a result.[12]

Whether Meade knew at the time or his captain-son was covering his tracks after the fact, by 1:00 p.m. that afternoon both of Buford's brigades were riding south toward Westminster. His troopers left "the Infantry to fight it out at Gettysburg while we looked after the Reb. cavalry," complained a trooper of the 3rd Indiana Cavalry, who was still itching for a fight.[13] Although no one could have known it at the time, their exodus from the field ended their role in the battle of Gettysburg.

Buford's troopers rode 14 miles to Taneytown, Maryland, where they camped for the evening. The next day, July 3, they covered the remaining

11 Ibid.

12 The order to withdraw Buford's troopers and the failure by Pleasonton to make arrangements for other cavalry forces to guard the Union left flank triggered years of controversy and recriminations. Well-known historian Edward G. Longacre, for example, insinuated that Buford abandoned the field of battle when he wrote, "About 9:00 a.m., Gamble's troopers turned their backs to the enemy and marched south to Taneytown. Devin's people would follow a few hours later." He continued, "After spending the night in Taneytown, Buford guided his two brigades toward the railroad supply base at Westminster, the sounds of battle growing ever fainter behind him." Longacre, *The Cavalry at Gettysburg*, 206. For a detailed discussion of this controversy, see Eric J. Wittenberg, "The Truth about the Withdrawal of Brig. Gen. John Buford's Cavalry, July 2, 1863," *Gettysburg Magazine: Articles of Lasting Historical Interest*, (July 2007), Issue 37, 71-82.

13 Bellamy, Diary, July 2, 1863.

distance to Westminster, where they spent the balance of the battle awaiting further orders. "We marched to Westminster. Rain very heavy—camped in woods West of town," recounted Edward C. Reid of the 3rd Indiana Cavalry.[14] Although the troopers had left the active field of battle, it did not mean their travails were at an end. In addition to their exhaustion and that of their animals, explained the regimental historian of the 8th New York, "Our horses about starved."[15]

"I suppose the reason we were called away on the second day was that ourselves and horses had lived five days on two days' rations," declared orderly Sgt. Charles Van Dusen of the 8th New York, echoing the sentiment observed in the regimental history, "but we did well enough, for we bought bread and butter, and had plenty of coffee and sugar, and I bought oats at a farm house for my horse, but the majority of the horses had lived on nothing but grass, and were very near used up."[16]

Colonel Chapman of the 3rd Indiana Cavalry also confirmed the hungry state of man and beast alike. "We are after supplies for men & horses," explained the officer, "both having been on short allowance four days."[17] A trooper of the 9th New York Cavalry penned a similar letter home that day, one describing not only their food plight but losses as well. "I am alive and well although I have had several narrow escapes," he wrote. "We have had a number of skirmishes and lost quite a number in our regt. Our Division was ordered back to this place where are not to recruite our horsess a little they have been saddled every day and nearly every night for 4 weeks and not mutch grain for them to eat." He concluded, "The hardest Battle of the war is being fought now."[18]

"We are now encamped two miles from the village, engaged in the double duty of picketing and protecting our supply trains, and recruiting ourselves and horses, for constant service and short rations had, to use a common phrase in camp, nearly 'played us out,'" admitted a trooper of the 8th New York Cavalry. "We are anxiously awaiting news from the front, as the battle was raging

14 Edward C. Reid, Diary, July 3, 1863.

15 Norton, *Deeds of Daring*, 69.

16 *Rochester Daily Union and Advertiser*, July 22, 1863.

17 Chapman, Diary, July 3, 1863.

18 Taylor, *Saddle and Saber*, 95.

yesterday with fury. However, we shall undoubtedly soon have an opportunity of renewing our experience, whether our army is defeated or victorious."[19]

One member of the 8th Illinois cavalry recalled, "we remained here during the days the battle was going on [July 2-3], and many regretted they could not be there to help."[20] A comrade agreed: "Here we have been for two days listening to the roar of a tremendous battle that is being fought a few miles to our front. The thunder of battle was heard all day yesterday and this afternoon. It has now ceased. How we have ached to take part in it."[21] The thunder of the great cannonade preceding Pickett's Charge on July 3 was plainly heard by the troopers at Westminster, and the lack of any reliable information as to what was transpiring on the battlefield frustrated them.[22] Still, they remained optimistic. "Buford's men felt that Meade's army was winning the fight," was how one New Yorker remembered it.[23]

While Buford's men waited for orders, a large contingent of Confederate prisoners passed through the railroad junction at Westminster, triggering further speculation among the essentially unemployed troopers. Without much to do, they anxiously awaited news of the fate of their comrades. However, the Gettysburg campaign was not over. John Buford and his weary troopers still had a great deal of important work left to do during the pursuit of Robert E. Lee's Army of Northern Virginia during its retreat to Virginia after its crushing defeat at Gettysburg.[24]

19 "Genesee," "From the 8th Cavalry."

20 *Aurora Beacon*, August 20, 1863.

21 *The Chicago Tribune*, November 22, 1863.

22 Chapman, Diary, July 3, 1863.

23 Cheney, *History of the Ninth New York Cavalry*, 116.

24 John E. Hoffman, Diary, July 3, 1863. For a detailed discussion of the critical role played by John Buford and the First Cavalry Division during the retreat from Gettysburg and the pursuit of Lee's Army of Northern Virginia, see Eric J. Wittenberg, J. David Petruzzi, and Michael F. Nugent, *One Continuous Fight: The Retreat from Gettysburg and the Pursuit of Lee's Army of Northern Virginia, July 4-14, 1863* (El Dorado Hills, CA, 2008).

Conclusion

An Assessment of John Buford's Performance in the Battle of Gettysburg

John Buford's men played a major role at Gettysburg. They outdid themselves throughout the first day of the battle, and performed well in their limited role on the second. They held off more than twice their number of veteran Confederate infantry on July 1. Their stout stand extracted a high price from Heth's division, forcing the brigades of James Archer and Joe Davis to deploy in a variety of ways several times. This, in turn, took them two and one-half hours to cover the two miles between Marsh Creek and Willoughby Run. It was this valuable time that allowed John Reynolds to bring up his First Corps infantry, deploy for battle, and secure the crucial defensive terrain. Their conduct that morning was valiant and their courage conspicuous. Even the Confederates grudgingly admitted as much. One acknowledged that Buford's precision deployments and withdrawals "practically neutralized Archer's gallant brigade."[1] As Col. William Markell of the 8th New York Cavalry put it, "When we consider that two divisions of Hill's Corps were held in check for three hours by so small a cavalry force, it become unnecessary to say anything more about their gallantry and fighting qualities."[2]

Their service in the afternoon phase of the first day's fighting, although often overlooked, was arguably as important. Gamble's stand with his embattled brigade along the stone wall below the Fairfield Road helped hold a crumbling position in the face of assaulting waves of Rebels and saved hundreds and perhaps thousands of infantrymen from being flanked and captured, or killed and wounded. "The stand we there made against the enemy

---

1 Shue, *Morning on Willoughby Run*, 205.

2 Markell, "Dedication of Monument," 3:1145.

prevented our left flank from being turned," Colonel Markell accurately recalled, "and saved a division of our infantry."[3] This stand also helped bring the Confederate advance to a grinding halt. "General Lane of the extreme right, being annoyed by a heavy force of dismounted cavalry on his right flank, which kept up a severe enfilade fire, was so much delayed thereby that he was unable to attack the enemy in front excepting in meeting a force of them posted in the woods," reported Dorsey Pender's adjutant general after the battle, grudgingly acknowledging the role played by Gamble's troopers in slowing down and softening the push toward Seminary Ridge.[4]

The feinted mounted charge of Gamble's and Devin's weary brigades during the late afternoon phase of the battle probably contributed to the Confederate decision not to launch an all-out attack on East Cemetery Hill. "My brigade fought well under disadvantageous circumstances against a largely superior force," reported Gamble. "Every officer and soldier did his duty." He concluded, "This brigade had the honor to commence the fight in the morning and to close it in the evening."[5] Tom Devin's troopers also performed well, buying enough time during the retreat through town for Generals Buford, Howard, Hancock, and Warren to forge their strong defensive position atop Cemetery Hill, preserving the strategic high ground for the Army of the Potomac.

Years after the war, Capt. William C. Hazelton of the 8th Illinois Cavalry summed up the feelings of the men of the First Cavalry Division. "Pleasonton says that Buford was the hero of that battle; that the position he held was of vital importance," he wrote. "That he held the position was due to that his cavalry fought that morning as never before."[6] The performance of these troopers impressed the Cavalry Corps commander. "This division continued in the fight throughout the day, displaying great obstinacy in holding all their positions, and splendid courage and skill in their treatment of the rebels," reported Alfred Pleasonton.[7]

---

3   Ibid.

4   *OR* 27, pt. 2, 657.

5   Ibid., pt. 1, 935.

6   Hazelton, "An Address Made at a Regimental Reunion."

7   *OR* vol. 27, pt. 1, 914.

The artillery fighting with Buford also performed exceptionally well. Calef's gunners were among those who did magnificent duty at Gettysburg. Engaging more than twice their number for most of the morning on July 1, these talented Regular artillerists enabled Buford and his troopers to hold on during those nearly three long, bloody hours that first morning. "All behaved nobly," declared a proud Calef. "The battery did well, and I was highly gratified by the compliments paid it by General Buford . . . and Colonel Gamble." Calef reported that he lost 12 men badly wounded and 13 horses killed in "a very severe" engagement. He went on to praise "the coolness and intrepidity" of the three chiefs of sections.[8] His achievements that day earned Calef a well-deserved brevet to captain for his fine work at Gettysburg and what would follow during the pursuit of the Army of Northern Virginia to come.[9] Without the fine work of Calef and his men, it is doubtful that Gamble's and Devin's troopers could have hung on long enough for the First Corps infantry to arrive.

As noted throughout this monograph, Buford demonstrated the appropriateness of his nickname "Old Steadfast" by his calm and courageous stand in the face of heavy odds throughout his short stay in Pennsylvania, and especially for fighting where and how he did on July 1. Once he decided to stay and fight at Gettysburg, he did so with grim determination until the infantry arrived. Utterly fearless, despite intense pain from crippling arthritis, he rode his lines on his mount Grey Eagle, rallying his troops and encouraging them to stand tall and keep fighting. He designed and fought a classic delaying action in textbook fashion. Alert to his surroundings, Buford held the commanding high ground and interior lines of communication, forcing the Confederates to adopt longer, less advantageous lines.

"It was [Buford's] foresight and energy," wrote one of Reynolds' staff officers, Lt. Joseph Rosengarten, "his pluck and self-reliance in thrusting forward his force, and pushing the enemy [on June 30] and thus inviting, almost compelling their return, that brought on the engagement of the first of July."[10] And yet, what he achieved on July 1 was only made possible by Buford's careful arrangements on the night of June 30. This did not become obvious until after the end of the battle. Brigadier General Theophilus F. Rodenbough, the

8 *OR* 27, pt. 1, 1032.

9 Cullum, *Biographical Register*, 2:582.

10 Bean, "Who Fired the Opening Shots!"

commander of the 2nd U.S. Cavalry of Wesley Merritt's brigade at Gettysburg, penned what is perhaps the most concise and accurate summary of what Buford's sound decisions and superb tactics managed to accomplish on July 1:

> The dispositions made by him the night before to meet a formidable onset of infantry; the complete nature of his methods of obtaining information of the enemy's movements; the skillful concentration of his limited force between the town and two hostile army corps, approaching from different directions; the good judgment of the officer in charge the first skirmish line in opening fire at the extreme range of his carbines; the gallant and effective handling, by Lieutenant Calef, of his two sections under the concentrated fire of twelve field-guns at close quarters; the characteristic tenacity with which the dismounted cavalrymen held their ground, having "to be literally dragged back a few hundred yards to a position more secure;" the real love of fighting shown by some of the Third Indiana Cavalry, who "found horseholders, borrowed muskets and fought side by side with the Wisconsin regiment that came to relieve them;" these all go to show the superiority of such cavalry methods with a fine personnel to direct and execute.[11]

The Confederates recognized Buford's accomplishments as well. Colonel Edward Porter Alexander, an artillery battalion commander in Longstreet's First Corps, was an especially astute observer. Alexander candidly and honestly noted that Heth (and to a lesser degree, Pender), who launched the ill-advised attacks against Buford's troopers that day, got "a genteel whipping, by the . . . force they had inadvertently pitched into."[12] One must wonder whether Buford might not have had the measure of his old comrade-in-arms. He and Harry Heth had served together in the Old Army and during the First Sioux War at the September 1855 battle of Ash Hollow. They would have ridden together, camped together, and known one another fairly well. Gettysburg marked Heth's first engagement as a division commander, and he did not handle his troops well. Buford likely knew Heth was inexperienced at division command in 1863, and that the Virginian was not known for his intellectual prowess. Buford may well have had the full measure of his opponent and used that familiarity to his advantage on July 1. The Union general was fortunate to have faced Heth's division that morning at the outset and not one of the Army of Northern Virginia's better-led divisions.

11 Theophilus F. Rodenbough, "Cavalry War Lessons," *Journal of the United States Cavalry Association* (1889), 2:115.

12 Gary W. Gallagher, ed., *Fighting for the Confederacy: The Personal Recollections of General Edward Porter Alexander* (Chapel Hill, NC, 1989), 232.

Buford also deserves credit for choosing the battlefield at Gettysburg. He knew Meade wanted to fight a largely defensive engagement, and so carefully selected the ground, designed and executed a brilliant delaying action, and in doing so bought the time needed for the Army of the Potomac to consolidate on that terrain to wage that defensive battle on ground of its own choosing.

"It is no more than justice to claim that the North owes to the soldierly instincts, energy, and tenacity of John Buford the possession of the position at Gettysburg, and the fortunate issue of that decisive conflict," wrote Gen. John Watts DePuyster, one of America's leading military historians of the nineteenth century. "He and Reynolds were the heroes of the first day's fight."[13] Captain William L. Heermance of the 6th New York Cavalry agreed, observing, "Buford alone selected the ground to be held, seeing on his arrival the day previous the advantage of its position," a position echoed by General Hancock and a number of other Gettysburg historians.[14] General Pleasonton, Buford's senior in the chain of command, remarked, "To the intrepidity, courage, and fidelity of General Buford and his brave division, the country and the army owe the battle-field at Gettysburg. His unequal fight of four thousand men against eight times their numbers, and his saving of the field, made Buford the true hero of the battle."[15]

General John Gibbon, who led a division of infantry in Hancock's Second Corps and was also one of the heroes of the battle, acknowledged the trooper's actions. "The concentration of Meade's Army and the retention of [Cemetery] Ridge," wrote Gibbon, "was rendered possible by Buford's measures on the 30th of June and the brave stand he took and fought on till the arrival of Reynolds on the 1st of July. History, even if it desired to perpetuate anything but the truth, cannot wrest that proud boast from Buford's great record."[16]

Major Chapman Biddle, whose First Corps brigade was one of those saved from being flanked by the feinted charge of the 8th Illinois Cavalry, declared,

13 DePuyster, *Decisive Conflicts of the Civil War*, 29.

14 William L. Heermance, "The Cavalry at Gettysburg," Military Order of the Loyal Legion of the United States, New York Commandery, *Personal Recollections of the War of the Rebellion*, A. Noel Blakeman, ed. (New York, 1907), 201.

15 DePuyster, *Decisive Conflicts of the Civil War*, 29. This figure overstates the size of Buford's division by more than 1,000 men, making the accomplishments of his two brigades all the more remarkable.

16 John Gibbon, "The John Buford Memoir."

"Buford had . . . faithfully discharged his whole duty in the face of heavy odds. He had tenaciously kept his position, and thus rendered it possible for the Union, in its hour of peril, to find its deliverance through the Army of the Potomac. To the boldness, persistence, and gallantry of John Buford, on this and other fields, his country owes his memory a vast debt of gratitude."[17]

General Francis A. Walker, the official historian of the Hancock's Second Corps, also agreed on the important role performed by the cavalry on July 1:

> Here at Gettysburg, the intrepid, vigilant, enterprising Buford, searching every avenue by which the enemy might approach, suddenly experienced the onset of Heth, coming in from Chambersburg on his left, the first of Lee's widely scattered divisions to arrive in a general movement of concentration at that point ordered on the 29th of June, in ignorance of Meade's advance northward. Hastily sending word to Reynolds, Buford proposed to hold the enemy back until the Union infantry could come up. Twelve months earlier a Confederate division would have driven the Union cavalry before them like chaff; but the mounted service had now reached the same degree of hardiness, tenacity and endurance which the infantry acquired a year earlier. Posting his men along the banks of Willoughby Run, a mile or more to the northwest of Gettysburg, Buford, with the utmost courage and address, holds back the advancing Confederates until the head of the infantry corps, under Reynolds in person, comes up rapidly to the sound of the firing.[18]

Characteristically, "Honest John" Buford modestly gave all the credit to his men. In his after-action report, Buford proudly proclaimed, "The zeal, bravery, and good behavior of the officers and men on the night of June 30, and during July 1, was commendable in the extreme. A heavy task was before us; we were equal to it, and shall all remember with pride that at Gettysburg we did our country much service."[19]

It bears repeating that Buford did extraordinary work gathering intelligence about the dispositions of the Confederates throughout the Gettysburg campaign. "From the day upon which the Army of the Potomac left its cantonments on the Rappahannock until Reynolds relieved Buford's Cavalry Division on the battlefield at Gettysburg," wrote one observer, "the Federal cavalry had performed its difficult and arduous duties with a resolution, intelligence, and efficiency which deserved, and has received, the highest

---

17 Chapman Biddle, *The First Day of the Battle of Gettysburg* (Philadelphia, 1889), 26.

18 General Francis A. Walker, *General Hancock* (New York, 1894), 103.

19 *OR* 27, pt. 1, 927.

praise."[20] Captain Charles Howard, the younger brother of Eleventh Corps commander Maj. Gen. Oliver Otis Howard, declared of Buford's intelligence gathering on June 30, "Never was cavalry more on the alert or more efficient in ascertaining the movements of the enemy."[21] Buford's troopers performed this vital duty better than anyone in the Union cavalry had done to date.

John Buford did not have time to bask in any glory. When the fighting ended on July 3 and Lee began retreating that night and the following day, Buford and his men were called upon once more. What followed was 10 days of intense riding and fighting during the retreat south to the Potomac River, and more fighting along the Rappahannock River in central Virginia during the first part of August—including another battle of Brandy Station fought over the same ground and by the same adversaries. During the latter fight, Buford's command encountered coordination problems with Maj. Gen. Henry W. Slocum's Twelfth Corps. The cavalry general's frustration erupted and he complained to General Pleasonton in one of the most angry and direct messages to a superior officer written during the entire war. "I am disgusted and worn out with the system that seems to prevail. There is so much apathy, and so little disposition to fight and co-operate that I wish to be relieved from the Army of the Potomac," complained Buford. "I do not wish to put myself and soldiers in front where I cannot get a support short of 12 miles. The ground I gain I would like to hold. . . . I am willing to serve my country, but I do not wish to sacrifice the brave men under my command."[22]

While on leave in Kentucky on August 10, 1863, Buford penned a letter to his friend General Burnside. "[The Army of the Potomac] is in about the same state as when you left it," he shared in his typical sardonic humor. "The same faults exist among corps commanders as has always existed. Too much apathy, too much cold water."[23]

20 George B. Davis, "The Strategy of the Gettysburg Campaign," Read before the Military Historical Society of Massachusetts, *Campaigns in Virginia, Maryland and Pennsylvania, 1862-1863* (Boston, 1903), 410.

21 Charles H. Howard, "The First Day at Gettysburg," *War Papers*, Military Order of the Loyal Legion of the United States (Chicago, 1896), 4:317.

22 *OR* 27, pt. 1, 935. The problem arose when Devin, whose command had gone forward to picket the Rappahannock, was ordered back by Slocum, and Buford became aggravated by the seeming lack of coordination and communication.

23 John Buford to Ambrose Burnside, August 12, 1863, George Hay Stuart Papers, collection 913, Manuscripts Division, Library of Congress. The circumstances underlying this letter

Buford left the division for 10 days of well-deserved leave on August 8, with General Merritt in command during his absence. While he campaigned that summer, Buford's family lost a daughter, a sister-in-law, and his father-in-law. Seeking to put his affairs in order, Buford returned to the family home in Georgetown, Kentucky, for a few days. The loss of his beloved five-year-old daughter took a lot of the starch out of the tough old cavalryman, who was never quite the same again.[24]

After his leave, Buford resumed his post and engaged in routine patrolling punctuated by frequent outbreaks of fighting between the Rappahannock and the Rapidan rivers. The grueling pace continued into the Bristoe Station campaign in mid-October. Colonel Theodore Lyman, a volunteer aide serving on Meade's staff, was very fond of John Buford and appreciated the cavalryman's sense of humor. "General Buford came in today," Lyman wrote to his wife on October 22, "cold and tired and wet. 'Oh,' he said to me, 'do you know what I would do if I were a volunteer aide? I would just run home as fast as I could, and never come back again!' The General takes his hardships good-naturedly."[25]

The Union high command may have believed Buford's tactics were the best hope of coping with Maj. Gen. Nathan Bedford Forrest's Confederate cavalry, which operated in the Western Theater. In late October 1863, upon the specific request of Maj. Gen. William S. Rosecrans, Buford was assigned to command the Cavalry Corps of the Army of the Cumberland.[26] This could have created an interesting confrontation, as his first cousin Abraham would take command of a division of Forrest's Rebel cavalry early the next year. Unfortunately for John Buford, the opportunity to command the mounted arm of one of the Union's premier armies was not to be.

---

provide another fascinating view of the deep schisms in Kentucky brought about by the Civil War. John Buford was married to a woman whose maiden name was Duke. Her first cousin was Col. Basil Duke, one of John Hunt Morgan's Raiders, then incarcerated in the Ohio Penitentiary. Buford was writing to Maj. Gen. Ambrose Burnside, the commander of the Department of the Ohio, to seek permission for his mother-in-law to visit Duke at the prison to facilitate settlement of the estate of Buford's father-in-law, who was Colonel Duke's uncle. The author does not know whether the requested permission was granted.

24 Hard, *Eighth Cavalry Regiment*, 269.

25 Agassiz, *Meade's Headquarters*, 35.

26 Cullum, *Officers and Graduates of the U.S. Military Academy*, 2:355.

On November 19, Colonel Lyman announced, "We find the cavalry chief afflicted with rheumatism, which he bore with his usual philosophy."[27] Unfortunately, rheumatism was not all that plagued Buford. The rigors of so many years of hard marching and fighting had taken their toll on the cavalryman, who had contracted typhoid fever "from fatigue and extreme hardship" after all the marching and fighting that finally compelled Lee's Army of Northern Virginia to abandon its line along the Rappahannock and retire behind the Rapidan on November 7-8. Tired, ill, and in pain, Buford took a leave of absence and returned to Washington, D.C., on November 20.[28]

By now terribly ill, Buford traveled to the home of his good friend, Maj. Gen. George Stoneman. His intent was to find a quiet place to rest and recuperate. Stoneman, who had commanded the Army of the Potomac's Cavalry Corps under Joe Hooker, was living in the District of Columbia because of his appointment to command the Cavalry Bureau, which was headquartered there. The host did what he could to make sure his old friend had the best care possible. Buford realized he was becoming more ill by the day, and on November 26, arranged for a telegram to be sent to his brother James back in Rock Island: "Get Patsy to leave Duke and to come on train. I fear I am going to be really sick. She will find me at Gen. Stoneman's on Pa. Avenue between 21 & 22. Telegraph when she will arrive here."[29]

For a time Buford seemed to improve under the care of an army surgeon. He even felt well enough to entertain a few visitors. In early December, he learned that Capt. George B. Sanford of the 1st U.S. Cavalry was in Washington on business. Sanford missed most of the Gettysburg campaign because he contracted typhoid fever that nearly took his life. When he received a message that the Kentuckian wanted to see him, Sanford made straight for Stoneman's house. "It was evident that he was a very sick man," recalled Sanford, "and I who had so lately recovered from this same dreadful disease, felt very anxious about him." Buford, observed Sanford, seemed bright and cheerful, and indicated he had been anxious to see an officer of his command. When the ill general asked Sanford whether he knew he had been offered command of the Cavalry Corps of the Army of the Cumberland, Sanford indicated that he was

27 Agassiz, *Meade's Headquarters*, 50.

28 Keogh, "Etat de Service of Major Gen. Jno. Buford."

29 John Buford to his brother, November 26, 1863, Telegrams Collected by the Secretary of War, Microfilm Group 504, Roll 119, Frame 899, NARA, Washington, DC.

not aware of that development. "Well it is true," replied Buford. "I have been offered the command of all the cavalry in the West and I have replied that I will accept it on one condition, viz: that I may be allowed to take with me my own brigade." Buford, of course, was referring to the Reserve Brigade. "Now I want you to give this news to the brigade," he continued, "and have it understood that I wish no promotion that will separate me from them." After the Kentuckian passed along some personal messages for Sanford to take back to Merritt and some other officers, General Stoneman, who was present, motioned to Sanford that it was time for him to say goodbye.[30]

Buford's improvement proved fleeting and his condition quickly deteriorated. It soon became apparent that he would not survive. On December 16, President Lincoln sent a note to Secretary of War Edwin M. Stanton—who was said not to trust anyone with Southern antecedents, and who disliked most of the officers associated with John Pope's Army of Virginia—requesting the gravely-ill Buford, whom Lincoln did not expect to survive the day, be promoted to major general. The promotion was more than deserved, but Stanton permitted it only when he was certain Buford was dying.[31] The promotion was made retroactive to July 1, 1863, in tribute to his service at Gettysburg.[32]

Buford was indeed expiring. Much of the time he lapsed in and out of delirium, unknowingly criticizing his loyal black servant between fits of consciousness. Someone managed to communicate that fact to Buford, who roused himself sufficiently to call him to his bedside. "Edward," began the dying Kentuckian, "I hear that I have been scolding you. I did not know what I was saying. You have been a faithful servant, Edward." A witness to this

---

30 E. R. Hageman, ed., *Fighting Rebels and Redskins: Experiences in Army Life of Colonel George B. Sanford 1861-1892* (Norman, OK, 1969), 214.

31 Abraham Lincoln to Edwin M. Stanton, December 16, 1863, Manuscripts Collection, United States Military Academy, West Point, New York.

32 See Buford's oath of office, dated December 16. 1863, Micro- film M1064, Letters received by the Commissions Branch of the Adjutant General's Office, 1863-1870, roll 9, file no. Bi 115 CB 1863, NARA. "Gen. Buford, however, was so thoroughly loyal a soldier as lived, but had to suffer, like to many others, for the sins of his relatives," observed Capt. George Sanford. "The War Secretary never trusted him, and his promotion came slowly and was given grudgingly. It is most painful to think that his commission as Major General of Volunteers only reached him on the day of his death, and that Mr. Stanton positively refused to allow it to be issued until assured that he was dying." Hageman, *Fighting Rebels and Redskins*, 215. The fact that the Bufords were staunch Democrats probably also hindered the dying cavalryman's prospects for promotion until it became obvious that his supposedly suspect loyalty was no longer a threat.

touching scene recalled that Edward "sat down and wept as though his heart was broken."[33]

As Buford slipped in and out of lucidity, several former comrades, including his aide Capt. Myles W. Keogh and General Stoneman, comforted him. Buford was enjoying a few clear moments when news of his major general's commission arrived. "Too late," he murmured. "Now I wish that I could live." Keogh helped him sign the necessary forms and executed the document as a witness, while Capt. Andrew J. Alexander, of the 1st U.S. Cavalry, who served on Pleasonton's staff, penned a letter to Stanton accepting the promotion.[34] Reflecting a Regular's loathing of skulkers, Buford's last intelligible words were, "Put guards on all the roads, and don't let the men run back to the rear."[35] He died in Keogh's arms on the afternoon of December 16, 1863.[36] Ironically, this was also Harry Heth's 38th birthday. His wife Patsy was unable to make it in time to be with her husband.

Merritt, who succeeded Buford in command of the First Division, prepared general orders lamenting the death of the popular division commander:

> His master mind and incomparable genius as a cavalry chief, you all know by the dangers through which be has brought you, when enemies surrounded you and destruction seemed inevitable. . . . The profound anguish which we all feel forbids the use of empty words, which so feebly express his virtues. Let us silently mingle our tears with those of the nation in lamenting the untimely death of this pure and noble man, the devoted and patriotic lover of his country, the soldier without fear and with out reproach.[37]

The division's staff officers prepared resolutions of regret, mourning Buford's death and resolving that the members of the First Division would

33 "Anecdotes of General Buford," *The National Tribune*, February 18, 1882.

34 See letter to Edwin M. Stanton, December 16, 1863, written for Buford by Capt. A. J. Alexander. Microfilm M1064, Letters received by the Commissions Branch of the Adjutant General's Office, 1863-1870, roll 9, file no. B1115 CB 1863, NARA.

35 Ibid. See also Richard Kehoe letter to Tom Keogh, January 1, 1864, National Library Microfilm.

36 See Buford's service record, and Buford's commission as a major general of volunteers, Microfilm Ml 064, Letters received by the Commissions Branch of the Adjutant General's Office, 1863-1870, roll 9, file no. B 15 CB 1863, NARA.

37 Hard, *Eighth Cavalry Regiment*, 287.

wear a badge of mourning for 30 days as a sign of respect for their fallen leader.[38] "He had the respect and esteem of every man in the army, and the cavalry loved him as a father," lamented his friend and fellow cavalryman Captain Sanford.[39] "The army and the country have met with a great loss by the death of . . . Buford. He was decidedly the best cavalry general that we had, and was acknowledged as such in the army," wrote another of Buford's peers in his diary. "[He was] rough in his exterior, never looking after his own comfort, untiring on the march and in the supervision of all the militia of his command, quiet and unassuming in his manners."[40]

The fallen horse soldier had two funerals, one in Washington, D.C., and a second at the United States Military Academy at West Point, where he was buried—a fitting final campground for a Regular and alumnus of the academy. The first was held on December 20, 1863, at the New York Avenue Presbyterian Church in the nation's capital. President Lincoln and Secretary Stanton both attended the funeral, as did the army's chief of staff, Maj. Gen. Henry W. Halleck. Eight general officers served as Buford's honorary pallbearers: John M. Schofield, Abner Doubleday, Daniel E. Sickles, Silas P. Casey, Samuel P. Heintzelman, Gouverneur K. Warren, Winfield Scott Hancock, and Christopher C. Augur. Sadly, Patsy Buford did not attend, "owing to severe indisposition."[41] Two of Buford's orderlies led his horse Grey Eagle during the funeral procession. According to one eyewitness, "The horse, a fine high-spirited gray, was fully caparisoned, having on the saddle and trappings of a Major-General, with the boots and spurs of the deceased attached." After the solemn state funeral, Buford's body was taken to the railroad station for its final journey to West Point, with Buford's beloved Irish

38 Ibid., 285-86.

39 Hageman, *Fighting Rebels and Redskins*, 215.

40 Stephen Z. Starr, *The Union Cavalry in the Civil War*, 3 vols. (Baton Rouge, LA, 1979), 2:77.

41 Patsy Buford's story is a tragic one. She had recently buried her beloved daughter, and now her husband was dead. She was a widow at 33 after only nine years of marriage. Their son Duke would not achieve adulthood, dying on April 5, 1874, at the age of 17 years, 8 months. The cause of his death is unknown. Patsy eventually remarried in 1873. Her second husband, a Methodist minister named Rev. B. H. McCown, died on August 29, 1881. Patsy lived until October 4, 1903. She died after a lengthy illness as a penniless invalid, needing a special act of Congress to restore the meager soldier's widow's pension of $30.00 per month that she gave up to marry Reverend McCown. Buford, *The Buford Family in America*, 127-128; Obituary, *Georgetown Times*, October 7, 1903. She was buried with her children, parents, and her maternal grandparents in the town Cemetery in Georgetown, Kentucky.

aide, Myles Keogh, and another of his staff officers, Capt. Craig Wadsworth, acting as its escorts.[42]

Buford's second funeral occurred at West Point two days later, on December 22. The superintendent of the military academy, all of the professors, officers, cadets, and the post's assigned detachments of cavalry and artillery attended, as did Keogh and Wadsworth. "The remains were conveyed to the Cadets Cemetery, where they were interred with distinguished honors," read an article in the *New York Times*.[43] In a tribute to their beloved commander, the men of the First Division raised money to erect a monument to Buford at his gravesite. Most members of the 9th New York contributed a dollar each to pay for the handsome monument that marks his gravesite.[44] The Kentuckian rests next to his fellow Gettysburg hero Lt. Alonzo Cushing, who was killed on July 3, 1863, while defending the Angle during Pickett's Charge—the "high ground" Buford had selected for the Army of the Potomac to hold.

John Buford's Legacy to the American Civil War

In many ways, Buford deserves credit for the Union victory at Gettysburg. He personally selected the battlefield and developed a strategy to hold it—despite the approach of the Confederates in overwhelming numbers on July 1. Buford and his men campaigned almost nonstop for 50 days, and their performance was superb throughout this period. As discussed, their stubborn and determined delaying action along the Chambersburg Pike bought just enough time for General Reynolds to reach the field, determine that the high ground south of the town was a strong defensive position worthy of defending, and decide that the Army of the Potomac should stand and fight there. But for Buford's successful fight for time, Reynolds never would have had the opportunity to make that decision, and the outcome of the Battle of Gettysburg might have been very different. Certainly it would have been fought on different terrain.

---

42 Washington *National Republican*, December 21, 1863.

43 *New York Times*, December 23, 1863.

44 William O. Hills, Diary, April 18, 1864, William O. Hills Papers, Collection 436, Library of Congress. Unfortunately, an ugly dispute arose over payment for this monument. Several rounds of correspondence were required before the bill was finally paid. See Commissions Branch file for this information.

Another of Buford's legacies was that many of his protégés advanced to higher levels of command within the Army of the Potomac's Cavalry Corps. Both Tom Devin and William Gamble were promoted to brigadier general, and Wesley Merritt served as commander of the First Division until after the surrender of Lee's army at Appomattox in April 1865. Merritt became the final commander of the Army of the Potomac's Cavalry Corps, and both Merritt and Devin continued their meritorious service in the postwar U.S. Army.[45]

Unlike many of his peers, John Buford earned the undying respect of both friends and enemies. Confederate Brig. Gen. Beverly H. Robertson, who had served with Buford in the old Second Dragoons and then defeated him at Lewis Ford on August 30, 1862, wrote this: "Look where we may and we will never find a more admirable or lovelier character than Buford. Quiet, modest, unassuming, affectionate, without any display; true to every trust; true to all his friends, sincere, honest, chivalrous and brave. No more can be said. He will be forever enshrined in the hearts of those who knew him best."[46] Frank C. Armstrong, another former comrade from the Second Dragoons who became a Confederate general and fought with Forrest in the Western Theater, wrote, "I knew John Buford personally . . . I held him in the highest esteem as an officer and a gentleman. The fortunes of war and circumstance placed us on different sides in the issue, but my love and admiration were never lessened for my old time comrade and friend. We of the 'Old 2nd Drags' knew him better than all others—and a truer, more gallant soldier or friend never buckled on a saber."[47]

"Probably no officer of the Cavalry Corps was more honored, respected, and loved than he; a most gallant and efficient officer, of a pleasant and genial

---

45 Merritt served in the Regular Army for 40 years. The zenith of his long career was commanding the expedition that captured Manila in the Philippines during the Spanish-American War. He was the U.S. Army's second-ranking officer at the time of his retirement in 1900. Warner, *Generals in Blue*, 322. Devin was eventually promoted to brevet major general of volunteers and was the final commander of the First Cavalry Division in 1865. In 1866, he was appointed lieutenant colonel of the newly-formed 8th U.S. Cavalry, and in 1877 became colonel of the 3rd U.S. Cavalry. He died in 1873. Warner, *Generals in Blue*, 124. Gamble was promoted to brigadier general and commanded the Army's Cavalry Bureau. He mustered out in 1866 and was appointed major of the 8th Cavalry in July 1866. While transiting west with his regiment in Nicaragua, Gamble contracted yellow fever and died of the disease on December 20, 1866. Warner, *Generals in Blue*, 166.

46 Beverly H. Robertson to the Buford Memorial Association, June 26, 1895, *Proceedings of the Buford Memorial Association*, 37-38.

47 Frank C. Armstrong to the Buford Memorial Association, July 2, 1895, *Proceedings of the Buford Memorial Association*, 38.

nature, cool in action, and always quick to see mistakes of the enemy and to take advantage of them," recalled an officer of the 6th New York Cavalry, Capt. Jerome B. Wheeler. "His movements were planned with deliberation and executed most brilliantly, but never coupled with rashness."[48] "Everyone knows that he 'in his day' was first and foremost," declared Lt. Aaron B. Jerome, who served as Buford's signal officer during the battle of Gettysburg, not long after the end of the war.[49] Another of his soldiers said Buford was "straight forward, honest, conscientious, full of good common sense, and always to be relied upon in any emergency...decidedly the best cavalry officer in the Army of the Potomac."[50] While no match for his rival Jeb Stuart in flair, Buford, in his tattered old hunting shirt and worn corduroys, was popular with his men, who firmly believed him to be the Union's best cavalry officer.[51]

When he learned that an effort was underway to erect a monument to Buford on the battlefield at Gettysburg, Buford's old roommate and friend John Gibbon declared, "I am ready to do anything in my power to perpetuate the memory of the best cavalryman I ever knew."[52] Colonel Richard I. Dodge, a West Point classmate of Buford's, wrote, "At West Point, Buford and I had a fight, when plebes, which was the foundation of a strong and lasting friendship. He was a noble man and a most gallant soldier."[53] Colonel Charles McK. Loeser, who served under Buford's command in the 2nd Dragoons, declared, "I am sure Buford deserves a monument as much as any and more than most. If he had never been in a fight he would deserve a monument for his modesty."[54]

48 Hillman A. Hall, ed., *History of the Sixth New York Cavalry* (Worcester, MA, 1908), 377.

49 David L. Ladd and Audrey J. Ladd, eds., *The Bachelder Papers: Gettysburg in Their Own Words*, 3 vols. (Dayton, OH, 1995), 1:202.

50 Edward G. Longacre, *The Cavalry at Gettysburg: A Tactical Study of Mounted Operations During the Civil War's Pivotal Campaign, 9 June-14 July 1863* (East Rutherford, NJ, 1986), 51.

51 A trooper of the 8th Illinois Cavalry declared, "General Buford . . . many of us claim, was the best cavalry officer ever produced on this continent." James A. Bell to Gusta Ann Halluck, July 11, 1863, Bell Papers, Huntington Library, San Marino, California. Lieutenant Colonel Lyman called him the "model commander." Agassiz, *Meade's Headquarters*, 21.

52 John Gibbon to the Buford Memorial Association, January 11, 1894, *Proceedings of the Buford Memorial Association*, 36.

53 Richard I. Dodge to the Buford Memorial Association, December 1, 1893, *Proceedings of the Buford Memorial Association*, 35.

54 Charles McK. Loeser to the Buford Memorial Association, October 23, 1893, *Proceedings of the Buford Memorial Association*, 34.

Perhaps most telling was this statement by an enlisted man of the First Cavalry Division: "We of the ranks of the old First Division, Cavalry Corps, loved John Buford; we trusted General Buford; we always held ourselves ready to do what he ordered; we wept when he died. We felt that our country as well as ourselves, had lost a friend, a comrade, a general."[55]

Buford's most important legacy, however, lay in the successes of the Cavalry Corps of the Army of the Potomac. It was during the Gettysburg campaign hat the Union horsemen first took on Jeb Stuart's vaunted cavaliers and fought them as equals. Their fighting at Brandy Station, coupled with Buford's perfectly executed delaying action at Gettysburg, demonstrated what these volunteer horse soldiers could accomplish with good leadership.

John Buford and his men deserve the accolades they received for their role in the Gettysburg campaign, for without their service the manner in which the Civil War progressed would have been very different. The devil gave John Buford a large bill to pay at Gettysburg, and Old Steadfast paid that it in full.

55 S. M. Finch to the Buford Memorial Association, April 9, 1894, *Proceedings of the Buford Memorial Association*, 37.

Epilogue

On July 1, 1895, an august group of former cavalrymen and other distinguished old soldiers gathered on McPherson's Ridge on the first day's battlefield at Gettysburg. These members of the Buford Memorial Association had come together to honor John Buford on the site of their hero's greatest accomplishment.[1] "On the platform facing the flag-draped statue, the most distinguished Cavalrymen of the country were gathered," noted a newspaper reporter assigned to cover the proceedings.[2] More than 1,000 spectators assembled to honor Buford's memory that morning.

Troop A of the 6th U.S. Cavalry led the procession at 9:00 a.m. that warm summer morning, carrying the battle flag of the old First Cavalry Division. Troop H of the 6th Cavalry came next, followed by Battery C, 3rd U.S. Artillery.

---

1   The committee that was responsible for the erection of the monument included: Maj. Gen. Wesley Merritt, Maj. Gen. James H. Wilson, Bvt. Maj. Gen. David M. Gregg, Bvt. Brig. Gen. John C. Tidball, Col. Charles McK. Loeser, Bvt. Col. Alexander C. M. Pennington, Col. W. H. Harrison, Maj. G. I. Whitehead, Maj. John H. Calef, Capt. W. W. Frazier, Lt. Osgood Welsh, Bvt. Brig. Gen. Charles G. Sawtelle, Col. Daniel S. Gordon, Bvt. Col. Rudulph Ellis, Bvt. Lt. Col. George G. Meade, Jr., Bvt. Col. Henry C. Weir, Maj. Jerome B. Wheeler, Bvt. Maj. Paul Quirk, Capt. William L. Heermance, and Brig. Gen. Theophilus F. Rodenbough, who was the driving force behind the formation of the committee. A disproportionate number of the members of the committee were alumni of the 6th Pennsylvania Cavalry, which was one of Buford's favorite regiments; Buford used to refer to the Keystone Staters as "my Seventh Regulars." This fine regiment's complement of officers included George Meade, Jr., the son of the former commander of the Army of the Potomac. Gregg served as chairman of the committee, Merritt as vice chairman, Rodenbough as secretary, and Loeser as treasurer. Each member of the executive committee made a financial contribution to the costs associated with the project. Minutes of the meeting of the Buford Memorial Association held on November 16, 1893, Eric J. Wittenberg Collection, Columbus, Ohio.

2   Styple, *Generals in Bronze*, 114.

The dais at the ceremony to dedicate the Buford memorial on McPherson's Ridge on July 1, 1896. Seated, from the left, are Col. John H. Calef, Thomas Jefferson Buford (younger brother of John Buford), Buford's West Point classmate, Gen. John C. Tidball, Bvt. Maj. Gen. David M. Gregg, Maj. Gen. Wesley Merritt, and Maj. Gen. James H. Wilson, who delivered the dedication address. Standing in the second row, from the left, are Maj. Jerome B. Wheeler, unknown, sculptor James E. Kelly, unknown, and Col. Alexander C. M. Pennington. Seated between Merritt and Wilson is Brig. Gen. Theophilus F. Rodenbough, who was the president of the Buford Memorial Association. No more distinguished gathering of Civil War cavalrymen had occurred since 1865. *William B. Styple*

"The admirably equipped body of 170 trained horsemen was the picturesque feature of the occasion," editorialized one newspaper, "moving with absolute precision, its excellent band playing a spirited air, and the red and yellow plumes touching with a bright color the somber landscape—it was most inspiring; it only needed the stained and tattered battleflag of Buford's Division, borne with evident pride by a picked color guard of young cavalry sergeants, to raise the enthusiasm of the spectators to the highest pitch. In the rear of the escort followed twelve carriages, containing the committee and their guests."[3]

3 "Unveiling of the Buford Memorial," undated newspaper clipping included in John Buford's file, Microfilm M1064, Letters received by the Commissions Branch of the Adjutant General's Office, 1863-1870, roll 9, file no. B 1115 CB 1863.

Wesley Merritt, one of Buford's protégés and now a major general and the chairman of the association, led the procession of dignitaries onto the dais. Other attendees included: Brig. Gen. David M. Gregg, Maj. Gen. James H. Wilson, Brig. Gen. John C. Tidball (Buford's West Point classmate), Brig. Gen. Theophilus F. Rodenbough (Medal of Honor recipient who commanded Buford's old regiment, the 2nd U.S. Cavalry, at Gettysburg), Brig. Gen. Alexander C. M. Pennington, Col. George G. Meade (the son of the army commander), and Maj. John H. Calef (who was still on active duty as an artillerist). Buford's brothers, Thomas Jefferson Buford and James Monroe Buford, also attended the ceremony, as did several of the general's nephews, including Capt. J. C. Watson of the U.S. Navy. Distinctly absent was his widow Patsy, who had remarried a minister named McCown. She was in poor health and evidently could not withstand the long journey to attend the dedication ceremony.[4]

At a dinner held in New York City on June 9, 1890, the 27th anniversary of the battle of Brandy Station, a number of former officers of the Reserve Brigade convened to begin the process of erecting a monument to John Buford on the Gettysburg battlefield. Their efforts did not bear fruit until the summer of 1893, when the committee was empowered to raise funds to pay for the proposed monument. Thereafter, these men organized the Buford Memorial Association in November 1893.[5] Twenty-five members made up the executive committee of the Buford Memorial Association, including Gregg as chairman, Merritt as vice-chairman, Rodenbough as secretary, and Col. Charles McK. Loeser, with whom Buford had served in the Second Dragoons, as treasurer. "A movement is on foot to erect a monument on the spot from which the first gun was fired by the Union forces at Gettysburg in memory of that distinguished General and typical American cavalryman, John Buford, and the achievements of the cavalry corps in the Gettysburg Campaign," noted a New York newspaper.[6]

Jerome B. Wheeler, who had been a captain in the 6th New York Cavalry at Gettysburg, married well after the war. His wife was a member of the Macy mercantile family, and Wheeler was a partner in Macy's Department Store in New York City. This association allowed him to grow fabulously wealthy as a

4   Ibid. There is no record to suggest that Patsy Buford was even invited to the ceremony.

5   *The Proceedings of the Buford Memorial Association*, 31.

6   "Monument for General Buford," *New York World*, November 18, 1893.

A post-war image of Maj. Jerome B. Wheeler of the 6th New York Cavalry. The very wealthy Wheeler, patron of sculptor James E. Kelly, was the primary donor for the erection of the Buford memorial on McPherson's Ridge. *Aspen Times*

result.[7] Wheeler had befriended a talented sculptor named James E. Kelly, and he commissioned Kelly to create a handsome monument to Buford. Wheeler donated a large portion of the nearly $4,000.00 price for the creation of the monument, while the balance was raised through contributions of individuals wanting to honor John Buford.[8] The statue was cast at the Henry-Bonnard bronze foundry on West Sixteenth Street in New York City.[9]

Kelly interviewed a number of veterans to ensure he got the likeness of Buford right. Captain John W. Blunt of the 6th New York Cavalry provided

7 "Once Again for Jerome B. Wheeler," *The Aspen Times*, December 19, 1985. Wheeler's military career was noted for his courage under fire, but he was also broken from the rank of colonel for insubordination. He used the Macy's money to finance banks, railroads, and silver mines. Wheeler helped found the resort town of Aspen, Colorado, investing nearly $6,000,000 into the town. A number of commercial buildings (including a hotel and an opera house) in Aspen are named in his honor. Unfortunately, when the price of silver plummeted in 1893, investors in Wheeler's silver mines sued him for millions and he lost his entire fortune as a result. Wheeler declared bankruptcy in 1903. Fortunately, he lost his fortune after paying for the sculpting of the Buford monument. His story is both interesting and serves as a cautionary tale. For a more detailed biographical sketch of Wheeler, see Eric J. Wittenberg, "Bvt. Maj. Jerome B. Wheeler," http:// civilwarcavalry./?p=3864.

8 Approximately 180 former officers of the Army of the Potomac's Cavalry Corps donated money for the erection of the monument. Among the larger donors were Bvt. Brig. Gen. Charles Francis Adams, the great-grandson and grandson of two presidents of the United States, Maj. Gen. Daniel E. Sickles, Buford's brother Thomas Jefferson Buford, the family of Maj. Gen. John F. Reynolds, and his former staff officers and numerous others. The number of donors demonstrates the esteem in which his old comrades in arms held Old Steadfast. *The Proceedings of the Buford Memorial Association*, 45-49.

9 "Statue of Gen. Buford," *Rock Island Argus*, June 4, 1895.

Kelly with the following description: "According to my recollection [Buford] stood with his left hand resting on his saber (after dismounting from his horse) and his right hand extended; right foot slightly in advance of left. I think he wore a black soft hat with stiff brim, and had his coat buttoned up. And I well remember as he stood, he bore as prompt and soldierly an appearance as one could hope to see, as any one who saw him could vouch for."[10]

Kelly made the controversial decision to depict Buford dismounted rather than mounted, sculpted precisely as Captain Blunt described him. Tidball and several other members of the committee visited Kelly's studio to see how the statue was coming along. When Rodenbough turned to Tidball and asked, "Now, General, here's your old friend and classmate—what do you think of him?" Tidball took a close look and declared, "That's Buford!" He circled the monument and continued, "I knew Buford at West Point; I . . . saw him at Gettysburg. The proportions are good—the character is good. That's Buford!"[11]

Meanwhile, back on the battlefield in 1895, Merritt made a few brief remarks before introducing General Wilson to deliver the dedication speech. Wilson was only 23 in 1863, hardly knew Buford, and never served under his command. However, he became an outstanding cavalryman in his own right. "The oration by Gen. Wilson was a model for such an occasion," confirmed a newspaper account. "It gave due proportion to biographical and historical details, and was delivered with great eloquence; the tribute came from unusual force from one who himself has helped to make cavalry history."[12]

Since the monument was Wheeler's idea, he got the honor of unveiling it. The battery fired a salute to honor Buford as he pulled the massive flag away from the monument. As the flag fell away, "the cavalry presented sabers, all colors were drooped, and the first gun of a major general's salute broke the still air."[13] It made for quite a sight. "The Battery smoke rolled over the ground like a heavy cloud, circling around the base, obscuring it and the General, then caught by the breeze, it swirled in a complete circle around the bronze which

10 Styple, *Generals in Bronze*, 110.

11 Ibid., 111.

12 "Unveiling the Buford Memorial."

13 Ibid.

A close-up of the figure of John Buford from his monument.

glowed in brilliant relief against the deep blue sky," as Kelly vividly described the scene.[14]

14 Styple, *Generals in Bronze*, 114.

In 1864, Calef's Battery A, 2nd U.S. Artillery, was rearmed, and Calef turned in "four of the rifled three-inch wrought-iron guns which had formed a part of it since it was organized as a horse battery at the beginning of the Civil War," as the young battery commander remembered years after the end of the war. "The four guns to be turned in being parked, something impelled me—probably the sentiment of parting with old friends—to make a record of the identifying marks on those pieces, their weight, numbers, initials of inspector, etc., not dreaming that thirty-one years after my memoranda would come into use." Calef forgot about these notes until discussions about erecting a monument to Buford began in earnest. He "suggested that the very guns that opened the battle might appropriately be incorporated into the memorial." Locating his diary, which had turned "yellow with age," Calef tracked down the four guns by their serial numbers. This bit of sleuthing proved to be no small task, as two of the guns had "wandered" as far as the Pacific Coast.[15] In fact, it took the intervention of the army's chief of ordnance to locate the gun that fired the first Union artillery shot of the battle of Gettysburg, stored "among scores of other abandoned cannon at the Presidio, San Francisco." Once the cannon was identified, the Army brought it east to its final resting place on McPherson's Ridge.[16]

Calef continued: "Four of them now repose at the foot of the Buford monument, their muzzles in the direction of the cardinal points, the 'opening gun,' number 233, pointing up the Chambersburg Pike in almost the same spot it occupied on July 1, 1863, when it notified the Confederates they reached the limit of their northern invasion, and signaled the beginning of a battle which sealed the fate of a southern Confederacy."[17] Calef rose, walked over to the gun that had fired the first shot, drove a spike into the touchhole, and declared, "I spike this gun that it may speak no more."[18]

15 Calef, "Gettysburg Notes," 54.

16 "Where the Fight Began: A Monument to Gen. Buford on Gettysburg's Battleground," *New York Times*, July 1, 1895.

17 Calef, "Gettysburg Notes," 53-54. The serial numbers of the four gun tubes are 233 (cast in 1862), 244 (1862), 632 (1863), and 756 (1864). Obviously gun 756 would not have been at Gettysburg, but its significance as a relic of Calef's outstanding service at Gettysburg makes it noteworthy.

18 Styple, *Generals in Blue*, 114.

The John Buford monument located on McPherson's Ridge.

Tidball, Buford's sole surviving West Point classmate, placed a wreath at the base of the monument and saluted his old friend.[19] Most of the other dignitaries on the dais also laid wreaths at the base of the monument, which was soon littered with flowers. Merritt introduced Kelly, who modestly declined to make a speech. "His work, however, bears eloquent testimony to his genius and the occasion was a great professional triumph for him," correctly commented the newspaper account of the ceremony.[20]

"Old Steadfast" remains vigilant standing atop his chosen defensive position on the western slope of McPherson's Ridge, peering intently off to the west as Henry Heth's Confederate division tramps toward him. John Calef's guns surround him, just as they did that fateful day in 1863, ready to defend the ridge and the high ground beyond with Buford until John Reynolds' infantry could arrive. Frozen in time, Buford waits, his binoculars at the ready, his trusty pipe tucked into the pocket of his battered old hunting jacket, fully prepared to pay the large bill handed to him by the devil that warm July morning so many years ago.

19 Ibid.

20 "Unveiling the Buford Memorial."

Order of Battle
Battle of Gettysburg
9:00 a.m., July 1, 1863

UNION FORCES
ARMY OF THE POTOMAC
Maj. Gen. George G. Meade

Cavalry Corps

Brig. Gen. Alfred Pleasonton

1st Cavalry Division

Brig. Gen. John Buford

1st Brigade, Col. William Gamble

8th Illinois Cavalry (Maj. John L. Beveridge)

8th New York Cavalry (Lt. Col. William L. Markell)

3rd Indiana Cavalry (6 cos.) (Col. George H. Chapman)

12th Illinois Cavalry (8 cos.) (Capt. George W. Shears)

1,596 officers and men

2nd Brigade, Col. Thomas C. Devin

6th New York Cavalry (5 cos.) (Maj. William E. Beardsley)

9th New York Cavalry (Col. William Sackett)

17th Pennsylvania Cavalry (Col. Josiah H. Kellogg)

3rd West Virginia Cavalry (2 cos.) (Capt. Seymour B. Conger)

1,108 officers and men

Horse Artillery Battalion

Battery A, 2nd U.S. Artillery (Lt. John H. Calef)

81 officers and men

Total Strength, 2,795 officers and men

Casualties: 22 killed, 21 mortally wounded, 86 wounded, 53 missing=182 (6.5%)

CONFEDERATE FORCES
ARMY OF NORTHERN VIRGINIA

Gen. Robert E. Lee

Ewell's Corps

Lt. Gen. Richard S. Ewell

Rodes' Division

Maj. Gen. Robert E. Rodes

Iverson's Brigade, Brig. Gen. Alfred Iverson

5th North Carolina Infantry (Capt. Speight Brock West)

12th North Carolina Infantry (Lt. Col. William S. Davis)

20th North Carolina Infantry (Lt. Col. Nelson Slough)

23rd North Carolina Infantry (Col. Daniel H. Christie)

Hill's Corps

Lt. Gen. A. P. Hill

Heth's Division

Maj. Gen. Henry Heth

Pettigrew's Brigade, Brig. Gen. James J. Pettigrew

11th North Carolina Infantry (Col. Collett Leventhorpe)

26th North Carolina Infantry (Col. Henry K. Burgwyn, Jr.)

47th North Carolina Infantry (Col. George H. Faribault)

52nd North Carolina Infantry (Col. James K. Marshall)

Brockenbrough's Brigade, Col. John M. Brockenbrough

40th Virginia Infantry (Capt. Thomas E. Betts)

47th Virginia Infantry (Col. Robert M. Mayo)

55th Virginia Infantry (Col. William S. Christian)

22nd Virginia Battalion of Infantry (Maj. John S. Bowles)

Archer's Brigade, Brig. Gen. James J. Archer

5th Alabama Battalion (Maj. Sebastian Van De Graff)

13th Alabama Infantry (Col. Birkett D. Fry)

1st Tennessee (Provisional Army) (Lt. Col. Newton J. George)

7th Tennessee Infantry (Col. John A. Fite)

14th Tennessee Infantry (Lt. Col. James W. Lockett)

Davis's Brigade, Brig. Gen. Joseph R. Davis

2nd Mississippi Infantry (Col. John M. Stone)

11th Mississippi Infantry (Col. Francis M. Green)

42nd Mississippi Infantry (Col. Hugh R. Miller)

55th North Carolina Infantry (Col. John K. Connally)

Artillery Reserve

Maj. William J. Pegram

Crenshaw's Battery, Richmond (VA) Artillery (Capt. William G. Crenshaw)

Marye's Battery, Fredericksburg (VA) Artillery (Capt. Edward A. Marye)

Brander's Battery, "Letcher" Richmond (VA) Artillery (Capt. Thomas A. Brander)

Zimmerman's Battery, Pee Dee (SC) Artillery (Lt. William E. Zimmerman)

McGraw's Battery, "Purcell" (VA) Artillery (Capt. Joseph McGraw)

Appendix B

The Myth of the Spencers

One of the most persistent myths of the battle of Gettysburg is that John Buford's troopers carried Spencer rifles or carbines into battle on July 1, 1863.

The Spencer rifle was the first magazine weapon to see combat in the Civil War. It employed an interchangeable tube that held seven rim-fire bullets that could be rapidly loaded and even more rapidly fired because it did not require a cartridge or powder because everything required was included in the bullet's casing. The weapon enabled soldiers to lay down a tremendous rate of fire, which in turn prompted Confederates to say, "you'ns load in the morning and fire all day." At the same time, the Spencer had a voracious appetite for ammunition, which is why Brig. Gen. James W. Ripley, the U.S. Army's chief of ordnance, resisted their adoption.[1]

When novelist Shelby Foote published his epic trilogy on the American Civil War, he wrote, "Buford's two brigades were formidable in their own right, being equipped with the new seven-shot Spencer carbine, which enabled a handy trooper to get off twenty rounds a minute, as compared to his muzzle-loading adversary, who would be doing well to get off four shots in the same span."[2] This was just one of a number of Gettysburg narratives that repeated the claim that Buford's horse soldiers were armed with Spencer repeating weapons on July 1, 1863.

---

1   D. Alexander Watson, "The Spencer Repeating Rifle at Gettysburg," *Gettysburg Magazine: Articles of Lasting Historical Interest* (July 1996), Issue No. 15, 24-30.

2   Shelby Foote, *Fredericksburg to Meridian, The Civil War: A Narrative*, 3 vols. (New York, 1963), 2:465.

Even Edward G. Longacre's award-winning 1986 book *The Cavalry at Gettysburg: A Tactical Study of Mounted Operations during the Civil War's Pivotal Campaign, 9 June-14 July 1863* erroneously claims Buford's troopers carried Spencers: "All told, fewer than six hundred members of the Cavalry Corps possessed a Spencer rifle; they were scattered through the 8th and 12th Illinois, 3rd Indiana, 8th New York, and 1st West Virginia regiments."[3] As we shall see below, while Longacre more or less accurately stated the number of Spencer rifles in the Army of the Potomac's Cavalry Corps as of July 1, 1863, he has them distributed to the demonstrably wrong regiments.

Christopher M. Spencer invented the eponymous weapon in the late 1850s, and patented the rifle in 1859. His revolutionary weapon could lay down a tremendous rate of fire and be very quickly reloaded. He shopped the rifle to the U.S. Army in 1861, but it took time for it to win approval from the slow-moving bureaucracy. Some of them finally found their way into service in 1863 when Col. John T. Wilder's brigade of mounted infantry serving with the Army of the Cumberland was armed with them. The weapons made an immediate impact on the battlefield, but ongoing resistance by the War Department, which remained unconvinced, forced Wilder's men to purchase their own rifles.[4]

In the spring of 1863, nearly all of the 5th Michigan Cavalry and two companies of the 6th Michigan Cavalry were issued Spencer rifles. These regiments were part of what became the Army of the Potomac's Third Cavalry Division at the end of June, and comprised one-half of the Michigan Cavalry Brigade. The June 30, 1863, quarterly ordnance returns for the 5th Michigan Cavalry indicate the regiment was completely fitted out with 479 Spencer rifles, while the 6th Michigan boasted 93 of the weapons. These Spencer rifles are the *only* Spencer repeating weapons reported by the June 30 ordnance returns for the Army of the Potomac's entire Cavalry Corps.[5]

---

3   Edward G. Longacre, *The Cavalry at Gettysburg: A Tactical Study of Mounted Operations during the Civil War's Pivotal Campaign, 9 June-14 July 1863* (Rutherford, NJ, 1986), 60.

4   Joseph G Bilby, *A Revolution in Arms: A History of the First Repeating Rifles* (Yardley, PA, 2006), 67-82. Bilby's fine book provides the sort of detailed history of the development of the Spencer rifle that strays far beyond the scope of this study, and the author commends it to the reader for that purpose.

5   RG 56, Section 110, Quarterly Statements of Ordnance in Cavalry 1862-64, Returns for June 30, 1863, NARA.

A final note on Spencer repeating weapons is worth discussing. Although Shelby Foote claimed (as noted above) that Buford's men were armed with Spencer carbines at Gettysburg, this was simply not possible. The Spencer carbine did not go into mass production until September 1863, nearly 90 days after the battle. There may have been a few prototypes of the carbine floating around in July 1863, but there surely were not any being carried in the field. Foote's statement is therefore mythology.[6]

As a result, Buford's command was armed with single-shot breech-loading carbines on July 1, 1863. The Army of the Potomac's Cavalry Corps carried a variety of breech-loading carbines throughout the war, primarily the Sharps and the Burnside, with an assortment of other similar weapons by other manufacturers. Each fired a lead ball of approximately .56 caliber (although there was some variation here as well). Breech-loading carbines required loose powder and paper cartridges. Unlike muzzle-loading infantry rifles (where a proficient soldier could get off three rounds per minute), an efficient cavalryman could get off 5-7 rounds per minute. These guns typically traded a short range (of about 300 yards) for a more rapid rate of fire.

The June 30, 1863, ordnance returns for the Army of the Potomac's Cavalry Corps demonstrate the following distribution of weaponry for Gamble's and Devin's brigades:

Unit	Sharps	Burnside	Smith	Gallagher	Merrill
8th Illinois	311				
12th Illinois		86			
3rd Indiana	12			182	
8th New York	210				
6th New York	232				
9th New York	381		1		
17th Pennsylvania			127		108
3rd West Virginia				89	

6   Bilby, *A Revolution in Arms*, 111.

According to these returns, the distribution was: 1,146 Sharps, 86 Burnsides, 128 Smiths, 271 Gallaghers, and 108 Merrills. This means that of the 1,739 carbines reported as of June 30, 66 percent of the troopers of Buford's division carried Sharps carbines.[7] Admittedly, not all of the companies in Gamble's and Devin's brigades reported how they were armed, for the reported strengths of those two brigades on that date totaled 2,704. Therefore, it is theoretically possible that a handful of Buford's men *might* have been armed with Spencer rifles at the time of the battle, but there is no firsthand evidence to demonstrate that.

In 1995, Richard S. Shue's *Morning at Willoughby Run* included a chapter discussing a number of the controversies swirling around the morning of the first day's fighting at Gettysburg. Shue claims:

> Yet, at Manassas Junction fifteen days earlier, Buford received an allotment of these rifles, and a "limited distribution" was made. Just how many companies were involved is unknown, but the lucky troopers with the new improved rifles had the chance to break them in the next day, June 17, in the fighting at Aldie, Virginia. Sergeant Joseph A. McCabe of Company A, 17th Pennsylvania, left no doubt about their effectiveness and reliability: "The field was literally covered with dead and wounded—our Spencer rifles never failed us."

> Assuredly, then, this company fired Spencer rifles at Gettysburg. The "limited distribution" may have included one or two additional companies in the 17th Pennsylvania. As to the other regiments, all evidence points to their not having Spencers.

> So, even though the Spencer repeating rifle played only a minor role, it made a vivid impression on at least one Rebel. Captured in the morning's battle, he remarked to his Yankee captors, "What you all do—load on Sunday and fire all week!"[8]

The source for his claim of a "limited distribution" is suspect. Shue's evidence is a 1927 book about the first day of the battle written by James K. P. Scott, the bugler for Company H of the 1st Pennsylvania Cavalry, part of David Gregg's Second Cavalry Division. Scott, however, was not at Gettysburg on July 1 and never served in Buford's division. The claim about a Confederate prisoner taken on July 1 comes from the same page (135) of Scott's book as the claim about the "limited distribution" of Spencer rifles. Given Scott's pedigree

---

7   Quarterly Statements of Ordnance in Cavalry, 1862-64, Returns for June 30, 1863.

8   Shue, *Morning at Willoughby Run*, 214.

and the lack of any other corroborating documentation, this source is unreliable.

Sergeant McCabe's statement appears in the regimental history of the 17th Pennsylvania Cavalry,[9] part of a postwar reminiscence written by McCabe for inclusion in the regimental history. Unfortunately, it is filled with errors. McCabe claimed Buford's troopers took part in the battle of Aldie, which was not the case. McCabe apparently confused Aldie with the June 21, 1863, battle of Upperville, which McCabe placed on the wrong day. McCabe's account states this action was fought on June 20. This account is also unreliable and appears to have been tainted by the passage of time. However, this single statement by McCabe appears to be the basis for Shue's claim that at least one company of the 17th Pennsylvania Cavalry carried Spencer rifles into battle at Gettysburg.

Given that only 64 percent of the companies in Gamble's and Devin's brigade filed their quarterly returns on June 30, 1863, it is possible a handful of Spencer repeating rifles were present at Gettysburg. However, other than that single sentence in Sergeant McCabe's postwar reminiscences, there is not a shred of credible evidence to suggest there were any of them present. In the absence of such evidence, it appears safe to conclude that none of Buford's troopers carried Spencer repeating rifles at Gettysburg on July 1, 1863.

The lack of Spencer rifles makes what Buford and his determined troopers accomplished on July 1, 1863, all the more remarkable. His heavily outnumbered troopers laid down a heavy enough fire to persuade Henry Heth that he faced infantry, a fact that demonstrates the effectiveness of the defense designed and implemented by Buford. The rapid fire of the breech-loading carbines carried by his troopers more than compensated for their lack of effective range, and enabled the Union horsemen to hold off Heth's infantry just long enough for Reynolds and the First Corps to arrive on the battlefield.

---

9 Moyer, *History of the 17th Pennsylvania*, 328.

Appendix C

What was the Nature of John Buford's Defense at Gettysburg?

As described in Chapters 4, 5, and 6, Buford designed and implemented a textbook defense at Gettysburg, one that is still regularly taught to West Point cadets and serving line officers. The question of the precise nature of Buford's defensive scheme is worth exploring. Was it a defense in depth, or was it a covering force action?[1]

A defense in depth, explains a modern U.S. Army field manual,

> is normally the commander's preferred option. Forces defending in depth absorb the momentum of the enemy's attack by forcing him to attack repeatedly through mutually supporting positions in depth. Depth gives the commanders fire support assets time to generate devastating effects and affords him multiple opportunities to concentrate the effects of overwhelming combat power against the attacking enemy. This also provides more reaction time for the defending force to counter the attack. The commander gathers more information about the attacking enemy's intentions before the enemy commits to a [course of attack]. This reduces the risk of the enemy force quickly penetrating the main line of defense.

The same army field manual explains that the "commander positions his units in successive layers of battle positions along likely enemy avenues of approach when he conducts a defense in depth." This tactic is usually used when the terrain does not favor a defense that is well forward, and there is better terrain in the area of operations. The area of operations is usually deeper than it is wide, and significant depth is available. Most importantly, a defense in depth

---

1 Even though the definitions used here employ modern parlance and anticipate modern weaponry, they still apply equally well to Civil War tactics. Hence, this analysis will incorporate the modern definitions against the historical context.

is usually most effective when the enemy has several times the combat power of the defender.[2]

A defense in depth is: "The siting of mutually supporting defense positions designed to absorb and progressively weaken [the] attack, prevent initial observations of the whole position by the enemy, and to allow the commander to maneuver the reserve."[3] In other words, a defense in depth requires that a defender deploy his resources, such as fortifications, field works, and military units, both at and well behind the front line, falling back from one defensive position to another, with the purpose of drawing the enemy in so that he exposes his flanks to attack. The strategy is especially effective against an attacker who is able to concentrate his forces to attack a small number of places along an extended defensive line. It employs the deployment of force in mutually supportive positions. In other words, the idea is to force the enemy to drive the defender from each chosen position and inflict casualties upon him in the process.

The American Revolution offered two inspirational examples of defenses in depth for Buford to draw upon. The first was the January 17, 1781, battle of Cowpens in South Carolina, when Brig. Gen. Daniel Morgan used skirmishers in his front rank and militia in his second rank to draw in the British soldiers. Rather than order his militia to stand and fight, which they would not do in the face of advancing enemy professionals, Morgan told them to simply fire two volleys and retreat in order around the left of the last line, which was composed of Regulars. This successful tactic, combined with other factors, resulted in a crushing Patriot victory against the aggressive British attackers.[4] The second example came two months later on March 15, 1781, when Maj. Gen. Nathanael Greene duplicated this tactic on a larger scale at the battle of Guilford Court House near Greensboro, North Carolina. Greene organized his American army in three consecutive lines of battle, with each falling back on the next in order to draw the British into his killing zones and exhaust them. Although Greene was eventually driven from the field, British commander Gen. Charles Lord Cornwallis won a tactical victory but suffered a crushing strategic defeat. His army of some 2,000 men lost 532 killed, wounded, and missing, prompting a

---

2   Field Manual 3-90, *Tactics* (Washington, DC, 2001), 9-9.

3   Ibid.

4   For a detailed micro-tactical discussion of Morgan's fight, see Lawrence E. Babits, *A Devil of a Whipping: The Battle of Cowpens* (Chapel Hill, NC, 1998).

British politician to call Guilford Court House "that sort of victory which ruins an army and the Carolinas, like all America, are lost in rebellion."[5] When he learned of the pyrrhic nature of Cornwallis' triumph, another British politician observed, "Another such victory would ruin the British army."[6] Cornwallis had little choice but to withdraw to the coast at Wilmington, North Carolina, refit his army, and develop a different strategy. His change of course led him to Virginia and his final engagement and surrender at Yorktown on October 19, 1781.

Confederate Lt. Gen. William J. Hardee designed and implemented a classic defense in depth nearly two years after Gettysburg at the March 16, 1865, battle of Averasboro during the Carolinas campaign. Hardee's tactics were very similar to—and some say inspired by—Daniel Morgan's defense in depth at Cowpens. With fewer than 10,000 men, Hardee managed to hold off about one-half of Maj. Gen. William T. Sherman's much larger army for an entire day. He used three prepared defensive positions to do so, falling back from each one as he was driven from it until he ultimately reached the third and final line. By that time it was dark and Sherman did not have the stomach to attack the last prepared position, leaving Hardee the time he needed to pull out during the night. Hardee's battle offers a classic example of a much smaller force tying up a much larger one through the use of defense in depth tactics.[7]

The other option that might describe Buford's tactics at Gettysburg is a covering force action. A recent U.S. Army manual defines a covering force action thusly:

> The covering force operates independently from the main body. The purpose of covering force operations is to develop the situation early and deceive, disorganize, and destroy enemy forcing. However, unlike screening and guard forces, a covering force is tactically self-contained and often seeks to become decisively engaged with the enemy. Cover operations are performed in the offense or defense and can be conducted by either the [Armored Cavalry Regiment, or ACR] or separate brigade.

---

5   Lawrence E. Babits and Joshua B. Howard, *Long, Obstinate, and Bloody: The Battle of Guilford Courthouse* (Chapel Hill, NC, 2009), 187.

6   Franklin and Mary Wickwire, *Cornwallis and the War of Independence* (London, 1970), 311.

7   For a detailed discussion of Hardee's tactics at Averasboro, see Mark A. Smith and Wade Sokolosky, *No Such Army Since the Days of Julius Caesar: Sherman's Carolinas Campaign from Fayetteville to Averasboro* (Celina, OH, 2006).

There is no clear line between the covering force battle and the main battle. Covering forces continue to operate in some areas, while the main battle is pursued in others. Throughout the operation, battles shift from defensive action in one locale to offensive action. That is why the ACR or separate brigade conducting a covering force mission must be prepared for either mission [emphasis added].

When a covering force action begins, the main body generally is not engaged. Depending on how much warning it gets, and the mission of the main body, the covering force can be heavily augmented with engineers, [Military Intelligence, or MI], and artillery before the battle begins. With less warning, support arrives with the battle already underway. In any event, the covering force is expected to continue resistance until the corps has had time to deploy. Because it operates independently from the corps main body, the MI company must be able to move all of its personnel, systems, and equipment with its own organic assets.[8]

In other words, the idea behind a covering force action is to trade time for space, thereby allowing a detached forward unit (usually cavalry) to delay the advance of the enemy long enough to permit the main body to come up and engage. The covering force operates independently of the main body.

A careful analysis of the tactical scheme John Buford designed and implemented at Gettysburg makes it clear that he waged a covering force action. In fact, it was so well done that, as noted elsewhere, the army regularly teaches it as a staff ride to this day. Buford's purpose was to trade three ridgelines worth of space for enough time to permit John Reynolds and the First Corps to come up and engage. Buford's brilliantly designed and implemented tactic delayed the Confederate advance for nearly five hours on the first day at Gettysburg.[9]

A further analysis of Buford's plan reveals its classic nature. His deployments were intended to deceive the enemy as to force type, size, disposition, intent, and dispositions, and force the Confederates to buy every foot of ground at the highest cost possible. He also intended to trade time for ground by forcing the enemy to deploy his forces, thereby identifying the type, size, disposition, intent, and location of Henry Heth's division. All of this, in

---

8   Field Manual 34-35, *Armored Cavalry Regiment and Separate Brigade Intelligence and Electronic Warfare Operations* (Washington, DC, 1990), Ch. 4.

9   Colonel Robert H. G. Minty effectively designed and implemented the same tactics on the first day of the battle of Chickamauga on September 19, 1863, when his delaying action held off a significant portion of the Confederate Army of Tennessee at Reed's Bridge. For a comparison between Minty's and Buford's tactics, see Laurence D. Schiller, "A Taste of Northern Steel: The Evolution of Federal Cavalry Tactics 1861-1865," *North & South* (January 1999), No. 2, 2:30-46.

turn, completely disrupted the Virginian's operating plans for the morning of July 1, 1863.

The definition of covering force action set forth above comes from a modern army tactics manual for armored cavalry. While the horses and single-shot carbines have been traded in for tanks, Bradley armored fighting vehicles, and automatic weapons, the role and mission of cavalry remains identical. During the Cold War, before the fall of the Berlin Wall, NATO expected any potential Soviet invasion of western Europe to pass through a narrow mountain pass in central (what was then West) Germany to the east of Frankfurt called Fulda Gap, which Napoleon used to retreat after the 1813 battle of Leipzig. NATO doctrine held that armored cavalry would conduct a covering force action at Fulda Gap long enough for the main body of the allied forces to come up and engage and halt the Soviet invasion.[10] The NATO tactics were identical, adjusted only for advances in technology. The mission was identical. Perhaps this is why West Point still teaches Buford's textbook example of a covering force action at Gettysburg to its cadets.

10 For more on NATO doctrine and tactics during the Cold War, see Ingo Trauschweizer, *The Cold War U.S. Army: Building Deterrence for Limited War* (Lawrence, KS, 2008).

Did James Lane's Confederate Brigade form Infantry Squares in Echelon on the Afternoon of July 1, 1863?

Chapter 8 of this book discusses the stand made by John Buford's two brigades near Cemetery Hill during the final phase of the fighting on July 1, 1863. A variety of Confederates, including a pair of brigades under Col. Abner Perrin and Brig. Gen. James H. Lane, both of Dorsey Pender's division, helped drive the survivors of the Union First Corps off Seminary Ridge and back into the streets of Gettysburg. It appeared as though nothing could stop the advancing Rebels as their juggernaut reached Seminary Ridge.

The Union high command, meanwhile, was desperately cobbling together a makeshift defensive position on Cemetery Hill, but was not ready to receive an attack. Something had to be done to halt or at least slow down the steady Confederate advance. On Buford's order, the troopers of his two brigades ostentatiously prepared to unleash a mounted charge against the enemy. They assumed a position in the valley between Cemetery Hill and Seminary Ridge. Something stopped Lane's attack, which halted on Seminary Ridge and did not advance any farther. When he halted, there was nothing in front of him but Buford's two brigades, drawn up in line of battle, with their sabers drawn and glinting in the afternoon sun. The question is whether Lane's men stopped to form hollow squares to defend against the feinted mounted charge.

The tactic known as "forming square" is a classic Napoleonic technique for infantry to defend against mounted cavalry attacks. Each side of a square was four or six ranks deep, with the front rank kneeling while holding their muskets out, their bayonets thereby forming an intimidating wall of sharp points. These squares themselves were relatively small, with considerable gaps between them, which in turn forced charging cavalry to veer away in order to avoid crashing into them. Their ability to repel enemy cavalry relied upon presenting a solid impenetrable front rather than overwhelming firepower. They required the soldiers manning them to demonstrate tremendous discipline while they held their position—and their fire—awaiting the oncoming horse soldiers thundering toward them. As long as they held their formation, squares were nearly invincible against cavalry charges. This task was infinitely easier said than done.[1]

"It is an awful thing for infantry to see a body of cavalry riding at them at full gallop," recounted a Napoleonic soldier. "The men in the square frequently begin to shuffle, and so create some unsteadiness. This causes them to neglect their fire. The cavalry seeing them waver, have an inducement riding close up, and in all probability succeed in getting into the square, when it is all over."[2] The development of rifled muskets, which significantly extended the effective range of infantry weapons, made mounted charges by cavalry against infantry far less common. However, the tactic of forming squares remained established army doctrine until well after the Civil War. Hence, the square would have been the standard tactic used against a mounted charge in 1863.

An 1862 field manual for staff officers states, "When threatened by cavalry, infantry will, therefore, quickly adopt the formation in square, in order to be in condition to open fire on all sides. Squares formed by single battalions are the best. A square or column should be sparing of its fire in presence of cavalry, for it is its chief resource. The best fire is that of a whole front. If one or more horsemen enter the squares, the non-commissioned officers must at once bayonet the horses."[3]

The tactic plays out like this: "If a charge of cavalry is made, the first line forms squares, and in a plain, the second does likewise. Use then the formation of battalion squares, arranged checkerwise, at eighty paces, or form in echelon squares, resting those of the head and tail upon inert obstacles, or supporting them with cavalry, artillery, and skirmishers. . . . Squares of four battalions are

1   Rory Muir, *Tactics and the Experience of Battle in the Age of Napoleon* (New Haven, CT, 1998), 130-132.

2   Quoted in Brent Nosworthy, *With Musket, Cannon and Sword: Battle Tactics of Napoleon and His Enemies* (New York, 1996), 311.

3   William P. Craighill, *The Army Officer's Pocket Companion; Principally Designed for Staff Officers in the Field* (New York, 1862), 76.

still formed, with good reserves. Generally, however, the more numerous the squares, the more thorough is the flank defense."[4]

Forming squares in echelon would have been the appropriate response for Lane's brigade if it was threatened by a cavalry charge by Buford's two brigades on July 1. The question is whether they actually did so.

Captain Eminel P. Halstead of Abner Doubleday's staff, who carried the order to Buford to try to slow down Lane's advance, recounted, "the enemy, seeing the movement, formed squares in echelon, which delayed them and materially aided in the escape of the First Corps if it did not save a large portion of the remnant from capture."[5] This is one of two known sources that specifically state Lane's brigade formed square that afternoon. Sure of what he witnessed, Halstead added, "The formation of squares by the enemy that day has been doubted by nearly every one with whom I have conversed upon the subject, and not until the meeting of the survivors of the first corps at Gettysburg, in May 1885, was I able to satisfy Colonel [John B.] Bachelder [the official government historian of the battle], who has made a study of the battle, of the correctness of my statements, and only then after it had been corroborated by two of Buford's officers who were in the engagement." Unfortunately, Halstead did not identify either officer, and no accounts from Buford's command have been found that corroborate Halstead's claims.

General Lane's report sheds no light on this question. According to Lane, he ordered the 7th North Carolina:

> to deploy, as a strong line of skirmishers some distance to my right and at right angles to our line of battle, to protect our flank, which was exposed to the enemy's cavalry; Pettigrew's and Archer's brigades were in the first line, immediately in our front. We were soon ordered forward again after taking this position, the Seventh being instructed to move as skirmishers by the left flank. In advancing we gained ground to the right, and on emerging from the woods I found that my line had passed Archer's, and that my entire front was unmasked.

> We then moved about a mile, and as the Seventh Regiment had been detained a short time, Colonel Barbour threw out forty men to keep back some of the enemy's cavalry which had dismounted and were annoying us with an enfilade fire. We moved across this open field at quick time, until a body of the enemy's cavalry and a few infantry opened fire upon us from the woods, subsequently occupied by Pegram's battalion of

---

4   Ibid., 180.

5   Halstead, 8.

artillery, when the men gave a yell and rushed forward at double-quick—the whole of the enemy's force beating a hasty retreat to Cemetery Hill.[6]

Thus, Lane's report is vague and does not help to answer the question. Writing years after the war, Judge John Purifoy, a Confederate veteran, boldly declared, "Of all the facts that have been brought forward no evidence is found in the official reports on either side to indicate that the Federal cavalry present and active during the battle of the 1st of July, 1863, attempted to make a show of aggressiveness on horseback against their Confederate antagonists, hence there was no necessity for the formation of a hollow square by the Confederate soldiery on that date." Instead, the author speculates that Col. Abner Perrin's maneuver of splitting his column into two parts, facing each other, when Perrin's infantry finally drove Gamble's troopers away from the stone wall on Seminary Ridge *prior to* the episode where Lane's brigade formed square was misconstrued as forming squares.[7] This is possibly correct.

However, there are numerous problems with this claim. First, and foremost, the author was a member of the 6th Virginia Cavalry and was somewhere on the south side of the Potomac River when these events occurred. Second, the analysis is based exclusively upon the author's review of the official reports of the participants. As we have already seen, none of those accounts mention forming square anywhere. Finally, it is clear Judge Purifoy failed to understand that nobody ever claimed Perrin's brigade formed square on July 1. Purifoy's vehement denials simply are not credible. There are no other known Confederate accounts that address this episode one way or the other.

Finally, we have a vague reference by a member of the 7th North Carolina published in a Charlotte newspaper in 1894. Part of this was quoted in Chapter 8 of this book. "Lane's brigade marched from South Mountain without opposition until across a small stream northwest of Gettysburg. Here it formed line of battle in supporting distance of Heth's Division on the left of the Chambersburg road. In this order the two lines advanced and drove the enemy back several hundred yards, then halted, and Lane's Brigade was withdrawn

6   *OR*, pt. 2, 27:665.

7   John Purifoy, "The Myth of the Confederate Hollow Square", *Confederate Veteran* (February, 1925), 23:55; See, also, *OR* 27, pt. 2, 662, where Perrin describes the maneuver where the two halves of his brigade drove Gamble's dismounted troopers from their strong position behind the stone wall. This fighting is described in Chapter 7.

from the center and placed on the right of Pender's Division," recalled a Tar Heel. "Here the Seventh Regiment, Major Turner commanding, was sent to watch the movements of the enemy's cavalry, with instructions to move by the left flank 'as skirmishers,' so as to cover the right of the brigade in its advance. About 4 o'clock in the afternoon there was a general advance, and after desperate fighting the enemy was driven through and beyond the town. On account of the threatening attitude of the cavalry, the Seventh was detained, but subsequently rejoined the brigade on Seminary Ridge, near McMillan's house."[8] This account does not say that Lane's brigade formed square in response to Buford's threatened charge, but it plainly indicates that it interrupted and even halted the advance of Lane's infantry.

Since the Confederate accounts do not say for certain, we are thus left to examine the few Union accounts of this episode to try to determine the truth. Sadly, none of Buford's, Gamble's, or Devin's reports mention this episode one way or the other.

"A little [after 4:00 p.m.] we were marching leisurely to the College, where most of our prisoners captured had been confined for want of men to escort them to the rear, and subsequently were forgotten," recalled an officer of the 45th New York Infantry of the 11th Corps. "We made preparations to defend the College, and as the enemy in our front pressed very feebly forward expected to make a stubborn stand there, although we saw the left of the First Corps broken to pieces and pursued by overwhelming numbers of the enemy making for the left of the town. We also saw some of the enemy forming squares against some of our cavalry to the left."[9] The problem with this account is that the men of the 45th New York were in the vicinity of Pennsylvania (Gettysburg) College, which sits on the plain below Oak Ridge. It would have been very difficult for these men to have a clear view of Lane's position on the far right of the Confederate line.

An early history of the Army of the Potomac claimed that Buford's troopers, "by threatening to charge with Gamble's brigade of cavalry . . . compelled Lane to form square, which greatly impeded the advance of the enemy's right, which he intended to swing around and thus cut off the retreat of the Iron Brigade. . . . Buford deserves to have a monument erected on the spot where he defied Lane to advance, thereby greatly frustrating the well-conceived

8 "The Record of the Seventh."

9 "Historical Sketch by Regimental Committee," in *New York at Gettysburg*, 2:380.

designs of the enemy."[10] However, the source of this account is unknown. It is also not entirely accurate, as more than Gamble's brigade was involved.[11]

There are also several ambiguous accounts. The wording of these accounts suggests the Confederates definitely changed their deployment in response to the threat, but do not state that Lane's men actually formed square. Colonel Charles Livingston of Doubleday's staff claimed he could see Lane's cautious advance toward Seminary Ridge, and said he could see them "also forming against cavalry." We do not know what he meant by "forming against cavalry." Livingston's statement is ambiguous and does not clarify the issue at all. Doubleday himself claimed, "The troops in front of the Seminary were stayed by the firm attitude of Buford's cavalry, and made a bend in their line, apparently with a view to form square."[12] This is closer, but it does not say that they actually formed squares—only that they may have intended to do so.

One very significant fact lends credence to the conclusion that Lane's Brigade did not form square on July 1. Brigadier General Lawrence O'Bryan Branch commanded that brigade during the summer of 1862, including during the August 9 battle of Cedar Mountain, while Lane commanded the 28th North Carolina that day. Late in the day, as the Confederates began pressing their advantage, Maj. Gen. Nathaniel P. Banks, the Federal commander, ordered a mounted charge by a battalion of troopers of the 1st Pennsylvania Cavalry. The rifled muskets of the Confederate infantry shredded the foolish but heroic charge of the Pennsylvanians. Branch's Brigade—including Lane's 28th North Carolina—received and ultimately repulsed that brave but doomed charge. Therefore, having witnessed the carnage of the failed charge of the 1st Pennsylvania Cavalry at Cedar Mountain, both Lane himself, as well as his men, well knew that a Napoleonic cavalry charge stood little chance against infantry armed with rifled muskets. Given that experience, it seems unlikely that Lane would have ordered his troops to form square that day. However, there is no evidence one way or the other, but these troops' prior success in defending against a cavalry charge without forming square logically suggests that they may

10 James H. Stine, *History of the Army of the Potomac* (Philadelphia, 1892), 481.

11 Interestingly, author David G. Martin claims that there were two different instances where Lane's brigade may have formed square that afternoon. He insists that the episode described by Halstead is a different one from the one described above. However, this seems highly unlikely, and the evidence does not support his contention. See Martin, *Gettysburg July 1*, 428-29.

12 Doubleday, *Chancellorsville and Gettysburg*, 149.

not have done so in this instance, even though the mounted force that they faced at Gettysburg was substantially larger than the one that they faced at Cedar Mountain 11 months earlier.[13]

It appears that we will never know the answer to this question. In the end, its answer, while fascinating, is not important. Regardless of whether the feinted charge actually caused Lane to halt and form square, something unquestionably halted Lane's advance that day. While we do not know for certain, the sight of two full brigades of cavalry—roughly 2,700 troopers—mounted, in line of battle, with sabers drawn, awaiting the order to charge, undoubtedly helped Lane in deciding to obey the order not to attack and to halt on Seminary Ridge. But there is no evidence that Lane actually gave the order to form squares by echelon, and, other than the Halstead account, there is no evidence that they actually did so. Instead, it appears that the feint was enough. Lane's advance halted, allowing sufficient time for the Union infantry to fall back safely from its very exposed position on Seminary Ridge to the strong defensive positions that Maj. Gen. Winfield S. Hancock and Brig. Gen. Gouverneur K. Warren, the Army of the Potomac's chief engineer, had prepared on East Cemetery Hill.

---

13 Obviously, a detailed discussion of the specifics of the foolhardy but heroic charge of the 1st Pennsylvania Cavalry at Cedar Mountain strays far beyond the scope of this study. For those readers interested in learning more about this episode, see Robert K. Krick, *Stonewall Jackson at Cedar Mountain* (Chapel Hill, NC, 1990), 258-63. By contrast, the regimental history of the 1st Pennsylvania Cavalry claimed that the "advance of the enemy was completely checked by this daring charge, and the battery saved." William P. Lloyd, *History of the First Reg't Pennsylvania Reserve Cavalry from Its Organization, August 1861, to September 1864, with List of Names of All Officers and Enlisted Men* (Philadelphia, 1864), 24.

John Buford at Gettysburg:
A Walking and Driving Tour

This walking and driving tour will guide you to most of the prominent sites associated with John Buford's time at Gettysburg. If you desire, the GPS coordinates I provide can be programed into your GPS unit, and you can allow it to direct you from place to place as you enjoy the tour. The numerous modern-day photographs will assist you in locating the spots described herein. Please feel free to stop, get out, and walk around at most of the stops on the tour, but always be careful. Some of these locations are subject to heavy automobile traffic. Enjoy the tour![1]

The Tour Begins

We begin our tour at the National Park Service Visitor Center (GPS BENCHMARK 1). Depart from the Taneytown Road exit. Turn right onto the Taneytown Road (GPS BENCHMARK 2). Proceed 0.6 miles to the intersection of the Taneytown Road and the Emmitsburg Road (GPS BENCHMARK 3). Proceed north. The Taneytown Road becomes Washington Street on the north side of the intersection. Drive another 0.6 miles north on Washington Street to the intersection of Washington Street and Chambersburg Street (GPS BENCHMARK 4). As you sit at the intersection, you will see a 7-11 store to your right front. The store marks the original site of Tate's Blue Eagle Hotel, which served as John Buford's headquarters on the night of June 30,

---

1   The author is grateful to Jennifer Goellnitz, whose excellent photographs grace the pages of this tour.

A modern-day view of Schmucker Hall on the campus of the Lutheran Seminary.

1863. The 7-11 was built after the Blue Eagle Hotel burned down. Turn left onto Chambersburg Street.

Continue 0.3 miles until you come to a Y-intersection (GPS BENCHMARK 5). Take the right fork of the Y, which is Buford Avenue. As you proceed west on Buford Avenue, you will get a clear view of Schmucker Hall, which is topped by the cupola used by John Buford and by his signal officer, Lt. Aaron B. Jerome, to observe the situation on the morning of July 1, 1863. Schmucker Hall has recently been turned into a Civil War museum open to the public, and is a worth a visit.

The First Shot Marker

Drive another 2.7 miles west along Buford Avenue and you will come to the intersection of Knoxlyn Ridge Road and the Chambersburg Pike (GPS BENCHMARK 6). The white house on the north side of the Chambersburg Pike was the Wisler blacksmith shop. The small monument there is the marker to the first shot of the battle of Gettysburg, fired by Lt. Marcellus Jones of the 8th Illinois Cavalry. Be careful visiting the First Shot Marker. Traffic on the Chambersburg Pike can be quite heavy and it can be dangerous to cross the road there. If you wish to proceed a bit farther west, you will descend Knoxlyn

Top: The First Shot Marker, located at the Ephraim Wisler house on Knoxlyn Ridge.
Bottom: A modern-day view of the Ephraim Wisler house and the First Shot Marker,
located in the yard of the house, atop Knoxlyn Ridge.

The plaque atop the gun tube that fired the first artillery shot of the Battle of Gettysburg.

Ridge to Marsh Creek. The small knoll overlooking Marsh Creek on the west side of the creek is the spot where Capt. William Marye unlimbered his gun to fire the first Confederate artillery shot of the battle. This is private property, so be careful not to trespass. Turn your car around and head back east on the Chambersburg Pike toward town. You will descend into a valley and then head

Monument to Battery A, 2nd U.S. Artillery.

A present-day view of the McPherson barn.

up another ridge, which is Herr Ridge. This ridge was the position chosen by John Buford as his second line of battle, and the spot where Union resistance stiffened.

Buford's Main Position on McPherson's Ridge

From the First Shot Marker, you will drive east for another mile (GPS BENCHMARK 7). The high ground where the church sits is Belmont School

8th New York Cavalry monument.

8th Illinois Cavalry monument.

House Ridge, which merges into Herr Ridge just to the south of the intersection of the Herr Ridge Road and the Chambersburg Pike. Proceed east for another 0.1 miles. Directly in front of you will be the Herr Tavern (GPS BENCHMARK 8). As you continue east for another 0.4 miles, you will descend into a valley bisected by Willoughby Run (GPS BENCHMARK 9). Proceed up the hill (the western slope of McPherson's Ridge) for another 0.2 miles and turn right onto Stone Avenue (GPS BENCHMARK 10). Park your car in the parking lot of the small ranger station there. Carefully cross the Chambersburg Pike and visit the monument to John Buford. There are four cannon tubes on the corners of the base of the monument. All four of those tubes were with Calef's battery at Gettysburg. The one on the southwest corner, with the brass plate on the top, is gun number 233, which fired the first artillery shot of the battle of Gettysburg. The two guns of Hall's Maine battery between the Buford and John F. Reynolds

12th Illinois Cavalry monument.

monuments are on the precise location where one section of Calef's guns fought during the battle. The other section is directly across the Chambersburg Road, where the other two cannon are placed. Feel free to visit them, but be careful crossing the road. Return to your car and then turn right onto Stone Avenue from the ranger station.

Proceed 0.2 miles to the monument to John Burns that will be on your left (GPS BENCHMARK 11). Burns is the civilian who cut the unfortunate Cyrus James of the 9th New York Cavalry from his stirrup after his body was dragged into Gettysburg after he fell near the Samuel Cobean farm. Burns, a

Monument to the 1st Cavalry Division.

Marker for Gamble's First Cavalry Brigade.

septuagenarian veteran of the War of 1812, grabbed his squirrel rifle and headed out to join the Army of the Potomac's infantry fighting the Confederates on McPherson's Ridge. Burns was wounded multiple times that afternoon.

Continue on for another 0.6 miles until you come to the dead end (GPS BENCHMARK 12). Look right and you will see two cannons about 150 yards away. These mark the position of Sergeant Roder's two-gun section of Calef's battery. Note how far away from the other four guns of the battery these two guns were placed. You will get a much closer look at them later in the tour. The

3rd Indiana Cavalry monument.

monument directly in front of you on the other side of Reynolds Avenue is to the 8th New York Cavalry. Turn right on Reynolds Avenue.

Continue north for 0.3 miles, and you will come to the monument to the 8th Illinois Cavalry (GPS BENCHMARK 13). Continue straight to the traffic light (GPS BENCHMARK 14). Cross the Chambersburg Pike and proceed north for 0.2 miles to the monument to the 12th Illinois Cavalry (GPS BENCHMARK 15). Proceed another 0.1 miles and you will see the monument to the 3rd Indiana Cavalry on the right (GPS BENCHMARK 16). Proceed north for another 0.2 miles to the dead end (GPS BENCHMARK 17).

Devin's Positions

Turn left onto Buford Avenue and proceed for another 0.5 miles. You will then find the monument to the 3rd West Virginia Cavalry on your right (GPS BENCHMARK 18). Proceed another 0.1 miles north to the large handsome monument to the 6th New York Cavalry (GPS BENCHMARK 19). James E. Kelly, the same sculptor who designed the John Buford monument, designed

3rd West Virginia Cavalry monument.

and sculpted this monument. On the front of the monument is a depiction of Col. Thomas C. Devin leading a cavalry charge at Five Forks on April 1, 1865, and a bust of Devin can be found on the back on the monument. A number of years ago, this structure received a direct lightning strike that nearly destroyed it.

6th New York Cavalry monument.

9th New York Cavalry monument.

Fortunately, it was repaired and restored to good condition. Continue another 0.1 miles north to the monument to the 9th New York Cavalry (**GPS BENCHMARK 20**). Then proceed another 0.1 miles north to the intersection of Buford Avenue and the Mummasburg Road. The monument to the 17th Pennsylvania Cavalry will be on your right (**GPS BENCHMARK 21**). The Forney farm buildings were located here. The Forney house sat just across the road from the 17th Pennsylvania's monument at the current road intersection.

Most visitors never realize that the 17th Pennsylvania's monument should not be situated where it is, because none of the Pennsylvanians fought on Oak

Hill. Their monument should have been erected in the valley below, near the Samuel Cobean farm, which is where these troopers fought on July 1.

The Samuel Cobean Farm and the Fight against Rodes

Turn right onto the Mummasburg Road and drive 0.7 miles to Howard Avenue. Along the way, you will move down Oak Hill and cross some railroad tracks. You will then turn left onto Howard Avenue (**GPS BENCHMARK 22**). Proceed 0.4 miles on Howard Avenue to its intersection with Carlisle Street, which is also Pa. Route 34 (**GPS BENCHMARK 23**). Turn left onto Carlisle Street. As you head north, you will pass a carwash at a Y-intersection. That carwash was the location of the headquarters of the 17th Pennsylvania Cavalry on the morning of July 1. Proceed north on Carlisle Street for 0.7 miles and then turn left onto the driveway for the Samuel Cobean farm (**GPS BENCHMARK 24**). Drive 0.3 miles down the driveway to the loop (**GPS BENCHMARK 25**).

17th Pennsylvania Cavalry monument.

Top: A present-day view of the Samuel Cobean farmhouse. This home presently serves as the
Gettysburg National Military Park's administrative offices.
Bottom: A present-day view of the Samuel Cobean barn and out buildings.

The Cobean farm property houses the administrative offices for the Gettysburg
National Military Park, and park personnel occupy the house. Be respectful of
their privacy and of their property. Much of the fighting between Devin's
brigade of troopers and the infantry of Robert E. Rodes' Confederate division

occurred on the Cobean farm. (This was where Cyrus W. James, who was dragged into town by his horse, as mentioned earlier, was shot and killed.) Proceed 0.3 miles back to Carlisle Street (GPS BENCHMARK 26), turn right onto Carlisle Street, and drive 0.7 miles back to Howard Avenue (GPS BENCHMARK 27). Turn right onto Howard Avenue and go another 0.4 miles to the intersection of Howard Avenue and the Mummasburg Road (GPS BENCHMARK 28).

Turn right onto the Mummasburg Road and proceed west for 0.9 miles to the stop sign at the intersection of the Mummasburg Road and Herr Ridge Road (GPS BENCHMARK 29). Turn left onto Herr Ridge Road.

As you drive south on the Herr Ridge Road, be sure to look to your left and get a good view at Devin's position on the western slope of McPherson's Ridge. You will be impressed by the strength of Devin's position. Once you have traveled 0.4 miles, you will see a farm on the west side of the Herr Ridge Road. The small knoll that you see there was occupied by Confederate artillery for much of the first day of the battle of Gettysburg (GPS BENCHMARK 30). Proceed another 0.4 miles south to the traffic light (GPS BENCHMARK 31). Turn left onto the Chambersburg Pike and continue east.

The Afternoon Phase of the Fighting

After 1.1 miles, turn right onto Seminary Ridge Road (GPS BENCHMARK 32). The yard behind the white house at the corner was where Robert E. Lee maintained his headquarters for the second and third days of the battle of Gettysburg. Thankfully, this was recently purchased by the Civil War Trust and will be preserved. Proceed another 0.2 miles and Schmucker Hall will be on your left (GPS BENCHMARK 33). The cupola on the top of Schmucker Hall was the one used by both John Buford and Aaron B. Jerome, and the initial meeting between John F. Reynolds and Buford occurred right where your vehicle presently sits. Drive on another 0.3 miles to the traffic light (GPS BENCHMARK 34). The stone wall that you see in front of you, across the road from the Shultz House, marks the northern end of the position occupied by most of William Gamble's brigade of cavalry during the afternoon of July 1. Their position extended south along that stone wall for approximately 0.25 miles to the McMillan House.

Turn right onto Middle Street, which was called the Fairfield Road in 1863. Continue for 1.0 mile to Cumberland Township building on the hill on the south side of the road (GPS BENCHMARK 35). This is the position occupied by Maj. John Beveridge and the 8th Illinois Cavalry, and is where Beveridge feinted the mounted charge that caused the 52nd North Carolina Infantry of Pettigrew's brigade to halt and form a hollow square in response to that mounted feint. Turn around in the parking lot of the municipal building and turn right onto Middle Street.

Continue east for 0.4 miles and then turn left onto Reynolds Avenue (GPS BENCHMARK 36). Proceed north for 0.2 miles to the monument and guns of Sergeant Roder's section of Calef's battery (GPS BENCHMARK 37). Again, note how far away from the other two sections of Calef's battery these two guns were placed. This was done to create the illusion that Buford had more than six cannons available to him that morning. Also, if you look to your left, you will see the large red barn of the Herbst farm. The swale between the barn and the higher ground of McPherson's Ridge is the area where the 52nd North Carolina Infantry formed square in response to the feinted charge of the 8th Illinois Cavalry at the location you visited on your last stop. Continue on another 0.3 miles and then turn right onto Buford Avenue, which is also Route 30 (GPS BENCHMARK 38).

"Unshaken and undaunted"

Proceed east for 1.0 mile to the Y intersection (GPS BENCHMARK 39) and bear left onto Chambersburg Street. Continue 0.2 miles to Washington Street (GPS BENCHMARK 40) and turn right onto Washington Street. Drive 0.6 miles and turn right onto Gettys Street (GPS BENCHMARK 41). The Gettysburg Hospital will be on your right. Continue 0.3 miles to the dead end at Long Lane (GPS BENCHMARK 42). The recreational park in front of you marks the spot where Buford ordered Gamble's and Devin's brigades to deploy into a mounted line of battle to deter the advance of Brig. Gen. James H. Lane's Confederate brigade, which could have proceeded on to Cemetery Hill. Turn left onto Long Lane.

The Night of July 1 and the Morning of July 2

Continue on for 0.1 miles to Queen Street (GPS BENCHMARK 43), turn left onto Queen Street, and continue for 0.5 miles to the dead end (GPS BENCHMARK 44). Turn right onto Steinwehr Avenue and drive 1.6 miles

A modern-day view of the Joseph Sherfy barn and farmhouse along the Emmitsburg Road.

south on Steinwehr Avenue (known as the Emmitsburg Road in 1863) and continue on past the John Sherfy farm to the Wheatfield Road (GPS BENCHARK 45). Turn left onto the Wheatfield Road at the Peach Orchard. Buford's camps were in the field in front of you on the night of July 1-2, 1863, and his pickets extended from the Peach Orchard all the way to to Little Round Top in the distance. Devin's brigade deployed south along the Emmitsburg Road, and Calef's battery was deployed just to the south of the Peach Orchard during the morning skirmishing on July 2, 1863. Drive another 1.1 miles to the Taneytown Road (GPS BENCHMARK 46) and turn left onto the Taneytown Road.

Drive north on the Taneytown Road for 1.3 miles to the entrance to the National Park Service Visitor Center (GPS BENCHMARK 47). Turn right into the driveway for the Visitor Center, and return to the Visitor Center (GPS BENCHMARK 48). This concludes the tour of the primary points of interest for Buford's cavalry.

It is my hope that you will come away from this tour with a much greater appreciation for the defense designed and implemented by John Buford, his excellent use of terrain, and the ordeal faced by his embattled command at Gettysburg.

GPS BENCHMARKS:

BENCHMARK 1: N39° 48.659'
                W077° 13.451'
BENCHMARK 2: N39° 49.7841'
                W077° 14.105'
BENCHMARK 3: N39° 49.283'
                W077° 13.976'
BENCHMARK 4: N39° 49.828'
                W077° 14.000'
BENCHMARK 5: N39° 49.858'
                W077° 14.200'
BENCHMARK 6: N39° 51.042'
                W077° 16.830'
BENCHMARK 7: N39° 50.659'
                W077° 15.883'
BENCHMARK 8: N39° 552'
                W077° 15.719'
BENCHMARK 9: N39° 50.398'
                W077° 15.390'
BENCHMARK 10: N39° 50.272'
                W077° 15.117'
BENCHMARK 11: N39° 50.161'
                W077° 15.170'
BENCHMARK 12: N39° 50.009'
                W077° 15.050'
BENCHMARK 13: N39° 50.149'
                W077° 14.969'
BENCHMARK 14: N39° 50.187'
                W077° 14.944'
BENCHMARK 15: N39° 50.225'
                W077° 14.915'
BENCHMARK 16: N39° 50.277'
                W077° 14.877'
BENCHMARK 17: N39° 50.410'
                W077° 14.796'
BENCHMARK 18: N39° 50.617'
                W077° 14.877'

BENCHMARK 19: N39° 50.676'
                    W077° 14.831'
BENCHMARK 20: N39° 50.757'
                    W077° 14.767'
BENCHMARK 21: N39° 50.843'
                    W077° 14.732'
BENCHMARK 22: N39° 50.403'
                    W077° 14.213'
BENCHMARK 23: N39° 50.587'
                    W077° 13.876'
BENCHMARK 24: N39° 51.166'
                    W077° 14.027'
BENCHMARK 25: N39° 51.227'
                    W077° 14.427'
BENCHMARK 26: N39° 50.587'
                    W077° 14.027'
BENCHMARK 27: N39° 50.587'
                    W077° 13.876'
BENCHMARK 28: N39° 50.404'
                    W077° 14.218'
BENCHMARK 29: N39° 51.270'
                    W077° 15.230'
BENCHMARK 30: N39° 50.831'
                    W077° 15.649'
BENCHMARK 31: N39° 50.550'
                    W077° 15.684'
BENCHMARK 32: N39° 50.074'
                    W077° 14.690'
BENCHMARK 33: N39° 49.927'
                    W077° 14.683'
BENCHMARK 34: N39° 49.970'
                    W077° 14.644'
BENCHMARK 35: N39° 49.460'
                    W077° 15.686'
BENCHMARK 36: N39° 49.620'
                    W077° 15.170'
BENCHMARK 37: N39° 49.921'
                    W077° 15.069'

BENCHMARK 38: N39° 50.183'
W077° 14.942'
BENCHMARK 39: N39° 49.852'
W077° 14.194'
BENCHMARK 40: N39° 49.853'
W077° 14.001'
BENCHMARK 41: N39° 49.400'
W077° 13.998'
BENCHMARK 42: N39° 49.451'
W077° 14.231'
BENCHMARK 43: N39° 49.366'
W077° 14.314'
BENCHMARK 44: N39° 49.240'
W077° 14.023'
BENCHMARK 45: N39° 48.093'
W077° 14.996'
BENCHMARK 46: N39° 47.652'
W077° 13.869'
BENCHMARK 47: N39° 48.750'
W077° 13.882'
BENCHMARK 48: N39° 48.659'
W077° 13.451'

Bibliography

PRIMARY SOURCES

NEWSPAPERS

Army-Navy Journal
The Aspen Times
Aurora Beacon
Boston Sunday Globe
Brooklyn Eagle
Charlotte Observer
The Chicago Tribune
The Daily Courier (Jefferson County, Indiana)
The Fort Wayne Journal-Gazette
The Galveston Daily News
Georgetown Times (Georgetown, Kentucky)
Gettysburg Compiler
Gettysburg Star and Sentinel
National Republican (Washington, D.C.)
The National Tribune
The New York Times
New York Tribune
New York World
Paris Kentuckian-Citizen
Philadelphia Press
Philadelphia Weekly Times
Raleigh Daily Progress
Richmond Enquirer
Rochester Daily Union and Advertiser
Rock Island Argus
Rock Island Daily Union
The Vevay Reveille

MANUSCRIPT SOURCES

Archives, Emmitsburg Historical Society, Emmitsburg, Maryland:
  Captain Albert M. Hunter's account of the War Between the States
Archives, Gettysburg National Military Park, Gettysburg, Pennsylvania:
  John B. Bachelder Papers
  Sarah Broadhead Diary
Account of Capt. Benjamin F. Little, Co. F, 52nd North Carolina Infantry
  William Gamble letter to William L. Church, March 10, 1864
  W. B. Murphy Letters
John Slentz Claims Reparation Files
  Charles H. Veil letter to David McConaughy, April 7, 1864
  Charles S. Wainwright diary transcript
Archives, Huntington Library, San Marino, California:
  James A. Bell Papers
  Joseph Hooker Papers
Illinois State Archives, Springfield, Illinois:
  Various election papers
Archives, Illinois State Historical Society, Springfield, Illinois:
  Edward C. Reid Diary for 1863
Archives, Indiana State Historical Society, Indianapolis, Indiana:
  George H. Chapman Diary
Archives, Indiana State Library, Indianapolis, Indiana:
  Flavius Bellamy Papers
Musselman Library, Gettysburg College, Gettysburg, Pennsylvania:
  Civil War Collection
    Joseph Hooker to Maj. Gen. E. D. Townsend, September 28, 1875
Manuscripts Division, Library of Congress, Washington, D.C.:
  Samuel J. B. V. Gilpin Diary for 1863
  William O. Hills Papers
  George Hay Stuart Papers
The National Archives and Records Administration, Washington, D.C.:
  John Buford Appointments, Commissions and Pension File
  Abner Doubleday Diary
  RG 94, 8th Illinois Cavalry Order and Log Books
  RG 109 Compiled Service Records of Confederate and Staff Officers and
    Non-regimental Enlisted Men
  RG 156, Section 110, Quarterly Statements of Ordnance in Cavalry 1862-1864, Reports
    for June 30, 1863
  RG 393, Entry 3980, Army of the Potomac, 1861-1865, Miscellaneous Letters, Reports,
    and Lists Received
  RG 393I, Entry 3980, Army of the Potomac, 1861-1865, Bureau of Military Information
    Microfilm M1064, Letters received by the Commissions Branch of the Adjutant
    General's Office, 1863-1870, roll 9, file no. B 1115 CB 1863
  Telegrams Collected by the Secretary of War, Microfilm Group 504, Roll 119, Frame 899

Archives, National Library, Dublin, Ireland:
    Keogh Family Papers
Archives, New York Historical Society, New York, New York:
    James E. Kelly Papers
    William Henry Shelton Autobiography
Archives, New York State Library, Albany, New York:
    John Inglis Papers, Collection No. SC22716
    John Muldoon Papers, Collection No. SC12337
Archives and Military Collection, North Carolina Division of Archives and History,
    Raleigh, North Carolina:
    J. B. Oliver, "My Recollections of the Battle of Gettysburg"
Archives, Pennsylvania Historical Society, Philadelphia, Pennsylvania:
    "The John Gibbon Memoir," John Gibbon Papers
Perrin-Wheaton Chapter, National Society of the Daughters of the American Revolution,
    Wheaton, Illinois:
    The Marcellus E. Jones Journal
Rochester Public Library, Rochester, New York:
    Daniel W. Pulis Letters
Southern Historical Collections, Wilson Library, University of North Carolina, Chapel Hill,
    North Carolina:
    Bryan Grimes Papers
United States Army History and Education Center, Carlisle, Pennsylvania:
    Civil War Miscellaneous Collection:
        Eugene Blackford Memoirs
        Abner B. Frank Diary
    Civil War Times Illustrated Collection:
        Jasper Chaney Diary
    Robert Brake Collection:
        F.J. Bellamy Papers
        Diary of Lt. John E. Hoffman
        Augustus C. Weaver Diary
Archives, United States Military Academy, West Point, New York:
    Abraham Lincoln letter to Edwin M. Stanton of December 16, 1863
    John Buford, Jr. Cadet Records
    Myles W. Keogh, "Etat de Service of Major Gen. Jno. Buford from his promotion to
        Brig. Gen'l. to his death"
Special Collections, Alderman Library, University of Virginia, Charlottesville, Virginia:
    William H. Redman Papers
Eric J. Wittenberg Collection, Columbus, Ohio:
    Minutes of the Buford Memorial Association

PUBLISHED SOURCES

"A Day With Buford", *The National Tribune*, July 5, 1888.

"A Present to the Post," *Rock Island Argus*, May 26, 1897.

Agassiz, George R., ed. *Meade's Headquarters 1863-1865: Letters of Colonel Theodore Lyman from The Wilderness to Appomattox*. Boston: Atlantic Monthly Press, 1922.

Alleman, Tillie Pierce. *At Gettysburg, or What a Girl Saw and Heard of the Battle*. New York: W. Lake Borland, 1889.

"Anecdotes of General Buford," *The National Tribune*, February 18, 1882.

Baker, John. "The First Man Killed at Gettysburg," *The National Tribune*, September 12, 1901.

Beaudot, William J. K. and Lance J. Herdegen, eds. *An Irishman in the Iron Brigade: The Civil War Memoirs of James P. Sullivan, Sergt., Company K, 6th Wisconsin Volunteers*. New York: Fordham University Press, 1993.

Beale, James. *From Marsh Run to Seminary Ridge*. n.p., 1891.

Bean, Lt. Col. Theodore W. "Address at the Dedication of the 17th Pennsylvania Cavalry Monument of September 11, 1889." *Pennsylvania at Gettysburg*. 2 vols. Harrisburg: William Stanley Ray Printers, 1904, 2:874-884.

——. "Who Fired the Opening Shots! General Buford at Gettysburg—The Cavalry Ride into Pennsylvania and the Choice of the Field of Battle—The First Day on the Outposts Before the Arrival of the Infantry." *Philadelphia Weekly Times*, February 2, 1878.

Beidler, Peter G., ed. *Army of the Potomac: The Civil War Letters of William Cross Hazelton of the Eighth Illinois Cavalry Regiment*. Seattle: Coffeetown Press, 2013.

Belo, Alfred H. *Memoirs of Alfred Horatio Belo: Reminiscences of a North Carolina Volunteer*. Ed. by Stuart Wright. Gaithersburg, MD: Olde Soldier Books, n.d.

——. "The Battle of Gettysburg: Reminiscences of the Sanguinary Conflict Related by Col. A. H. Belo, of the Fifty-fifth North Carolina Infantry, before the Sterling Price Camp, of Dallas, Tex., January 20, 1900." *Confederate Veteran* 8 (April 1900): 165-167.

Benedict, John F. "First Shot at Gettysburg," *The National Tribune*, September 3, 1914.

Bentley, Wilber G. "Dedication of Monument. 9th Regiment Cavalry—'Westfield Cavalry,'" included in *New York at Gettysburg*. 3 vols. Albany: J.B. Lyon Co., 1902, 3:1149-1156.

Beveridge, John L. "Address of Bvt. Brig. Gen. John L. Beveridge at the Dedication of the Monument of the 8th Illinois Cavalry," *Illinois Monuments at Gettysburg*. Springfield: H.W. Rokker, 1892: 17-22.

——. "The First Gun at Gettysburg." *War Papers*. Military Order of the Loyal Legion of the United States, Illinois Commandery. Vol. 2. Chicago: McClurg, 1894: 79-98.

——. "First Shot at Gettysburg," *The National Tribune*, July 31, 1902.

Biddle, Chapman. *The First Day of the Battle of Gettysburg*. Philadelphia: J. B. Lippincott, 1889.

Bingham, J.C. "Undated Letter," *Confederate Veteran*, Vol. 5 (November 1897): 565.

Boland, E.T. "Beginning the Battle of Gettysburg," *Confederate Veteran*, Vol. 14 (July, 1906): 308.

Bonham, Jeriah. *Fifty Years' Recollections with Observations and Reflections on Historical Events Giving Sketches of Eminent Citizens—Their Lives and Public Services*. Peoria, IL: J. W. Franks & Sons, 1883.

Brown, Samuel W. "One Who Was There," *The National Tribune*, January 27, 1910.

Brown, Varina Davis, ed. *A Colonel at Gettysburg and Spotsylvania*. Columbia, SC: The State Co., 1931.

Buell, Augustus C. "Story of a Cannoneer," Part III, *The National Tribune*, October 24, 1889.

Caldwell, J. F. J. *The History of a Brigade of South Carolinians, Known First as "Gregg's" and Subsequently as "McGowan's Brigade."* Philadelphia: King & Baird, 1866.

Calef, John H. "Gettysburg Notes: The Opening Gun", *Journal of the Military Service Institute of the United States*, Vol. 40 (1889), 40-58.

Calkins, Homer. "First to Fall at Gettysburg," *The National Tribune*, April 27, 1911.

Catalogue of the Corporation, Officers, and Students of Knox Manual Labor College, July 1842. Peoria, IA: William E. Butler & Co. Printers, 1843.

Chamberlaine, William W. *Memoirs of the Civil War Between the Northern and Southern Sections of the United States of America 1861-1865.* Washington, DC: Press of Byron S. Adams, 1912.

Cheney, Newell. *History of the Ninth Regiment, New York Volunteer Cavalry.* Poland Center, NY: privately published, 1901.

Clark, S. W. "Killed Between the Lines. Corp. James, 9th N. Y. Cav., was the First Man to Lose His Life at Gettysburg," *The National Tribune*, August 1, 1901.

Clark, Walter, ed. *Histories of the Several Regiments and Battalions from North Carolina in the Great War, 1861-65.* 5 vols. Goldsboro, NC: 1901.

Clarke, Augustus P. "Historical Sketch of the Sixth Cavalry Regiment, New York," *Final Report on the Battlefield of Gettysburg (New York at Gettysburg)* by the New York Monuments Commission for the Battlefields of Gettysburg and Chattanooga. 3 vols. Albany, NY: J.B. Lyon Company, 1902, 3:1136-1140.

Craighill, William P. *The Army Officer's Pocket Companion; Principally Designed for Staff Officers in the Field.* New York: D. Van Nostrand, 1862.

Davis, George B. "The Strategy of the Gettysburg Campaign," A paper read before the Military Historical Society of Massachusetts, *Campaigns in Virginia, Maryland and Pennsylvania, 1862-1863.* Boston: Griffith-Stillings Press, 1903: 376-414.

Dawes, Rufus R. *Service with the Sixth Wisconsin Volunteers.* Marietta, OH: E. R. Alderman and Sons, 1890.

Day, Thomas G. "First Shot at Gettysburg," *The National Tribune*, October 30, 1902.

——. "Opening the Battle of Gettysburg", *The National Tribune*, July 30, 1903.

dePuyster, J. Watts. *Decisive Conflicts of the Civil War.* New York: McDonald & Co., 1867.

Dickinson, Bvt. Brig. Gen. Joseph. "A Gettysburg Incident", included in *The Proceedings of the Buford Memorial Association.* New York: privately published, 1895, 23-25.

Dodge, H. O. "Opening the Battle: Lieut. Jones, the 8th Ill. Cavalryman, Fired the First Shot at Gettysburg," *The National Tribune*, September 24, 1891.

Doubleday, Abner. *Chancellorsville and Gettysburg.* New York: Charles Scribner's Sons, 1882.

Dyer, Frederick H. *A Compendium of the War of the Rebellion.* 2 vols. Des Moines: The Dyer Publishing Co., 1908.

Field Manual 3-90, *Tactics.* Washington, DC: Department of the Army, 2001.

Field Manual 34-35, *Armored Cavalry Regiment and Separate Brigade Intelligence and Electronic Warfare Operations.* Washington, DC: Department of the Army, 1990.

"Fifty-fifth North Carolina: History of Regiment and Officers—Positions Occupied at Gettysburg." *The Galveston Daily News*, June 21, 1896.

Foster, Alonzo. *Reminiscences and Record of the 6th New York V.V. Cavalry.* New York: privately published, 1892.

Fremantle, Arthur. *Three Months in the Southern States April-June 1863.* New York: John Bradburn, 1864.

Fulton, William Frierson, II. *The War Reminiscences of William Frierson Fulton, II.* Gaithersburg, MD: Butternut Press, Inc., 1986.

Gallagher, Gary W., ed. *Fighting for the Confederacy: The Personal Recollections of General Edward Porter Alexander.* Chapel Hill: University of North Carolina Press, 1989.

Gardner, J. M. "Union vs. Rebel Cavalry: The Superiority of the Former Proved on Many Bloody Fields," *The National Tribune*, May 24, 1888.

Gates, Theodore B. *The "Ulster Guard" and the War of the Rebellion.* New York: Benjamin H. Tyrrel, 1879.

"General Buford's Statue Unveiled," *New York Tribune*, July 2, 1895.

"Gen. John L. Beveridge. The Republican Candidate in Illinois for Congressman at Large," *New York Times*, September 24, 1871.

"Gettysburg. Great Speech of General Sickles on the Battlefield July 2," *The National Tribune*, July 15 and July 22, 1886.

Gibbon, John. *The Artillerists' Manual, Compiled from Various Sources, and Adapted to the Service of the United States.* Washington, DC: U.S. Government Printing Office, 1860.

Hageman, E. R., ed. *Fighting Rebels and Redskins: Experiences in Army Life of Colonel George B. Sanford 1861-1892.* Norman: University of Oklahoma Press, 1969.

Hall, Hillman A., ed. *History of the Sixth New York Cavalry.* Worcester, MA: The Blanchard Press, 1908.

Halstead, Eminel P. "Incidents of the First Day at Gettysburg," included in Robert U. Johnson and C. C. Buel. eds., *Battles and Leaders of the Civil War.* 4 vols. New York: Century Publishing Co., 1884-88, 3:284-285.

———. "The First Day of the Battle of Gettysburg," War Papers, District of Columbia Commandery, Military Order of the Loyal Legion of the United States, Read March 2, 1887, 1-10.

Hamlin, Percy Gatlin, ed. *The Making of a Soldier: Letters of General R. S. Ewell.* Richmond, VA: Whittet & Shepperson, 1935.

Hancock, Winfield S. "Gettysburg: A Reply to General Howard," included in Peter Cozzens, ed., *Battles and Leaders of the Civil War.* Vol. 5. Chicago: University of Illinois Press, 2002, 348-364.

Hans, Francis H. "First Shot at Gettysburg," *The National Tribune*, August 29, 1912.

Hard, Abner N. *History of the Eighth Cavalry Regiment Illinois Volunteers, During the Great Rebellion.* Aurora, IL: privately published, 1868.

Hardman, Asa Sleath. "As a Union Prisoner Saw the Battle of Gettysburg", *Civil War Times Illustrated* (July 1962), 46-50.

Harries, William H. "The Iron Brigade in the First Day's Battle at Gettysburg." *Glimpses of the Nation's Struggle.* Military Order of the Loyal Legion of the United States, Wisconsin Commandery. Vol. 4. St. Paul, MN: Collins, 1898: 337-350.

Hazelton, W.C. "An Address Made at a Regimental Reunion", *Gettysburg Star and Sentinel*, September 1, 1891.

Heermance, William L. "Oration at the Dedication of the Monument to the 6th New York Cavalry," included in *New York at Gettysburg.* 3 vols. Albany: J.B. Lyon Co., 1902, 3:1132-1136.

———. "The Cavalry at Gettysburg", Military Order of the Loyal Legion of the United States, NewYork Commandery, *Personal Recollections of the War of the Rebellion*, A. Noel Blakeman, ed. New York: G.P. Putnam's Sons, 1907: 196-206.

"Historical Sketch by Regimental Committee," included in *New York at Gettysburg*. 3 vols. Albany: J.B. Lyon Co., 1902, 1:378-381.

History of the 121st Regiment Pennsylvania Volunteers by the Survivors' Association. Philadelphia: Press of Burk & McFetridge Co., 1893.

Hodam, James P., ed. *The Journal of James Hodam: Sketches and Personal Reminiscences of the Civil War as Experienced by a Confederate Soldier*. Privately published; 1996.

Hoffsommer, Robert, ed. "The Rise and Survival of Private Mesnard, Part II," *Civil War Times Illustrated*, Vol. 24, No. 10 (February 1986): 10-46.

"Honors Its Hero: Grand Army Post Has a Memorial Entertainment," *Rock Island Argus*, March 10, 1896.

Howard, Charles H. "The First Day at Gettysburg." War Papers. Military Order of the Loyal Legion of the United States. Vol. 4. Chicago: McClurg, 1896: 238-264.

Howard, Oliver Otis. *Autobiography of Oliver Otis Howard Major General United States Army*. 2 vols. New York: The Baker & Taylor Co., 1907.

——. "The Campaign and Battle of Gettysburg," included in Peter Cozzens, ed., *Battles and Leaders of the Civil War*. Vol. 5. Chicago: University of Illinois Press, 2002, 314-348.

Hoyle, Joseph J. *"Deliver Us from this Cruel War": The Civil War Letters of Lieutenant Joseph J. Hoyle, 55th North Carolina Infantry*. Ed. by Jeffrey M. Girvan. Jefferson, NC: McFarland & Co., 2010.

Hunt, Henry J. "The First Day at Gettysburg," included in Robert U. Johnson and C. C. Buel. eds., *Battles and Leaders of the Civil War*. 4 vols. New York: Century Publishing Co., 1884-88), 3:254-284.

Hughes, Morgan. "People of Gettysburg. How They Inspired the Cavalry to Do Their Effective Work," *The National Tribune*, March 24, 1892.

Hyde, Bill, ed. *The Union Generals Speak: The Meade Hearings on the Battle of Gettysburg*. Baton Rouge: Louisiana State University Press, 2003.

Indiana at the Fiftieth Anniversary of the Battle of Gettysburg: Report of the Fiftieth Anniversary Commission, of the Battle of Gettysburg, of Indiana. State of Indiana: 1913.

Instructions for Officers and Non-Commissioned Officers on Outpost and Patrol Duty, and Troops in Campaign.In Two Parts. Washington, DC: U. S. Government Printing Office, 1863.

Ivy, William T. "At Gettysburg—Who was the Lone Cavalryman Killed Between the Lines?" *The National Tribune*, July 11, 1901.

"The Battle of Gettysburg." *The National Tribune*, March 21, 1901.

J. H. S. "Washington Letter," *The Fort Wayne Journal-Gazette*, November 29, 1885.

Jacobs, Professor Michael. *Notes on the Rebel Invasion of Maryland and Pennsylvania and the Battle of Gettysburg, July lst, 2nd, and 3rd, 1863*. Philadelphia: privately published, 1864.

Kelley, T. Benton. "First Shot at Gettysburg. It was Fired by Lt. E. M. Jones, 8th Illinois Cavalry," *The National Tribune*, October 15, 1908.

——. "Gettysburg. An Account of Who Opened the Battle By One Who Was There," *The National Tribune*, December 31, 1891.

Kelly, John. "The Spy at Frederick, Maryland", *The National Tribune*, February 9, 1888.

Kempster, Walter, M.D. "The Cavalry at Gettysburg", Military Order of the Loyal Legion of the United States, Wisconsin Commandery. Vol. 4. Milwaukee, WI: Burdick, Armitage & Allen, 1905: 397-429.

Ladd, David L. and Audrey J., eds. *The Bachelder Papers: Gettysburg in Their Own Words*. 3 vols. Dayton, OH: Morningside Press, 1995.

"Letter from General H. Heth," *Southern Historical Society Papers*, Vol. 4 (1877): 151-160.

Lloyd, William P. *History of the First Reg't Pennsylvania Reserve Cavalry from Its Organization, August 1861, to September 1864, with List of Names of All Officers and Enlisted Men*. Philadelphia: King & Baird, 1864.

Love, William. "Mississippi at Gettysburg." *Publications of the Mississippi Historical Society*. Vol. 9 (1906): 25-51.

Lowe, David W., ed. *Meade's Army: The Private Notebooks of Lt. Col. Theodore Lyman*. Kent, OH: Kent State University Press, 2007.

Mahan, Dennis H. *An Elementary Treatise on Advanced-Guard, Post, and Detachment Service of Troops and the Manner of Posting and Handling Them in the Presence of an Enemy*. New York: John Wiley, 1861.

Markell, Col. William L. "Historical Sketch of the 8th New York Cavalry", included in *New York at Gettysburg*. 3 vols. Albany: J.B. Lyon Co., 1902, 3:1142-1147.

Marye, Lt. John L. "The First Gun at Gettysburg, With the Confederate Advance Guard'", *The American Historical Register* (July, 1895), 1225-1232.

McCabe, J. E. "The Fist Shot at Gettysburg," *The National Tribune*, August 28, 1913.

McClellan, George B. *McClellan's Own Story*. New York: Charles L. Webster and Co., 1887.

Meade, George Gordon. *The Battle of Gettysburg*. Ambler, PA: privately published, 1924.

———. ed. *The Life and Letters of George Gordon Meade*. 2 vols. New York: Charles Scribner's Sons, 1913.

Meredith, Jaquelin Marshall. "The First Day at Gettysburg: Tribute to Brave General Harry Heth,Who Opened the Great Battle," *Southern Historical Society Papers* 24 (1896): 182-187.

Mills, Albert M. "Oration of Captain Albert M. Mills, U.S.V.," *In Memoriam James Samuel Wadsworth 1807-1864*. Albany, NY: J. B. Lyon Co., 1916: 48-56.

Mix, A. R. "Experiences at Gettysburg", *The National Tribune*, February 22, 1904.

"Monument to General Buford," *New York World*, November 18, 1893.

Moon, H.W. "Beginning the Battle of Gettysburg." *Confederate Veteran*, Vol. 23 (December 1925): 449.

Moore, A. H. "Heth's Division at Gettysburg." *The Southern Bivouac*. Vol. 3, No. 9 (May 1885): 383-395.

Moore, N. B. "The Opening at Gettysburg," *The National Tribune*, November 28, 1912.

Morgan, Gen. Charles H. "Narrative of the Operations of the Second Army Corps, from the time General Hancock assumed command, June 9, 1863, Until the Close of the Battle of Gettysburg", included in Almira Hancock, *Reminiscences of General Hancock by His Wife*. New York: Charles L. Webster & Co., 1887: 182-222.

Morrison, James L., ed. *The Memoirs of Henry Heth*. Westport, CT: Greenwood Press, 1974.

Mosby, John S. *The Memoirs of Colonel John S. Mosby*. Boston: Little, Brown & Co., 1917.

Moyer, Henry P. *History of the Seventeenth Regiment, Pennsylvania Volunteer Cavalry*. Lebanon, PA: n.p.,1911.

Nevins, Allan, ed. *A Diary of Battle, The Personal Journals of Colonel Charles S. Wainwright, 1861-1865*. New York: Harcourt, Brace & World, 1962.

Newhall, Frederic C. *With General Sheridan in Lee's Last Campaign*. Philadelphia: J. B. Lippincott, 1866.

Norton, Henry. *Deeds of Daring: or History of the Eighth New York Volunteer Cavalry*. Norwich, NY: Chenango Telegraph Printing House, 1889.

Norton, Walter B. "The Last Word About the First Shot," *The National Tribune*, April 24, 1884.

Official Register of the Officers and Cadets of the U.S. Military Academy, West Point, New York, June 1845. Washington, D.C.: U.S. Government Printing Office, 1845.

Official Register of the Officers and Cadets of the U.S. Military Academy, West Point, New York, June 1846. Washington, D.C.: U.S. Government Printing Office, 1846.

Official Register of the Officers and Cadets of the U.S. Military Academy, West Point, New York, June 1847. Washington, D.C.: U.S. Government Printing Office, 1847.

Official Register of the Officers and Cadets of the U.S. Military Academy, West Point, New York, June 1848. Washington, D.C.: U.S. Government Printing Office, 1848.

"Opened the Fight at Gettysburg," *Boston Sunday Globe*, December 5, 1909.

Patrick, Marsena Rudolph. *Inside Lincoln's Army: The Diary of Marsena Rudolph Patrick, Provost Marshal General, Army of the Potomac.* Ed. by David S. Sparks. New York: Thomas Yoseloff, 1964.

Perrin, Abner to Gov. Milledge L. Bonham, July 29, 1863. Ed. by Milledge L. Bonham. *Mississippi Valley Historical Review* (March 1938): 521-522.

Pickrell, W.N. *History of the Third Indiana Cavalry.* Indianapolis: Aetna Publishing Co., 1906.

Pope, Maj. Gen. John. "The Second Battle of Bull Run," included in Robert U. Johnson and C. C. Buel. eds., *Battles and Leaders of the Civil War.* 4 vols. New York: Century Publishing Co., 1884-88): 2:449-494.

Porter, Charles. "The First Shot at Gettysburg," *The National Tribune*, May 19, 1904.

The Proceedings of the Buford Memorial Association. New York: privately published, 1895.

Purifoy, John. "The Myth of the Confederate Hollow Square", *Confederate Veteran*, Vol. 33 (February, 1925), 53-55.

Redman, William H. "Address of W. H. Redman at the Dedication of the Monument to the 12th Illinois Cavalry." *Illinois Monuments at Gettysburg.* Springfield: H.W. Rokker, 1892: 31-33.

Robertson, John R. "Opening the Battle. How I Saw the First Shot Fired at Gettysburg," *The National Tribune*, April 2, 1903.

Rosengarten, Maj. Joseph G. "General Reynolds' Last Battle", included in *The Annals of the War*. Philadelphia: Times Publishing Co., 1879: 60-66.

Rodenbough, Theophilus F. "Cavalry War Lessons", *Journal of the United States Cavalry Association*, Vol. 2 (1889), 103-123.

Schurz, Carl. *The Reminiscences of Carl Schurz.* 3 vols. New York: Doubleday, Page & Co., 1907-1908.

Scott, James K. P. *The Story of the Battles at Gettysburg.* Harrisburg, PA: The Telegraph Press, 1927.

Shears, G. W. and S. Bronson, "The 12th Illinois Cavalry. Its Part in the Gettysburg Campaign," *The National Tribune*, February 5, 1891.

Skelly, Daniel A. *A Boy's Experiences During the Battles of Gettysburg.* Gettysburg, PA: privately published, 1932.

Skiff, Albert O. "The First Shot at Gettysburg," *The National Tribune*, May 13, 1915.

Smith, Thomas J. "Two Spies Instead of One," *The National Tribune*, May 1, 1884.

Smith, W. H. "Opening the Battle of Gettysburg," *The National Tribune*, June 5, 1913.

"Some Stories of the Great Battle," *Gettysburg Compiler*, January 14, 1903.

Stanford, Martha Gerber, ed. *Dear Rachel: The Civil War Letters of Daniel Peck.* Ashville, NY: Berrybook Press, 1993.

"Statue of Gen. Buford," *Rock Island Argus*, June 4, 1895.

Stevens, Charles A. *Berdan's Sharpshooters in the Army of the Potomac 1861-1865*. St. Paul, MN: privately published, 1892.

Styple, William B., ed. *Generals in Bronze: Interviewing the Commanders of the Civil War*. Kearny, NJ: Belle Grove Publishing, 2005.

——. *Writing & Fighting from the Army of Northern Virginia: A Collection of Confederate Soldier Correspondence*. Kearny, NJ: Belle Grove Publishing, 2003.

Supplement to the Official Records of the Union and Confederate Armies. 100 vols. Wilmington, N. C.: Broadfoot, 1995.

Swallow, W. H. "The First Day at Gettysburg," *Southern Bivouac* N.S. 1 (December 1885): 441-442.

Swett, Joel B. "The Eighth New York Cavalry at Gettysburg." *The National Tribune*, April 3, 1884.

Taylor, Dr. Gray Nelson, ed. *Saddle and Saber: The Letters of Civil War Cavalryman Corporal Nelson Taylor*. Bowie, MD: Heritage Books, 1993.

Taylor, Walter H. "The Campaign in Pennsylvania," included in *The Annals of the War*. Philadelphia: Times Publishing Co., 1879: 305-318.

Tevis, C. V. *The History of the Fighting Fourteenth: Published in Commemoration of the Fiftieth Anniversary of the Muster of the Regiment into the United States Service, May 23, 1861*. Brooklyn, NY: Brooklyn Eagle Press, 1911.

"The Fifty-Second Regiment. Its North Carolina Campaigns," *Charlotte Observer*, June 2, 1895.

"The Record of the Seventh," *Charlotte Observer*, May 12, 1895.

"The Soldiers' Reunion," *The Daily Courier*, October 15, 1885.

The War of the Rebellion: A Compilation of the Official Records of the Union and Confederate Armies, 128 vols. in 3 series. Washington, D.C.: U.S. Government Printing Office, 1889.

Tidball, John C. *The Artillery Service in the War of the Rebellion*. Ed. by Lawrence M. Kaplan. Yardley, PA: Westholme Publishing, 2011.

Tremain, Henry Edwin. *The Last Hours of Sheridan's Cavalry*. New York: Bonnell, Silver & Bowers, 1904.

Trotter, M.L. "Opening the Ball at Gettysburg," *The National Tribune*, January 31, 1884.

Turney, J.B. "The First Tennessee at Gettysburg", *Confederate Veteran*, Vol. 8 (December 1900): 535-537.

Walker, Maj. Gen. Francis A. *History of the Second Army Corps*. New York: Charles Scribner's Sons, 1886.

Weaver, Augustus C. *Third Indiana Cavalry*. Greenwood, IN: privately published, 1919.

Weld, Stephen Minot. *War Diary and Letters of Stephen Minot Weld, 1861-1865*. 2 vols. Boston: Riverside Press, 1912.

"Where the Fight Began: A Monument to Gen. Buford on Gettysburg's Battleground," *New York Times*, July 1, 1895.

Willett, Frank E. "Another Gettysburg. A Comrade Who Says the 8th New York Cavalry Opened the Great Battle," *The National Tribune*, December 1, 1892.

Wilson, James H. "Oration of Maj. Gen. James H. Wilson, July 1, 1895, at Dedication of Buford Monument at Gettysburg", *Journal of the United States Cavalry Association*, Vol. 8, No. 30. September, 1895, 171-183.

Wise, Jennings Cropper. *The Long Arm of Lee, or the History of the Artillery of the Army of Northern Virginia*. 2 vols. Lynchburg, VA: J. Bell Co., 1915.

Wood, George. "Capt. John Allen," *Confederate Veteran* 22 (1914), 35.

Young, Louis G. "Pettigrew's Brigade at Gettysburg, 1-3 July 1863," included in Walter Clark, ed. *Histories of the Several Regiments and Battalions from North Carolina in the Great War, 1861-65.* 5 vols. Goldsboro, NC: 1901, 5:113-135.

SECONDARY SOURCES

Acres, Mark. "Harry Heth and the First Morning at Gettysburg." *Gettysburg Magazine: Articles of Lasting Historical Interest*, No.46 (July 2012): 19-35.

Adams, William G., Jr. "Spencers at Gettysburg: Fact or Fiction." *Military Affairs* 29 (1965): 41-42, 56.

Babits, Lawrence E. *A Devil of a Whipping: The Battle of Cowpens.* Chapel Hill: University of North Carolina Press, 1998.

Babits, Lawrence E. and Joshua B. Howard, *Long, Obstinate, and Bloody: The Battle of Guilford Courthouse.* Chapel Hill: University of North Carolina Press, 2009.

Bates, Samuel P. *The Battle of Gettysburg.* Philadelphia: T. H. Davis & Co., 1875.

Bennett, Gerald R. *Days of Uncertainty and Dread.* Camp Hill, PA: Planks Suburban Press, 1994.

Bigler, David L. and Will Bagley. *The Mormon Rebellion: America's First Civil War, 1857-1858.* Norman: University of Oklahoma Press, 2011.

Bilby, Joseph G. *A Revolution in Arms: A History of the First Repeating Rifles.* Yardley, PA: Westholme Publishing, 2006.

Bishop, Randy. *The Tennessee Brigade.* Gretna, LA: Pelican Publishing Co., 2010.

Blackwell, Samuel M., Jr. *In the First Line of Battle: The 12th Illinois Cavalry in the Civil War.* DeKalb, IL: Northern Illinois University Press, 2002.

Brown, J. Willard. *The Signal Corps, U.S.A. in the War of the Rebellion.* Boston: U.S. Veteran Signal Corps Association, 1896.

Buford, Marcus Bainbridge. *History and Genealogy of the Buford Family in America.* LaBelle, Missouri, 1903.

Busey, John W. and David G. Martin. *Regimental Strengths and Losses at Gettysburg.* Hightstown, NJ: Longstreet House, 1994.

Carmichael, Peter S. *Lee's Young Artillerist: William R. J. Pegram.* Charlottesville: University Press of Virginia, 1995.

Casstevens, Frances H. *The 28th North Carolina Infantry: A Civil War History and Roster.* Jefferson, NC: McFarland & Co., 2008.

Coddington, Edwin B. *The Gettysburg Campaign: A Study in Command.* New York: Charles Scribner's Sons, 1979.

Cole, Philip M. *Civil War Artillery at Gettysburg.* Orrtanna, PA: Colecraft Industries, 2002.

Cullum, George W. *Biographical Register of the Officers and Graduates of the U.S. Military Academy*, 2 vols. New York: D. Van Nostrand. 1868.

Dalton, Andrew I. *Beyond the Run: The Emanuel Harmon Farm at Gettysburg.* Gettysburg, PA: Ten Roads Publishing, 2013.

Eddy, T. M. *The Patriotism of Illinois.* 2 vols. Chicago: Clarke & Co., 1865.

Fishel, Edwin C. *The Secret War for the Union: The Untold Story of Military Intelligence in the Civil War.* Boston: Houghton-Mifflin, 1996.

Foote, Shelby. *Fredericksburg to Meridian.* Vol. 2 of *The Civil War: A Narrative.* 3 vols. New York: Random House, 1963.

Gillispie, James. *Cape Fear Confederates: The 18th North Carolina Regiment in the Civil War.* Jefferson, NC: McFarland & Co., 2012.

Girardi, Robert I., comp. *The Civil War Generals: Comrades, Peers, Rivals in Their Own Words.* Minneapolis: Zenith Press, 2013.

Girvan, Jeffrey M. *The 55th North Carolina in the Civil War: A History and Roster.* Jefferson, NC: McFarland & Co., 2006.

Gottfried, Bradley M. *The Artillery of Gettysburg.* Nashville, TN: Cumberland House, 2008.

——. "To Fail Twice: Brockenbrough's Brigade at Gettysburg." *Gettysburg Magazine: Articles of Lasting Historical Interest,* No. 23 (July 2000): 66-75.

Gragg, Rod. *Covered with Glory: The 26th North Carolina Infantry at the Battle of Gettysburg.* New York: Harper Collins, 2000.

Haines, Douglas Craig. "Lee's Advance Along the Cashtown Road." *Gettysburg Magazine: Articles of Lasting Historical Interest,* Issue No. 23 (July 2000): 6-29.

Hall, Winfield Scott. *The Captain: William Cross Hazelton.* Riverside, IL: privately published, 1994.

Hardy, Michael C. *The Thirty-seventh North Carolina Troops Tar Heels in the Army of Northern Virginia.* Jefferson, NC: McFarland & Co., 2003.

Hassler, Warren W., Jr. *Crisis at the Crossroads: The First Day at Gettysburg.* Tuscaloosa, AL: University of Alabama, 1970.

Heitman, Francis E. *Historical Register and Dictionary of the United States Army.* 2 vols. Washington, D.C.: Government Printing Office, 1903.

Hennessy, John J. *Return to Bull Run.* New York: Simon & Schuster, 1992.

Herdegen, Lance J. *Those Damned Black Hats! The Iron Brigade in the Gettysburg Campaign.* El Dorado Hills, CA: Savas Beatie, 2008.

Hess, Earl J. *Lee's Tar Heels: The Pettigrew; Kirkland-MacRae Brigade.* Chapel Hill: University of North Carolina Press, 2002.

Hessler, James A. *Sickles at Gettysburg: The Controversial Civil War General Who Committed Murder, Abandoned Little Round Top, and Declared Himself the Hero of Gettysburg.* El Dorado Hills, CA: Savas Beatie, 2009.

History of Cumberland and Adams Counties, Containing History of the Counties, Their Townships, Towns, Villages, Schools, Churches, Industries, Etc., Portraits of Early Settlers and Prominent Men; Biographies. Chicago: Warner, Beers & Co., 1886

Hyde, Bill. "Did You Get There? Capt. Samuel Johnston's Reconnaissance at Gettysburg." *Gettysburg Magazine: Articles of Lasting Historical Interest,* No. 29 (July 2003): 86-93.

Imhof, John D. *Gettysburg Day Two: A Study in Maps.* Baltimore: Butternut & Blue, 1999.

Jones, J. Keith. *Georgia Remembers Gettysburg: A Collection of First-Hand Accounts Written by Georgia Soldiers.* Gettysburg, PA: Ten Roads Publishing, 2013.

Krick, Robert K. *The Fredericksburg Artillery.* Lynchburg, VA: H.E. Howard, 1986.

——. *Stonewall Jackson at Cedar Mountain.* Chapel Hill: University of North Carolina Press, 1990.

Kross, Gary M. "Fight Like the Devil to Hold Your Own", *Blue & Gray,* Vol. 12, Issue 3 (February, 1995), 9-24, 48-58.

Krumwiede, John F. *Disgrace at Gettysburg: The Arrest and Court Martial of Brigadier General Thomas A. Rowley.* Jefferson, NC: McFarland & Co., 2006.

Laino, Philip. *Gettysburg Campaign Atlas.* Dayton, OH: Gatehouse Press, 2009.

Lang, Theodore F. *Loyal West Virginia From 1861-1865.* Baltimore, MD: The Deutsch Publishing Co., 1895.

Langellier, John P., Hamilton Cox and Brian C. Pohanka, eds., *Myles Keogh: The Life and Legend of an "Irish Dragoon" in the Seventh Cavalry. Montana and the West* Series, vol. 9 El Segundo, California: Upton & Sons, 1991.

Lindsley, John Berrien, ed. *The Military Annals of Tennessee. Confederates. First Series: Embracing a Review of Military Operations with Regimental Histories and Memorial Roles, Compiled from Original and Official Sources.* Nashville: J. M. Lindsley & Co., 1886.

Longacre, Edward G. *General John Buford: A Military Biography.* Conshohocken, PA: Combined Books, 1995.

——. *The Cavalry at Gettysburg: A Tactical Study of Mounted Operations During the Civil War's Pivotal Campaign, 9 June-14 July 1863.* Rutherford, N. J.: Fairleigh-Dickinson University Press, 1986.

Martin, David G. *Gettysburg, July 1.* Conshohocken, PA: Combined Books, 1995.

McLean, James L. *Cutler's Brigade at Gettysburg.* Baltimore: Butternut & Blue, 1994.

Miers, Earl Schenck and Richard A. Brown, eds. *Gettysburg.* New Brunswick, NJ: Rutgers Univ. Press, 1948.

Miller, Francis Trevelyan, ed. *The Photographic History of the Civil War: Thousands of Scenes Photographed1861-65.* 10 vols. New York: Review of Reviews Co., 1911.

Miller, J. Michael. "Perrin's Brigade on July 1, 1863." *Gettysburg Magazine: Articles of Lasting Historical Interest*, No. 13 (July 1995): 22-32.

Mingus, Scott. *Flames Beyond Gettysburg: The Confederate Expedition to the Susquehanna River, June 1863.* El Dorado Hills, CA: Savas Beatie, 2011.

Muir, Rory. *Tactics and the Experience of Battle in the Age of Napoleon.* New Haven, CT: Yale University Press, 1998.

Murray, R. L. "Reynolds' 1st New York, Battery L, at Gettysburg." *Gettysburg Magazine: Articles of Lasting Historical Interest*, No. 47 (July 2012): 21-34.

Newton, George W. *Silent Sentinels: A Reference Guide to the Artillery at Gettysburg.* El Dorado Hills, CA: Savas Beatie, 2005.

Nolan, Alan. "Gettysburg's Hoosier Horsemen: The Third Indiana Cavalry." *Gettysburg Magazine: Articles of Lasting Historical Interest*, No. 25 (July 2001): 40-42.

Nosworthy Brent. *With Musket, Cannon and Sword: Battle Tactics of Napoleon and His Enemies.* New York: Sarpedon, 1996.

O'Brien, Kevin F. "'Give Them Another Volley, Boys': Biddle's Brigade Defends the Union Left on July 1, 1863," *Gettysburg Magazine: Articles of Lasting Historical Interest*, No. 19 (July 1998): 37-52.

"Once Again for Jerome B. Wheeler," *The Aspen Times*, December 19, 1985.

O'Neill, Robert F., Jr. *The Cavalry Battles of Aldie, Middleburg and Upperville: Small but Important Riots, June 10-27, 1863.* Lynchburg, VA: H. E. Howard, 1993.

Osborne, Seward R. *Holding the Left at Gettysburg: The 20th New York State Militia on July 1, 1863.* Hightstown, NJ: Longstreet House, 1990.

Paul, R. Eli. *Blue Water Creek and First Sioux War 1854-1856.* Norman: University of Oklahoma Press, 2004.

Petruzzi, J. David. "A Bloody Summer for Horsemen," *Civil War Times* (June 2013): 30-37.

——. "Cemetery Hill's Forgotten Savior: Union General John Buford and his Troopers Faced Down Richard Ewell's Infantry on the Afternoon of July 1 at Gettysburg," *Civil War Times* (October 2010): 50-51.

——. "John Buford by the Book," *America's Civil War* (July 2005): 24-28, 60.

——. "Opening the Ball at Gettysburg: The Shot that Rang for 50 Years," *America's Civil War* (July 2006): 30-36.

Petruzzi, J. David and Steven Stanley. *The Complete Gettysburg Guide: Walking and Driving Tours of the Battlefield, Town, Cemeteries, Field Hospital Sites, and other Topics of Historical Interest*. El Dorado Hills, CA: Savas Beatie, 2009.

——. *The Gettysburg Campaign in Numbers and Losses: Synopses, Orders of Battle, Strengths, Casualties, and Maps, June 9-July 14, 1863*. El Dorado Hills, CA: Savas Beatie, 2013.

Pfanz, Harry W. *Gettysburg—The First Day*. Chapel Hill: University of North Carolina Press, 2001.

——. *Gettysburg: The Second Day*. Chapel Hill: University of North Carolina Press, 1988.

Phipps, Michael and John S. Peterson *"The Devil's to Pay": General John Buford, USA*. Gettysburg, PA: Farnsworth House Impressions, 1995.

Powell, David A. "A Reconnaissance Gone Awry: Capt. Samuel R. Johnston's Fateful Trip to Little Round Top." *Gettysburg Magazine: Articles of Lasting Historical Interest*, No. 23 (July 2000): 88-99.

Powell, William H. *Officers of the Army and Navy Who Served in the Civil War*. Philadelphia: L.R. Hamersly & Co., 1893.

Ray, Fred L. *Shock Troops of the Confederacy: The Sharpshooter Battalions of the Army of Northern Virginia*. Asheville, NC: CFS Press, 2006.

Robbins, James S. *Last in Their Class: Custer, Pickett and the Goats of West Point*. New York: Encounter Books, 2006.

Rodenbough, Theophilus F. *The Bravest Five Hundred of '61*. New York: G.W. Dillingham, 1891.

Sauers, Richard A. *Gettysburg: The Meade-Sickles Controversy*. Washington, D.C.: Potomac Books, 2003.

Schiller, Laurence D. "A Taste of Northern Steel: The Evolution of Federal Cavalry Tactics 1861-1865," *North & South*, Vol. 2, No. 2 (January 1999): 30-46.

Shue, Richard S. *Morning at Willoughby Run*. Gettysburg, PA: Thomas Publications, 1995.

Shultz, David and Richard Rollins. "The Most Accurate Fire Ever Witnessed: Federal Horse Artillery in the Pennsylvania Campaign." *Gettysburg Magazine: Articles of Lasting Historical Interest*, No. 33 (July 2005): 44-81.

Skidmore, Warren and Donna Kaminsky. *Lord Dunmore's Little War of 1774: His Captains and Their Men Who Opened Up Kentucky & The West To American Settlement*. Berwyn Heights, MD: Heritage Books, 2002.

Smith, Mark A. and Wade Sokolosky. *No Such Army Since the Days of Julius Caesar: Sherman's Carolinas Campaign from Fayetteville to Averasboro*. Celina, OH: Ironclad Publishing, 2006.

Smith, Timothy H. *Farms at Gettysburg: The Fields of Battle*. Gettysburg, PA: Thomas Publications, 2007.

Stahl, Joseph. "Pvt. James H. Phillips, Company A, 12th Illinois Cavalry." *Gettysburg Magazine: Articles of Lasting Historical Interest*, Issue No. 35 (July 2006): 36-38.

Starr, Stephen Z. *The Union Cavalry in the Civil War*. 3 vols. Baton Rouge: Louisiana State University Press, 1979.

Stine, James H. *History of the Army of the Potomac*. Philadelphia: J. B. Rodgers Printing Co., 1892.

Storch, Marc and Beth. "'What a Deadly Trap We Were In': Archer's Brigade on July 1, 1863." *Gettysburg Magazine: Articles of Lasting Historical Interest*, No. 6 (January 1991): 13-28.

Tagg, Larry. *The Generals of Gettysburg: The Leaders of America's Greatest Battle*. Mason City, IA: Savas Publishing, 1998.

Thomas, Sarah Sites, Tim Smith, Gary Kross and Dean S. Thomas. *Fairfield in the Civil War*. Gettysburg, PA: Thomas Publications, 2011.

Trauschweizer, Ingo. *The Cold War U.S. Army: Building Deterrence for Limited War*. Lawrence: University Press of Kansas, 2008.

Venner, William Thomas. *The 7th Tennessee Infantry in the Civil War*. Jefferson, NC: McFarland & Co., 2013.

Walker, General Francis A. *General Hancock*. New York: D. Appleton & Co., 1894.

Warner, Ezra J. *Generals in Blue: Lives of the Union Commanders*. Baton Rouge: Louisiana State University Press, 1964.

———. *Generals in Gray: Lives of the Confederate Commanders*. Baton Rouge: Louisiana State University Press, 1959.

Watson, D. Alexander. "The Spencer Repeating Rifle at Gettysburg." *Gettysburg Magazine: Articles of Lasting Historical Interest*, No. 15 (July 1996): 24-30.

Welsh, Jack D., M.D. *Medical Histories of Union Generals*. Kent, OH: Kent State University Press, 1997.

Wert, Jeffry D. *Cavalryman of the Lost Cause: A Biography of J.E.B. Stuart*. New York: Simon & Schuster, 2008.

Wickwire, Franklin and Mary. *Cornwallis and the War of Independence*. London: Faber and Faber, 1970.

Williams, T. P. *The Mississippi Brigade of Brig. Gen. Joseph R. Davis*. Dayton, OH: Morningside House, 1999.

Winschel, Terrence J. "Part 1: Heavy Was Their Loss: Joe Davis's Brigade at Gettysburg." *Gettysburg Magazine: Articles of Lasting Historical Interest*, No. 2 (December 1989): 5-14.

Wittenberg, Eric J. "An Analysis of the Buford Manuscripts", *Gettysburg Magazine: Articles of Lasting Historical Interest*, No. 15 (July 1996): 7-24.

———. "And Everything is Lovely and the Goose Hangs High: John Buford and the Hanging of Confederate Spies During the Gettysburg Campaign," *The Gettysburg Magazine: Articles of Lasting Historical Interest*, No. 18 (January 1998): 5-14.

———. "John Buford and the Gettysburg Campaign." *Gettysburg Magazine: Articles of Lasting Historical Interest*, No. 11 (July 1994): 19-55.

———. *The Battle of Brandy Station: North America's Largest Cavalry Battle*. Charleston, SC: The History Press, 2010.

———. "The Truth About the Withdrawal of Brig. Gen. John Buford's Cavalry, July 2, 1863." *Gettysburg Magazine: Articles of Lasting Historical Interest*, No. 37 (July 2007): 71-82.

———. *The Union Cavalry Comes of Age: Hartwood Church to Brandy Station 1863*. Dulles, VA: Brassey's, 2003.

Wittenberg, Eric J. and J. David Petruzzi. *Plenty of Blame to Go Around: Jeb Stuart's Controversial Ride to Gettysburg*. El Dorado Hills, CA: Savas Beatie, 2006.

Wittenberg, Eric J., J. David Petruzzi and Michael F. Nugent. *One Continuous Fight: The Retreat from Gettysburg and the Pursuit of Lee's Army of Northern Virginia, July 4-14, 1863*. El Dorado Hills, CA: Savas Beatie, 2008.

Wynstra, Robert J. *The Rashness of That Hour: Politics, Gettysburg, and the Downfall of Confederate Brigadier General Alfred Iverson*. El Dorado Hills, CA: Savas Beatie, 2010.

WEBSITES

Caughey, Don. "Reserve Brigade Attrition in the Gettysburg Campaign," http://regularcavalryincivilwar.wordpress.com/2013/06/20/reserve-brigade-attrition-in-the-ge ttysburg-campaign/

Complete Sun and Moon Data for One Day, U.S. Naval Observatory, http://aa.usnonavy.mil/data/docs/RS_OneDay.php

Miller, John A. "The Skirmish of Fountaindale," http://southmountaincw.wordpress.com/2010/03/23/the-skirmish-of-fountaindale/

Petruzzi, J. David. "Faded Hoofbeats—Marcellus Jones, 8th Illinois Cavalry," http://petruzzi.wordpress.com/2007/05/31/faded-hoofbeats-marcellus-jones-8th-illinois-cav alry/
——."Faded Thunder," http://petruzzi.wordpress.com/2007/02/23/faded-thunder/

A. S. Van de Graff to his wife, July 8, 1863, http://historysites.com/civilwar/units/5albn/Vandegraaffltr.htm

Wittenberg, Eric J. "Bvt. Maj. Jerome B. Wheeler," http://civilwarcavalry.com/?p=3864

Index

Adams, Charles Francis, 200n

Aldie, battle of, 30, 32, 211

Alexander, Andrew J., 191

Alexander, Edward Porter, 184

Anderson, James Q., 96, 97, 98, *photo*, 98

Anderson, Richard H., 52, 60

Antietam campaign, 12, 14, 21, 24

Archer, James J., and his brigade, 48, 74n, 75, 75n, 76n, 104-107, 118, 133, 181, 207, 220; morning, July 1, 77, 79, 86-88; brigade pushes Wadsworth to Seminary Ridge, 119; captured, 119; *photo*, 76

Armstrong, Frank C., 194

Army of Northern Virginia, 27, 29-30, 43, 55, 68, 74n, 87n, 139n, 154, 162, 180, 183

Army of Tennessee, 5, 216

Army of the Cumberland, 188, 209

Army of the Mississippi, 2

Army of the Potomac, 12, 14n, 17, 26, 28n, 30, 32, 35-36, 46, 57, 70-70n, 86-87, 94, 109n, 111-113, 114-114n, 138n, 139n, 149, 155, 157, 160, 164, 168, 172, 182, 185-186, 194, 200n

Army of Virginia, 11, 12

Ash Hollow, battle of, 8-8n, 184

Augur, Christopher C., 192

Averasboro, battle of, 215

Bachelder, John B., 220

Baker, John, 97-98

Baker, Lafayette, 24n

Baltimore Pike, 163, 170n, 177

Banks, Nathaniel P., 11, 223

Baxter, Henry, 129

Beall, William N. R., 7

Bean, Theodore W., 40, 115, 158

Beardsley, William E., 47, 100, 205

Beck, Elias, 71

Bell, James A., 72, 195

Bellamy, Flavius J., 95, 117, 143

Belmont Schoolhouse Ridge, 54, 79, 90, 92, 94, 229

Belo Alfred H., 101; *photo*, 100

Bentley, Wilber, 115

Berdan, Hiram, 166-166n, 168

Betts, Thomas E., 207

Beveridge, John L., 18n, 33, 38, 80, 87, 104, 106, 116, 132-132n, 133, 137, 150, 152, 157, 205, 241; *photo*, 133

Beverly Ford, skirmish at, 32

Biddle, Alexander, 136

Biddle, Chapman, 132-133, 136-137, 143, 185

Big Round Top, 163

Blackford, Eugene, 128-129

"Bleeding Kansas," 9

Blocker's Schoolhouse, 83

Blunt, John W., 200-201

Boland, E. T., 78, 107

Boonsboro, Maryland, 32, 38, 39-39n

Booth, John Wilkes, 24n

Bouldin, Edwin E., 96

Bowles, John S., 207

Braddock, James, 2n

Bradshaw, William T., 164

Bragg, Braxton, 4

Branch, Lawrence O'Bryan, 223

Brander, Thomas A., 207

Brandy Station, battle of, 5n, 7n, 20, 28-28n, 37n, 161, 172, 187, 199

Brice's Cross Roads, battle of, 4

Bristoe Station campaign, 188

Broadhead, Sarah, 58

Brockenbrough, John, 74n, 76, 87-87n, 106, 207; *photo*, 88

Brown, Joseph, 142

Brown, Samuel W., 164

Bryan farmhouse, 148

Buck, Daniel, 80-81

Buell, Don Carlos, 3n

Buford Memorial Association, 197, 199-200; *photo*, 198

Buford, Abraham, 3n, 4, 5-5n, 8, 188; *photo*, 4

Buford, Anne Bannister Watson, 1, 5n

Buford, James Duke, John Buford's son, 8

Buford, James Monroe, 1, 199

Buford, John Jr., 3n, 11n, 38, 44n, 85, 110n, 112n, 119, 150, 152, 161, 168n, 170, 178n, 205, 240; born in Woodford County, Kentucky, 1; early years, 1, 5-6; Gibbon's "best cavalryman I ever saw" quote, 1; parents, 1; Napoleon Bonaparte Buford, 2; Abraham Buford, 3; Henry Heth, 4; Brandy Station, battle of, 5n,

7n, 28, 172; appointment to West Point, 6; class standing, 6-7; Knox College, 6; "Patsy" Duke, wife, 7, 8n, 188n; West Point, 7n; "Grey Eagle", 8; Ash Hollow, battle of, 8; dare-devil of a rider, 8; fond of riding, 8; quartermaster, Second Dragoons, 8; Sioux Punitive Expedition, 8; Camp Floyd, Utah, 9; Cavalry School for Practice at Carlisle, Pennsylvania, 9; decided to remain loyal to the Union, 9; Fort Riley, Kansas, 9; promoted to Captain, 9; Utah Expedition, 9; 2nd U.S. Cavalry, 11; appointed to the inspector general's office, 11; injury to right knee, 11; promoted to brigadier general of volunteers, 11; Second Bull Run campaign, 11-11n, 12; Antietam campaign, 12; one of a handful of Pope's senior commanders to remain in good standing, 12; commander 1st Division, Cavalry Corps, 13; assigned to McClellan's staff, 14; court-martial duty, 14, 15; Fredericksburg campaign, 14; assigned to command reserve brigade, 15; commander of 1st Division, Cavalry Corps, 15, 17; rheumatism, 15; hangs a spy, 16, 34, 35-35n; Lyman quote, 17; mutual respect with Devin, 22; Calef, 24; Wesley Merritt's Reserve Brigade, 25; Kupperville, 30; taught by Dennis Hart Mahan, 30; Aldie, battle of, 33; Leesburg, Virginia, 33; ordered by Pleasonton to hold Gettysburg, 35-36; hears Hooker is relieved of command, 36-37; detached his Reserve Brigade, 37; Merritt, 37; gathering intelligence, 39; march via Boonsboro, 39; Second Dragoons, 39; announced that both armies would concentrate at Gettysburg, 40; June 30, 42, 44, 47, 56, 57n, 58, 61; arrives at Emmitsburg, 46-46n; Fairfield, 46; meeting with Reynolds, 46n; arrives at Gettysburg, 47; Tate's Blue Eagle Hotel, 50, 52, 56, 68 -69, 81, 84, 109, 225; June 30 note to Reynolds, 52-53; Lutheran Seminary, 53, 56; has Gamble and Devin camp at the Lutheran Seminary, 54; hold until Reynolds' arrival, 55; plans delaying action north and west of Gettysburg, 55; has Gamble pick a defensive position, 56; reports Confederate infantry to Pleasonton, 60; night of June 30, 62, 64, 68, 70-71; vidette posts, 64; Dickinson, Joseph, 68; intelligence report to Reynolds, 68; Reserve Brigade, 68;

intelligence report from Buford, 69; morning, July 1, 74, 77, 84-85, 90, 96, 108; served with Heth in the Regular Army, 75, 184; has Jerome in the cupola of the lutheran Seminary, 81; meets with Wadsworth, 84; Belmont Schoolhouse Ridge, 92, 94; slows Confederate advance to a crawl, 93; gains two hours of time, 95; orders Devin to hold area north of the railroad cut, 101; "almost omnipresent", 103; "consummate generalship", 104; "where is Reynolds?" 108; observes Reynolds approaching, 109; "I recon I can.," 110; the "the devil's to pay!", 110; Reynolds arrives, 110; Reynold's validated decision to stand and fight, 111, 114; orders Gamble to withdraw from the Seminary, 117; finds Reynold's shot, 118; message to Meade about Reynold's arrival, 118; notice of Howard's arrival, 120; asks to relieve Calef's battery, 124; hung on just long enough, 130; requests Hancock come forward, 137; places Gamble's brigade along the Fairfield Road, 140; compliments the 8th New York Cavalry, 144; ordered to Doubleday's suppot, 148; orders Gamble to the Emmitsburg Road, 148; Seminary Ridge, 153; feinted charge, 154; East Cemetery Hill, 155; Gamble's men bore the brunt of the fighting, 155; every reason to be proud of his men, 156; stops at Calef's camp in the peach orchard, 156; night of July 1-2, 157-158, 160, 161-161n, 163; worries about the state of his command, 161; Pitzer's Woods, 167; Cemetery Ridge, 170; a bloody endeavor, 172; command is ordered to leave the battlefield, 174; ordered to Taneytown and Westminster, 174; ordered to Westminster by Pleasonton, 174, 176-177; pursuit of Lee's Army, 180; performance at Gettysburg, 181-183, 185-186; held the high ground, 183; nickname "Old Steadfast", 183, 196, 200n, 204; sound decisions, 184; compliments from Hancock, 185; compliments from Pleasonton, 185; credit for choosing the battlefield, 185; "Honest John", 186; Walker's commentary, 186; complaint to Pleasonton about Slocum, 187; did not have time to bask in glory, 187; Lee's retreat to Virginia, 187; on leave in Kentucky, 187; assigned to command the Cavalry Corps of the Army of the Cumberland, 188-190; departs on 10 days leave, 188; lost a daughter, 188; returns home to Georgetown, Kentucky, 188; sense of humor, 188; rheumatism plagued him, 189; takes a leave of absence, 189; terribly ill, 189; trying to get his wife to Washington D.C., 189; typhoid fever, 189; condidion deteriorates, 190; dying, 190-191; oath of office, 190n; died in Keogh's arms, 191; died on December 16, 1863, 191; last words, 191; funeral at West Point, 192; funeral in Washington, D.C., 192; honorary pallbearers in Washington, 192; buried at West Point, 193; legacy, 193-194, 196; West Point funeral, 193; deserves accolades, 196; Buford Memorial Association, 197-200; statue, 201; statue is dedicated, 201, 203, 204; Spencer rifles, 208-211; nature of defense, 213-216; Cemetery Hill, 218, 220; forming a square, 222; Schmucker Hall, 226; monument, 231; *photo*, as a captain, 10; *photo*, 13; *photo of statue*, 202, 204

Buford, Martha "Patsy" McDowell Duke, 7-8, 134, 191, 192-192n, 199; *photo*, 7

Buford, Napoleon Bonaparte, 2, 3-3n, 6; *photo*, 2

Buford, Pattie McDowell, Buford's daughter, 8

Buford, Simeon, 1-1n, 2n, 8

Buford, Thomas Jefferson, 1, 2n, 8, 199, 200n; *photo*, 198

Burgwyn, Jr., Henry K, 207

Burns, John, 98-98n, 233; *monument*, 232

Burnside, Ambrose E., 14, 187, 188n

Burrows, John, 160

Bushman's Hill, 161

Butterfield, Daniel, 174, 177

Calef, John H., 24, 40, 43, 86, 92-93, 95, 105, 108, 115, 120, 124, 126, 140, 144-145, 156, 164-164n, 167, 174, 184, 197n, 199, 203-204, 206, 233, 241; Antietam campaign, 24; Peninsula Campaign, 24; Second Bull Run campaign, 24; West Point, 24; battery, 67; posted along Chambersburg Pike, 90-91; observes Buford, 104; performance at Gettysburg, 183; spikes a gun, 203; *monument*, 231-232; *photo*, 23, 198

Camp Floyd, Utah, 9

Carlisle Road, 96, 97n

Carlisle, Pennsylvania, 56, 69, 120, 130

Casey, Silas P., 192

Cashtown Pass, 60

Cashtown, Pennsylvania, 32, 43-44, 46-46n, 47-48, 52, 55, 57n, 58-60, 64, 68, 116, 126

Cavalry School for Practice at Carlisle, Pennsylvania, 3, 9

Cavetown, Maryland, 39

Cedar Creek, battle of, 123

Cedar Mountain, 223, 224-224n

Cemetery Hill, 54, 110, 138n, 143, 145, 147-148, 150, 152-154, 157, 182, 218

Cemetery Ridge, 112, 163, 167, 170-170n, 171

Chamberlaine, William W., 60

Chambersburg Pike, 47, 56-58, 64, 66-67, 73-74, 77-78, 81-83, 85, 90-91, 96-97, 100-101, 108-109, 112, 114, 119-120, 126, 137, 138, 143, 193, 203, 221, 226, 228, 230-231, 232, 240; *photo*, 80

Chambersburg, Pennsylvania, 32, 54, 57, 60, 120, 186

Chancellorsville, battle of, 15, 26, 71n, 109n, 139n, 152n, 161

Chapman, George H., 42, 86, 145, 158, 167, 172, 179, 205; *photo*, 144

Cheney, Jasper, 167

Christian, William S., 207

Christie, Daniel H., 206

Clendennin, David, 18n

Cobean, Samuel, 98, 129, 240, 232, 238, 239, photo, 99

Coffin, Benjamin J., 163-164, 167

Confederate Military Units

Alabama
   5th Infantry Battalion, 86, 88, 90, 128, 207
   13th Infantry, 77-79, 86, 89, 107, 207

Louisiana
   Donaldson Artillery, 57

Mississippi
   2nd Infantry, 86, 115
   10th Infantry, 76n, 207
   11th Infantry, 207
   42nd Infantry, 42, 86, 115, 207

North Carolina
   1st Infantry, 152n
   3rd Infantry, 139n
   5th Infantry, 128, 206
   7th Infantry, 153, 220-221
   11th Infantry, 57, 59, 207
   12th Infantry, 56n, 206
   20th Infantry, 206
   23rd Infantry, 206
   26th Infantry, 57, 59, 207
   28th Infantry, 152n, 223
   37th Infantry, 152
   7th Infantry, 57, 59, 207

52nd Infantry, 42, 57n, 59, 105, 132-134, 207, 241

55th Infantry, 87, 100-100n, 101, 207

South Carolina
  1st Infantry, 143
  14th Infantry, 139n, 142
  Zimmerman's Battery, 207

Tennessee
  1st Infantry, 86, 105, 207
  7th Infantry, 48, 77, 86, 90, 92, 105
  14th Infantry, 86, 207

Virginia
  6th Cavalry, 221
  11th Infantry, 87
  14th Cavalry, 96
  22nd Infantry Battalion, 87, 207
  26th Infantry, 87
  35th Battalion of Cavalry, 32, 34
  40th Infantry, 87-87n, 207
  45th Infantry, 74n
  47th Infantry, 76, 87, 207
  52nd Infantry, 87
  55th Infantry, 207
  Brander's Battery, 207
  Crenshaw's Battery, 207
  Fredericksburg Artillery, 83, 86
  Marye's Battery, 207
  McGraw's Battery, 207

Conger, Seymour Beach, 23, 24n, 205; *photo*, 22

Connally, John K., 207

Cooke, Philip St. George, 3n, 8, 9n

Copeland, Joseph, 47

Corbett, Boston, 24n

Cornish, Daniel, 99

Cowpens, battle of, 214

Crenshaw, William G., 207

Culp's Hill, 155, 163, 176

Cumberland Valley, 40

Cushing, Alonzo, 193

Custer, George A., 34, 47

Cutler, Lynsander, 116; *photo*, 117

Dana, Henry E., 81, 103

Davis, Jefferson, 26, 76-77, 139n

Davis, Joseph, 42, 74n, 76-76n, 86-87, 100, 115, 120, 129, 181, 207; *photo*, 77

Davis, William S., 206

Day, Thomas G., 72, 82, 140, 145

Department of the Ohio, 188n

DePuyster, John Watts, 185

Devin, Thomas C., 23, 25, 33, 38, 41, 65, 96, 97n, 129, 148, 164, 166n, 187, 205, 237, 240;

commands Second Brigade, First Divison, 19-20; Antietam campaign, 21; commissioned colonel of 6th New York Cavalry, 21; Fredericksburg campaign, 21; promoted to lieutenant colonel, 21; mutual respect with Buford, 22; 72 skirmishes and battles, 23; Snickersville, Virginia, 32; June 30, 42; brigade, 50, 67, 128, 157, 241-242; camp at Lutheran Seminary, 54; Lutheran Seminary, 56; night of June 30, 66, 68, 71; vidette posts, 67; Herr ridge, 96; Samuel Cobean farm, 97; morning, July 1, 98, 100; moves to Seminary Ridge, 101; pulls off McPherson's Ridge, 101; hard pressed at the railroad cut, 115; withdraws to Cobean farm, 129; troops get a respite, 130; on Rock Creek, 145; abandons position because of Union shelling, 146; friendly fire from Wiedrich, 146; brigade inside Gettysburg, 147; pulls back to high ground, 147; Pitzer's Woods, 167; brigade departs for Westminster, 177-178; performance at Gettysburg, 182-183; promoted to general, 194; Spencer rifles, 210-212; forming a square, 222; *photo*, 19; *photo of monument*, 236

Dickinson, Joseph, 69, 70-70n; *photo*, 68

Diffenbaugh, David, 88

Ditzler, Eli, 38, 48

Dodge, H. O., 67

Dodge, Richard I., 195

Doubleday, Abner, 113-114, 118, 122, 129, 132-133, 148, 152-153, 192, 220, 223

Douglas, Stephen A., 5

Duke, Basil W., 8n, 188n

Dustin, Daniel, 18n

Early, Jubal A., 33, 47, 50, 56, 94n, 130, 146-147

East Cemetery Hill, 155, 163, 224

Edwards Ferry, 32-33

Ellis, Rudulph, 197n

Emmitsburg Road, 103, 109, 112, 144-145, 155, 157, 163, 164n, 166-168, 170-171

Emmitsburg, Maryland, 36, 39, 43-44, 47, 53, 55, 69, 225

Evans, Nathan G. "Shanks", 7

Evergreen Cemetery, 157

Ewell, Richard S., 3, 28, 32-33, 69, 96-97, 109, 123, 126, 138, 155n, 176, 206; *photo*, 29

Ewing, Hugh B., 7

Fairfield Gap, 43

Fairfield Road, 64, 86, 133, 140, 142-143, 181, 241

Fairfield, Pennsylvania, 40, 42-43, 46-46n, 47, 57n, 60

Falmouth, Virginia, 26

Faribault, George H., 207

Farnsworth, Elon J., 34

Farnsworth, John F., 18-18n, 20

Field, Charles, 87n

First Shot Marker, 229; *photo*, 227

Follett, Henry D., 106

Forney, John, farm, 67, 99-99n, 115; *photo*, 102

Forrest, Nathan Bedford, 4-5, 188, 194

Forsyth, George A., 18n

Fort Leavenworth, Kansas, 11, 18

Fort Riley, Kansas, 9

Fountaindale, Maryland, 39-39n, 43, 46n

Fowler, Edward B., 117

Frazier, W. W. , 197n

Frederick, Maryland, 34, 36

Fredericksburg campaign, 14, 20-21, 28, 152

Fremantle, Arthur, 3n

French and Indian War, 2n

Fry, Birkett D., 77-79, 86, 89, 207

Gamble, William, 18n, 19, 24, 47, 67, 85, 95, 138, 153n, 154, 205, 221, 240-241; commands First Brigade, First Division, 17, 20; Chicago Board of Public Works, 18; commissioned lieutenant colonel, 18; Fort Leavenworth, Kansas, 18; Indiana Street Methodist Church, 18; Brandy Station, battle of, 20; Fredericksburg campaign, 20; Malvern Hill, battle of, 20; Peninsula campaign, 20; promoted to colonel, 8th Illinois Cavalry, 20; camp at Lutheran Seminary, 54; Buford has him pick a defensive position, 56; night of June 30, 65, 68; skirmishers to Herr's Ridge, 90; Herr ridge, 95; pushed off Herr Ridge, 104, 106-107; engaged nearly three hours, 108; meets the Reynolds, 115; has to withdraw, 116-117; brigade fights with the infantry, 118; falls back to the Fairfield Road, 122; brigade held off infantry division for four hours, 123; description of his stand, 131; troops fall back to Gettysburg, 132; Biddle's brigade retires, 137; places Gamble's brigade along the Fairfield Road, 142; right flank exposed, 143; stand helped hold Seminary Ridge, 144; pulls back to Cemetery Ridge, 145; men borne the brunt of the fighting, 155; orders Calef to support the 6th New York, 166; Pitzer's Woods, 167; brigade departs for Westminster, 177-178; performance at Gettysburg, 181-183; promoted to general, 194; Spencer rifles, 210-212; forming a square, 222-223; *photo*, 16; *photo of brigade marker*, 233

Garnett, Richard S., 3n

Garnett, Robert S., 3n

Geary, John W., 155, 163; *photo*, 154

George, Newton J., 207

Gettysburg National Cemetery, 94n

Gibbon, John, 1, 7, 9, 15, 90, 185, 195

Gilpin, Samuel, 131

Gordon, Daniel S., 197n

Gorgas, Josiah H., 3n

Graff, A. S. Van de, 86, 88

Grant, Ulysses S., 2

Green, Francis M., 207

Greene, Nathanael, 214

Gregg, David M., 36, 44, 177, 197n, 199, 211; *photo*, 198

Grey Eagle, 85, 103, 148, 183, 192

Guilford Court House, battle of, 214-215

Hagerstown Road, 68, 120, 132

Haight, Willeet S., 107

Hall, James A., 64, 119-120, 124

Halleck, Henry W., 176, 192

Halstead, Eminel P., 148-149, 153-153n, 220, 223n

Hancock, Winfield Scott, 112n, 137, 138n, 150, 152, 155, 170, 182, 185-186, 192, 224; *photo*, 149

Hanley, Timothy, 98-99, 101

Hardee, William J., 215

Hardman, Asa, 85

Harmon, Amelia, 92

Harney, William S., 4, 8-8n, 9n

Harrisburg Pike, 130

Harrisburg, Pennsylvania, 32, 120, 130

Harrison, W. H., 197n

Harvey, John, 34

Hazelton, William C., 48, 82, 103, 182

Heermance, William L., 98, 146, 185, 197n

Heeth, Stockton, 76

Heidlersburg, 69, 109, 118, 126, 130

Heim, George, 64

Heintzelman, Samuel P., 192

Helena, Arkansas, 3

Henry-Bonnard foundry, 200

Herbst farm and woods, 107, 132

Herr's Tavern, 79, 230; *photo*, 91

Herr's Ridge, 54, 79, 81, 90, 92, 94-95, 106, 138, 229-230, 240; *photo*, 91

Heth, Henry, 3, 8-8n, 48, 74n, 138-139, 142, 181, 184, 91, 104, 206, 216, 221; division, 42, 56-57, 59, 76; June 30, 44, 61; Fairfield, 44; morning, July 1, 74-75, 77, 83, 86-87, 94-95, 97, 106, 108; first error of the battle, 75; second error of the battle, 75; served with Buford in the Regular Army, 75; third error of the battle, 76; pressing the attack, 104; *photo*, 75

Hill, Ambrose P., 28, 56, 60-61, 68, 74n, 75-76n, 108, 118, 137, 139n, 152n, 166, 206; *photo*, 55

Hodges, Alphonse, 66, 80n

Hoffman, John, 160

Hooker, Joseph, 12, 14-15, 26, 30, 32, 36, 37-37n, 189

Horner, William A., 39n

Hotopp, Henry J., 58

Houck's Ridge, 170

Howard, Charles H., 122, 187

Howard, Oliver O., 113, 120, 130, 138n, 145-146, 148-149, 154-155, 182, 187; *photo*, 121

Howe, Albion P., 3n

Howe, Edward,, 1

Hudson, Daniel L., 152

Hughes, Morgan, 67

Hunt, Henry J., 168, 177

Hunter, Albert M., 39n

Hunterstown, 52, 60

Hunterstown Road, 96-97

Iron Brigade, 76, 111, 113, 118-119, 133, 140, 222

Iron Springs Road, 42

Iverson, Alfred, 99n, 126, 128-128n, 206

Jack's Mountain, 40, 42

James, Cyrus, 97, 232

Jenkins, Albert G., 96-97; *photo*, 97

Jerome, Aaron B., 17, 53, 71-71n, 81, 107-110, 112, 117, 120, 130, 137, 195, 226, 240; *photo*, 72

Johnston, Albert Sidney, 9

Johnston, Samuel, 160, 161-161n

Joint Committee on the Conduct of the War, 170-171n

Jones, Marcellus e., 33, 79-79n, 80, 85, 95-96, 97n, 226

Jones, Samuel, 3n

Jones, William E. "Grumble", 7-7n

Keckler's Hill, 129n

Kelley, Thomas B., 49, 64, 66, 79, 81, 158

Kellogg, Josiah H., 128, 205

Kelly, James E., 200-202, 204, 236; photo, 198

Kelly, John, 35n

Kempster, Walter, 176

Keogh, Myles W., 191, 193

Kilpatrick, H. Judson, 36, 44-44n, 177

Knox College, 6

Knoxlyn Ridge, 54, 64, 78, 80-81, 85, 94, 226-227

Kress, John A., 84

Kyle, W. E., 43

Lafayette, Marquis de, 1n

Lamberson, George, 92

Lane, James, 138, 152-152n, 153-153n, 154, 182, 218, 221-222, 223n; brigade, 143-144, 153, 241; forming a square, 218-220, 223-224; *photo*, 150

Lee, Robert E., 26, 30, 32, 34, 36, 43, 53, 74n, 89, 138, 145, 155n, 157, 160-161, 174, 176, 180, 186-187, 189, 194, 206, 240; *photo*, 27

Leister, Lydia, 70n

Lemmon, Charles, 78, 82, 140; *photo*, 78

Leventhorpe, Collett, 207

Lewis Ford, engagement at, 194

Lincoln, Abraham, 18, 24n, 37n, 109n, 190, 192

Little Round Top, 154, 157, 161, 163, 168, 242

Little, Benjamin, 42

Livingston, Charles, 223

Lockett, James W., 207

Loeser, Charles McK., 195, 197n

Long, Henry F., 158, 176

Longstreet, James, 12, 28, 32, 69, 137, 164, 174, 184

Lord Dumore's War, 2n

Lott, Jacob, 80

Lutheran Seminary, 52, 54, 56, 71, 81, 102, 226; photo, 53

Lyman, Theodore, 16, 17-17n, 188-189

Lyon, Nathaniel, 3n

Macomber, Jonathan, 168

Mahan, Dennis Hart, 30

Malvern Hill, battle of, 20

Manchester, Maryland, 112n

Markell, William L., 94, 106, 142-143, 181-182, 205

Marriott, Edward, 109

Marsh Creek, 47, 52-54, 58-59, 64, 79-80, 83-84, 181, 228

Marshall, James K, 77, 132-134, 207; *photo*, 134

Marye, Edward A., 83-85, 94-95, 207

Marye, John, 83

Marye, William, 228

Mayo, Robert M., 76, 207

McCabe, Joseph A., 211-212

McClellan, George B., 12, 14, 113
McClure, William, 78
McCown, B. H., 192n
McDowell, Irvin, 8n, 12
McGowan, Samuel, 139n
McGraw, Joseph, 207
McLean, Nathaniel H., 7
McMillan house, 153
McPherson, Edward, 54-54n, 67
McPherson's barn; *photo*, 229
McPherson's Ridge, 54, 66, 82, 86, 95, 98n, 101, 106-108, 115-116, 118- 119, 137, 139, 197, 203-204, 230, 233, 241; *photo*, 91
McPherson's Woods, 64, 83, 91, 133
Meade, George G., 14, 16, 37-37n, 58, 69-70, 112-112n, 114n, 137, 149-150, 163, 166, 170, 171n, 172, 176-178, 180, 188, 205; *photo*, 173
Meade, Jr. George G., 197n, 199
Medill, William H., 95, 122, 134, 153n
Meredith, Jaquelin Marshall, 59, 76
Meredith, Solomon, 118; *photo*, 119
Merritt, Wesley, 25, 34, 37, 68, 178, 184, 188, 190-191, 194-194n, 197n, 199, 201, 204; *photo*, 198
Mexican War, 3, 75n, 128n, 139n
Middleburg, battle of, 30
Middletown, Maryland, 36
Miller, Hugh R., 207
Millerstown Road, 60, 163
Mills, Albert, 106
Minty, Robert H. G., 216
Mix, A. R., 67-68, 126, 164, 166
Mix, John, 34
Monterey Pass, 39, 43, 46n
Monterey Springs, 39
Moore, A. H., 48, 77
Morgan, Daniel, 214-215
Morgan, Edwin, 21
Morgan, John Hunt, 4, 188n
Mormon War, 9n
Morris, John, 86
Mosby, John S., 73n
Mummasburg Road, 67, 98-99, 101-102, 114, 126, 237-238, 240
Mummasburg, 44, 52, 60
Musselman, Peter, 42-42n
Nashville campaign, 5
National Park Service Visitor Center, 225
New York Avenue Presbyterian Church, 192
Newman, Joseph, 91, 120
Nichols, Perry, 99

Oak Hill, 86, 101, 115, 122, 126, 128-129, 238
Oak Ridge, 129n, 222
O'Neal, Edward A., 128
Peace Light Memorial, 102
Peck, Daniel, 164
Pegram, William J., 60, 83, 86, 95, 126, 207; photo, 84
Pender, William Dorsey, 68, 74n, 137-138, 139-139n, 142, 144, 148, 153, 182, 184, 218, 222; *photo*, 136
Peninsula Campaign, 20, 24
Pennington, Alexander C. M., 197n, 199; photo, 198
Pergel, Charles, 91
Perrin, Abner, 138, 139-139n, 142, 143, 148, 221, 221n; *photo*, 138
Perryville, battle of, 4
Pettigrew, James J., 42, 74n, 142; June 30, 56n, 57-59, 61; brigade, 56, 59-60, 132-133, 207, 241; morning, July 1, 87; *photo*, 57
Pickett-Pettigrew-Trimble charge, 3n, 70n, 164n, 180, 193
Pierce, Tillie, 51-52
Pipe Clay Creek, 176
Pipe Creek Circular, 112n
"Pipe Creek Line", 112n, 172, 176
Pitzer's Schoolhouse, 164
Pitzer's Woods, 166-166n, 167-168
Pleasonton, Alfred, 15, 21, 23, 33, 37, 39, 68, 70, 132n, 137, 174, 177- 178, 185, 187, 191, 205; Brandy Station, battle of, 28; Aldie, battle of, 32; Upperville, battle of, 32; orders Buford to Gettysburg to cover the army's left flank, 36; orders Gregg to guard the army's right flank, 36; orders Kilpatrick to guard the army's center, 36; June 30, 53, 60; intelligence report to Reynolds, 69; performance at Gettysburg, 182; *photo*, 35
Point Pleasant, battle of, 2n
Polk, Leondas K., 3n
Pope, Edwin M., 144
Pope, John, 11-11n, 12
Pulis, Danel, 142
Purifoy, John, 153n, 221
Raison, Henry, 90
Redman, William H., 50, 94-94n, 160
Reid, Edward C., 82, 143, 179
Reynolds, Gilbert, 124, 126
Reynolds, John F., 3n, 44, 47, 69-70, 108, 110n, 114n, 132, 148, 181, 185-186, 200n, 204, 216, 240; June 30, 46, 55, 60; meeting with

Buford, 46n; Buford's note on June 30, 52-53; night of June 30, 64; seen approaching Buford's position, 109-109n, 110; turns down offer to command the army, 109n; arrives and meets Buford, 110; received Buford's request for support, 110; validated Buford's decision to stand and fight, 111-112, 114; defends the town of Gettysburg, 112; meets with Buford, 113; sets up Wadsworth's division, 113; approaches the front, 115; men arrive on the the field, 117; shot, 118-119, 121; death, 137, 149; *monument*, 231; *photo*, 111

Richardson, Israel B., 3n

Richmond & Danville Railroad, 4

Riddler, Alex, 64

Ripley, James W., 208

Robertson, Beverly H., 194

Robertson, Walter H., 59

Robinson, Benjamin, 128

Robinson, John C., 105, 122, 124, 129, 133; photo, 122

Rock Creek, 130, 163

Rock Island, Illinois, 5

Rodenbough, Theophilus F., 183, 197n, 199, 201; *photo*, 198

Roder, John, 91, 241

Rodes, Robert E., 44, 69, 109, 126, 129, 206, 240; *photo*, 123

Rodman, Thomas, 3n

Rosecrans, William S., 2, 188

Rosengarten, Joseph G., 110, 183

Rowley, Thomas A., 122-122n, 124

Sackett, William, 96, 98, 205; *photo*, 96

Sandoe, George, 94n

Sanford, George B., 189, 190-190n, 192

Sawtelle, Charles G., 197n

Scales, Alfred, 138, 143

Schaffer, Levi, 79

Schmucker Hall, 102, 240; *photo*, 226

Schofield, John M., 192

Schurz, Carl, 114n

Scott, James K. P., 211

Scranton, W. A., 100

Second Bull Run campaign, 11-11n, 12, 24

Seddon, James A., 26

Seminary Ridge, 54, 58, 101, 115, 124, 133, 137-140, 145, 148, 153-154, 182, 218, 221-224, 240

Seminole Wars, 18

Seven Pines, battle of, 139

Shaffer, Levi, 64

Shears, George W., 205

Shenandoah Valley, 32

Shepard, Samuel G., 105

Shepherdstown, Maryland, 32

Sherfy, Joseph, farm, peach orchard, 155, 157-158, 161, 164, 170, 242; *photo*, 242

Sheridan, Phillip H., 23

Shippensburg, Pennsylvania, 57, 120

Shultz house and woods, 140, 142, 240

Sickles, Daniel, 155, 163, 167, 168-168n, 170, 177, 192, 200n; *photo*, 166

Sioux Punitive Expedition, 8

Slattery, Thomas, 120

Slentz, John, 54n, 67, 90

Slocum, Henry W., 187

Slough, Nelson, 206

Smith, Edmund Kirby, 4

Snicker's Gap, 32

Snickersville, skirmish at, 32

South Mountain, 33, 38-39, 52, 60, 78, 221

Spanish-American War, 194n

Sparks, Harry B., 47-48

Spence, E. B., 59

Spencer, Christopher M., 209

Stanton, Edwin M., 37n, 190-190n, 191-192

Steuart, Jr., George H., 7

Stevens, Isaac, 21

Stone, John M., 115, 207

Stone, Roy, 98n

Stoneman Raid, 32

Stoneman, George, 14, 14n, 15, 161, 189-191

Stuart, James E. B., 3n, 11-12, 17, 28, 30, 32, 44, 46-47, 196

Sully, Alfred, 3n

Swett, Joel, 116

Talbot, Will, 34, 36

Taneytown Road, 70n, 225

Taneytown, Maryland, 112n, 178

Tate's Blue Eagle Hotel, 52, 56, 68-69, 81, 84, 109, 225-226; *photo*, 50

Taylor, Walter, 75

Thomas, Edward, 138

Thoroughfare Gap, 12

Thurmont, Maryland, 37

Tidball, John C., 7, 30, 124, 197n, 199, 201, 204; *photo*, 198

Trevilian Station, battle of, 96

Tupelo, battle of, 4

Turner, J. McLeod, 153

Turner's Gap, 38

Turney, J. B., 105
United States Military Academy, 2, 3-3n, 6, 24, 30, 74n, 139n, 192, 213
United States Military Units
Berdan's Sharpshooters, 166, 168-168n
District of Columbia,
1st Cavalry, 24n
Illinois
2nd Cavalry, 16
8th Cavalry, 17n, 18-18n, 20, 33, 38, 42-43, 47-49, 58, 64-67, 72, 73-73n, 78, 79n, 80-83, 87-88, 91, 94-95, 103-104, 106-108, 114, 116, 122, 132-132n, 133-134, 137, 142-143, 150, 152, 153n, 157-158, 163, 176, 180, 182, 185, 195, 205, 209-210, 226, 234, 241; *photo of monument*, 230
8th Infantry, 79
12th Cavalry, 20, 20n, 50, 64, 83, 94, 107, 160, 205, 209-210, 234; *photo of monument*, 231
27th Infantry, 2
Indiana
3rd Cavalry, 19, 20-20n, 42, 47, 65, 71-72, 78, 82-86, 85, 88, 95, 117-118, 131, 140, 143-145, 158, 160, 167, 172, 178-179, 184, 205, 210, 235; *photo of monu- ment*, 234
3rd Infantry, 209
Maine
2nd Artillery, Battery B, 119
3rd Infantry, 168-168n
Maryland
1st Potomac Home Brigade, 39n
Michigan
5th Cavalry, 209
6th Cavalry, 209
Michigan Cavalry Brigade, 209
New Jersey
1st Infantry, 71n
New York
1st Artillery, Battery I, 145
1st Artillery, Battery L, 124, 126
1st State Militia Cavalry, 21
6th Cavalry, 17, 21-23, 42, 44, 47, 50, 98, 100, 115-116, 126, 146, 157-158, 160, 166, 185, 195, 199-200, 205, 210; *photo of monument*, 236
8th Cavalry, 20, 38, 64, 83, 91, 94, 105-106, 109, 122, 142, 144, 167, 179, 181, 205, 209-210, 234, *photo of monument*, 229
9th Cavalry, 33, 34, 36, 66-67, 71, 80n, 96-101, 115-116, 129-130, 146-147, 152, 158, 163-164, 168, 170-171, 179, 193, 205, 210, 232; *photo of monument*, 237

14th Brooklyn, 117
45th Infantry, 222
Pennsylvania
1st Cavalry, 211, 223
4th Cavalry, 224n, 177
6th Cavalry, 178, 197n
8th Cavalry, 23
17th Cavalry, 23, 38, 40, 96, 98, 101, 115, 128, 130, 132n, 147, 158, 163, 205, 210-212, 237, 238; *photo of monument*, 238
121st Infantry, 136
United States Regulars
1st Cavalry, 128n, 189, 191
2nd Artillery, Battery A, 23-24, 203, 206; *photo of monument*, 228
2nd Cavalry, 11, 15, 35n, 184
3rd Artillery, Battery C, 197
3rd Cavalry, 194n
5th Artillery, 24
6th Cavalry, 37, 197
8th Cavalry, 194n
First Dragoons, 3, 7, 17
Second Dragoons, 7-8, 9-9n, 10, 194-195, 199
West Virginia
1st Cavalry, 209
3rd Cavalry, 22-23, 24n, 160, 205, 210; *photo of monument*, 235
Wisconsin
2nd Infantry, 118
Upperville, battle of, 7n, 30, 32, 161
Ushuer, Ferdinand, 94-94n
Utah Expedition, 9
Van buren, Geoge M., *photo*, 105
Van De Graff, Sebastian, 207
Van Dusen, Charles, 179
Veil, Charles, 110
Vicksburg campaign, 2, 26
Virginia Military Institute, 87n, 152n
Wade, James, 37
Wadsworth, James, 84, 113, 116, 119, 122, 124, 126, 193; *photo*, 114
Wainwright, Charles S., 15, 124, 126; *photo*, 124
Waite, John, 18n
Wakerly, Henry J., 160
Walker, Francis A., 150, 186
Warren, Gouverneur K., 152, 155, 182, 192, 224
Washington, George, 2n
Watson, J. C., 199
Weaver, John E., 88
Weed, Thurlow, 21
Weir, Henry C., 197n

Weld, Stephen Minot, 112
Welsh, Osgood, 197n
West, Speight Brock, 206
Western Maryland Railroad, 174
Westminster, Maryland, 109, 112n, 166, 170n, 177-180
Wheeler, Jerome B., 17, 195, 197n, 199, 200-200n; *photo*, 198, 200
White, Elijah V., 34
Whitehead, G. I., 197n
Whitney, Charles, 34, 36
Wiedrich, Michael, 145-146
Wilcox, Cadmus M., 164, 166-167
Wilder, John T., 209
Williams, Alpheus, 163
Williamsport, Maryland, 36, 105
Willoughby Run, 54, 57, 86, 92, 104, 106-107, 119, 152, 181, 186, 230
Wilson, James H., 197n, 199, 201; *photo*, 198
Winchester, battle of, 28
Winchester, Virginia, 28
Wisler blacksmith shop, 226
Wisler, Ephraim, 54, 64, 85, 99, 227
Withrow, Thomas, 43-44
Wolf's Hill, 163
Woodford County, Kentucky, 1, 4
Worley, C. L. F., 90
Wright, Horatio G., 3n
York, Pennsylvania, 52, 69, 113, 120, 130
York Road, 147
Young, Brigham, 9
Young, Louis G., 56-59, 61
Zimmerman, William E., 207